Women and the Irish Diaspora

Women and the Irish Diaspora looks at the changing nature of national and cultural belonging both among women who have left Ireland and those who remain. It identifies new ways of thinking about Irish modernity by looking specifically at the lives of Traveller and settled women and examining their experiences of migration and diaspora. Based on original research with Irish women, both in the Republic of Ireland and in England, this book explores how questions of mobility and stasis are recast along gender, class, racial and generational lines. Through analyses of representations of 'the strong Irish mother', migrant women, the global Irish family and celebrity culture, Breda Gray further unravels some of the complex relationships between femininity and Irish modernity(ies).

Breda Gray is Senior Lecturer, Women's Studies, in the Department of Sociology at the University of Limerick.

Transformations: Thinking Through Feminism
Edited by
Maureen McNeil, Institute of Women's Studies,
Lancaster University
Lynne Pearce, Department of English, Lancaster University
Beverley Skeggs, Department of Sociology, Manchester University

Other books in the series include:

Women and the
Irish Diaspora

Breda Gray

Routledge
Taylor & Francis Group

LONDON AND NEW YORK

First published 2004
by Routledge
11 New Fetter Lane, London EC4P 4EE

Simultaneously published in the USA and Canada
by Routledge
29 West 35th Street, New York, NY 10001

Routledge is an imprint of the Taylor & Francis Group

Typeset in Times New Roman by
Florence Production Ltd, Stoodleigh, Devon
Printed and bound in Great Britain by
The Cromwell Press, Trowbridge, Wiltshire

British Library Cataloguing in Publication Data
A catalogue record for this book is available from the British Library

Library of Congress Cataloging in Publication Data
Gray, Breda.
    Women and the Irish diaspora/Breda Gray – 1st ed.
        p. cm. – (Transformations)
        1. Women – Ireland – Identity.   2. Women – Great Britain –
    Identity.   3. Ireland – Emigration and immigration.   4. Women
    immigrants.   5. Women – Ireland – Social conditions.   6. Women
    – Great Britain – Social conditions.   I. Title.   II. Series.
    HQ1600.3.G73 2004
    305.48′89162–dc21   2003010826

ISBN 0–415–26001–9 (hbk)
ISBN 0–415–26002–7 (pbk)

For Brigid and in memory of Frank

Contents

Acknowledgements

My first thanks are to all of the women in London, Luton and Ireland who took part in this project and who gave so generously of their ideas and time.

I am very grateful to Beverley Skeggs, Jackie Stacey and Celia Lury for all their guidance and encouragement. Sara Ahmed and Avtar Brah's helpful comments and inspiration are also very much appreciated. The questions that led to the research for this book were stimulated by the inspiring work of Ailbhe Smyth. A special thanks to Ginny Hardy and Louise Ryan for their enthusiasm, feedback and advice and to Maura Gray for her generosity and support. I am grateful to friends and colleagues at Lancaster University, including Emma Bulley, Jean Carroll, Anne Cronin, Kath Cross, Anne-Marie Fortier, Anne Harper, Janet Hartley, Cathy Holt, Rose Jack, Jane Kilby, Sharon Lambert, Wendy Langford, Yu Ying Lee, Ruth McElroy, Simon Pardoe, Fran Stafford and Kathleen Sullivan for the many discussions and exchanges. Friends and colleagues at the Irish Centre for Migration Studies and the Department of Sociology at the National University of Ireland, Cork – Piaras MacÉinrí, Clare Roche, Linda Connolly and Su-ming Khoo – provided invaluable help with translating my diasporic research 'back home'. I am indebted to Máiread Dunne, Lorna Siggins, Ronit Lentin, Liam Harte, Bronwen Walter, Colin Graham and Lisa Smyth for their many perspectives on and contributions to my project. I am grateful to Catherine Williams, Roz Cran and Gina Dowding for their friendship and for being the source of so many diversions! Thanks also to Mari Shullaw and Gerhard Boomgaarden at Routledge and to the series editors Maureen McNeil, Lynn Pearce and Beverley Skeggs. A special thanks to Alastair Christie.

An earlier version of Chapter 6 was first published in the *European Journal of Cultural Studies* (2002) 5(3): 257–74 as '"Whitely Scripts" and Irish women's racialized belonging(s) in England', Breda Gray © Sage 2002, reprinted by permission of Sage Publications Ltd.

Introduction

Women have left Ireland in search of life opportunities, sexual liberation and career advancement, to give birth and to have abortions, as a means of personal survival and of contributing to the survival of their families in Ireland. They have emigrated to escape difficult family circumstances, heterosexism, Catholicism and the intense familiarities and surveillances that have marked Irish society. They have left as migrants and as part of the nomadic way of life of Irish Travellers. They have left voluntarily and involuntarily, by chance and because others were leaving. They emigrated in greater numbers than men in most decades since the mid-nineteenth century and left mainly as single women rather than as part of a family.[1] They were often pioneers creating migration chains that facilitated the migration of others, primarily to Britain and the United States. They became domestic servants, factory workers, nurses, nuns, feminist activists, farm-workers, breeding stock, sex workers, businesswomen and professionals in many countries around the world. Women have also stayed in Ireland to do many of the same things.

This book is about women who left the Republic of Ireland in the 1980s for London and Luton and women who stayed put. It draws on original research with migrant and non-migrant[2] women to consider how changing formations of Irish modernity are gendered and to generate new and politically productive directions for thinking about women and the Irish diaspora. My analysis is informed by poststructuralist feminist and social theory (Ahmed 2000; Burchell *et al.* 1991; Butler 1990 and 1993; Felski 1995 and 2000; Foucault 1979, 1980, 1982; Grewal 1996; Kaplan 1996; Lowe 1996; Probyn 1993; Rose 1999a and b; Scott 1993 and Skeggs 1997) and recent theoretical interventions on 'the global', globalisation, diaspora and multiculturalism (Bhabha 1990 and 1994; Brah 1996; Franklin *et al.* 2000; Gilroy 1993a and 2000; Hall 1990; Robertson 1992 and Urry 2000). My goal is to offer a nuanced account of late twentieth-century women's migration and Irish modernity(ies) from the perspectives of women who stayed and women who left. Although located in the wider context of the Irish diaspora, the particular time space of the research discussed here is the Republic of Ireland/London and Luton in the 1980s and 1990s. The originality of this book's contribution lies in its transnational focus, which re-frames questions of Irish migration and the category 'Irish women' within complex migratory activities that link societies of origin and settlement. The approach of the book is also new to the extent that it renders women's experience paradigmatic in accounting for Irish modernity(ies).

Migration and Irish women

Irish women's migration did considerable ideological and cultural work in the constitution of Irish femininity in the new southern state following independence in the early 1920s.[3] Until the 1950s at least, women's migration was variously constructed as a loss of national breeding stock, a threat to women's 'purity', and potentially undermining of their national and religious identities (Ryan 2001; see also Lee 1989a; Miller 1985; Moser 1993; Nash 1993b; Travers 1995; Walter 2001). It was also accounted for in relation to the lack of social and cultural outlets for women in rural Ireland and the pull of US and British city life (Commission on Emigration 1954). The focus was largely on the consequences, rather than the causes or conditions of women's migration (Ryan 2001). Although primarily a response to economic necessity, Irish women's migration throughout the twentieth century was also a response to the regulation of women's sexuality and of pregnancy outside of marriage (Garrett 2000; Jackson 1963; Lambert 2001; Ryan 2001). Irish femininity was recognised only in so far as it was separated from the sexual (see Chapters 1 and 2), a separation that was enabled partly by the enforced migration of some women from the state. But it was not only sexually deviant women who were emigrating; the large numbers of women leaving until the middle of the twentieth century at least was humiliating for the country and contributed to a national sense of failed maleness (Akenson 2000).[4]

Much of the academic literature on Irish women's migration takes the view that 'Ireland became a place that women left' (Diner 1983: 29; see also Nolan 1989; O'Carroll 1990; Scheper-Hughes 1979 and Travers 1995). Irish women's migration is constructed as liberation from economic and sexual constraint 'at home', but also paradoxically, as a dutiful familial practice that facilitated family and cultural survival in Ireland (see Chapter 2). Those who have researched Irish women's experiences in the United States have frequently concluded that the experience of these women was an emancipatory one with migration representing liberation from the confines and oppression of a small, patriarchal and Catholic society. Yet, the act of migration itself was also constructed as a form of family loyalty because women saw themselves as being able to support their families (of origin) better from America (Diner 1983).[5] Most went into domestic service in the US[6] and, although duty bound to their families in Ireland, Diner argues that these women sought independence and economic opportunity through waged employment as an alternative to marriage.[7] Similarly, Íde O'Carroll suggests that Irish women migrating to the United States, by opting for domestic service and factory work, were rejecting 'family life and its inherent male power structure' (1990: 18). Women's migration in the late nineteenth century, she suggests, provided 'a network and a lifeline to relative freedom', thereby providing role models for Irish women in the twentieth century (ibid.). Choice and freedom are seen as shaping their migrant lives for the better through a language of autonomy and self-realization in this literature. Yet, as Nikolas Rose argues, choice and freedom have come to represent another set of regulatory ideals (1996: 319). In the case of Irish migrant women in the early twentieth-century US, these regulatory ideals might include the imperative to 'make something of oneself' and to achieve bourgeois American individual status.[8]

Another thesis is that Irish women's migration from Ireland between 1885 and 1920 represented an attempt to recover the loss of status experienced in post-Famine Ireland and to increase their chances of marrying and establishing families (Nolan 1989).[9] Domestic service in the US is seen as having enabled the transition from rural to urban life, from traditional to modern society, the achievement of 'social and economic modernization as women' and the assimilation of the second generation via 'the manners and mores of the middle class learned during migrant women's time in service' (ibid.: 94–5). Family and home emerge here as key sites of expulsion from 'traditional' Ireland, but as sites of 'modern' belonging in the US as these women are seen as facilitating the civilisation and modernisation of the Irish-American community (see also Casey 1996). Janet Nolan argues that these women's successful adaptation to urban society and employment enabled them to send remittances, which 'helped maintain obsolete patterns of life in rural Ireland that would have [otherwise] disappeared ...' (1989: 71). Ironically, their 'liberating' migration to cities in the United States is seen as sustaining the conditions of stasis and resistance to change 'at home' (ibid.). Instead of the dichotomous positioning of 'homeland' as static and migrant destination as progressive, it might be more accurate to suggest, as David Fitzpatrick does, that migration challenged 'home certainties and invite[d] reflections from both sides on the competing attractions of new and old worlds' (1994: 26).[10]

Diner argues that Irish 'matricentred families' shaped the American-born children of these immigrant women and that many Irish-American public figures grew up in 'female headed households' (1983: 69). These assertions beg questions of the relationship between US nation building and the roles that these 'white' immigrant Irish women were expected to play in the reproduction of 'white' US citizens.[11] These women were incorporated into nation-building and modernisation projects in Ireland (through migration, correspondence and remittances) and in the US (via their civilising of Irish America and the reproduction of ambitious 'white' US citizens). Through work in the privatised space of domestic service and the transfer of 'modern' US norms to their own families, these women might be seen as achieving the paradoxical status of 'controlled independence'.

While migration to the US in the nineteenth and early twentieth centuries involved permanent relocation for most Irish women migrants,[12] many of those going to Britain in the twentieth century harboured plans to return to Ireland.[13] After the 1930s, most Irish women's migration was to Britain, and to England in particular. Irish women immigrants to Britain after the Famine years settled mainly in large cities. They worked in factories and mills in Lancashire and West Scotland and as domestic servants, street vendors, doing needlework and pub work in London (Lees 1979; Lennon *et al.* 1988; Walter 1988).[14] By the 1950s, the numbers working in domestic work were falling as more Irish women went into nursing, factory and clerical work in England (Lennon *et al.* 1988; Walter 1988). Irish women's migration to England is also framed in the academic literature in terms of freedom and liberation (Jackson 1963: 28; Kennedy 1973), but equally as an ambivalent journey to a country that many had learned to fear (Lambert 2001: 89; Walter 2001). Most of the research on Irish women immigrants to England, unlike the US, focuses on their largely disadvantaged status in a gendered migrant labour market, their experiences of anti-Irish racism and, for Catholic women, their struggles to negotiate Irish and Catholic identities in England (Fielding 1993; Lambert 2001; Lennon *et al.* 1988; Walter 2001). The labour market positioning of some of these migrants as domestic servants is addressed less in relation to personal liberation than in terms of their relegation to the invisible space of the private English middle-class home (Walter 2001). They were rendered invisible by a cult of domesticity that relied on the hiding of women's work in the household from sight and a focus on 'the home' as a representation of a classless and private Englishness (ibid.: 102/109). In Sharon Lambert's study of women migrants to Lancashire between 1920 and 1960, women who worked in domestic service moved into alternative employment as soon as they could (2001: 17). While acknowledging regional differences in England, Bronwen Walter argues that Irish women were positioned as 'other' through discourses of colonial stereotyping, anti-Catholicism, racialisation, and by the denial of Irish particularity in the postwar period.

The 1980s represents the most recent period of mass out-migration from the Republic of Ireland. Almost 70 per cent of this generation of migrants went to the southeast of England and to London in particular. As for earlier generations of Irish women migrants, questions of liberation, self-actualisation, racialisation and the gendered labour market framed the experiences of women migrants in the 1980s with particular effects for both migrants and those women who stayed. This book builds on and nuances the existing literature on Irish women's migration by accounting for staying as well as going; by taking a transnational/translocal approach to the research and by discussing the complex 'technologies of the self' that produce the

Irish migrant and non-migrant woman's self in conditions of late twentieth-century global Irish modernity. Although there was also out-migration from Northern Ireland in this period, the conditions of this migration and public constructions of it were different from those in the south, so the research on which this book is based was confined to women in the Republic of Ireland, London and Luton.

The categories 'women', 'the Irish diaspora' and 'the global'

The title of this book indicates that it is about relationships between the two social categories of 'women' and 'the Irish diaspora'. The invocation of such categories produces an 'illusionary certainty' that these categories exist, are knowable and do not change (Scott 2001: 285). Categories of social identity are central to the constitution of Western/Irish modernity and are reproduced in and through practices of modernity including capitalism, industrialisation, post-industrialisation, nation-state building, science, globalisation, social and sexual divisions of labour, the public/private divide and so on (Hall 1991). To reject these categories would be to elide the effects of modernity and its drive to categorise and classify in ways that involve certain individuals coming to be seen and to see themselves in similar ways. Although individuals may identify with and make investments in particular categories and combinations of categories, they are never captured by these categories – there is always more.

Categories do not operate in isolation from one another, but in a complex and changing set of inter-connections with other categories. For example, 'Irish' and 'woman' are mutually constitutive categories. The Irish woman is a site of contradiction and ambivalence and it is often by rendering the divisions and antagonisms between national and gender categories visible that the Irish woman herself as a subject of history may become visible (Ahmed 1998). The conditions of possibility for the categories 'Irish', 'women', 'migrant', 'national' and 'diaspora' (and intersections between these) were shifting in the 1980s and 1990s. This book traces these shifting conditions of possibility and their effects for thinking about women and the Irish diaspora. The book does not produce a unified narrative, but examines the multi-located and overlapping practices and techniques by which women are made and render themselves national, migrant, ethnic, diasporic and gendered subjects. It focuses in particular on the discourses and practices that frame women's ways of describing, judging and directing their own conduct as subjects and selves (Rose 1996). It considers changing formations of belonging and the ways in which these are newly gendered through changing notions of the national, diasporic and global.

Belonging exceeds categories of identity because it 'expresses a desire for more than what is' (Probyn 1996: 6). If selves are understood as effects of particular modes of subjectification, performances and identifications, then it is important to see belonging as 'an achievement' rather than an ontological status (Bell 1999: 3). Belonging can be seen as an achievement in so far as the very idea that we belong to a particular sex, gender, nation or diaspora is always open to question (Butler 1990; Sedgwick 1994). National and gender identities can be seen as results of a 'collective agreement to perform, produce and sustain' (Butler 1990: 140) discrete gender, national and other identities as 'natural'. These identities involve 'complex incorporations' (Bell 1999: 3), self-identifications and recognition of membership of particular categories. But categories also shift, producing new modes of incorporation and identification. For example, the national as an emblematically modern category of belonging is refigured by the diaspora which now circulates as a category of deterritorialised belonging in global modernity.

Tololyan (1991) argues that for consciousness of diaspora to emerge, a discourse of diaspora must be produced by a small group of intellectuals and political leaders. A small number of academics and journalists, as well as the new President of Ireland, Mary Robinson, began to use the term diaspora in the 1990s as a means of disturbing apparently 'settled' notions of Irish identity. For the most part, the diaspora was invoked as a figure for rethinking the boundaries of the nation and how these might be more openly or progressively defined. What might be described as 'new diaspora theory' or 'diaspora studies' also emerged in the 1990s. Diaspora was introduced as an interpretative term to characterise new transnational public spheres, the transformation of everyday subjectivities, identifications beyond the time/space of the nation-state, a complex conception of sameness and a solidarity that recognises rather than represses difference (Appadurai 1996; Bhabha 1994; Brah 1996; Gilroy 1993a; Hall 1990). Some theorists see the social heterogeneity incorporated in the term 'diaspora' as progressive because of its critical theoretical challenge to racial, ethnic and nationalist absolutisms (Brah 1996; Clifford 1994; Gilroy 1993a and 2000).

Diaspora is conceptualised by Gilroy as 'an alternative to the metaphysics of "race", nation, and bounded culture coded into the body' and as problematising 'the cultural and historical mechanics of belonging' (2000: 123). He argues that diaspora

> might offer seeds capable of bearing fruit in struggles to comprehend the sociality of a new phase in which displacement, flight, exile and forced migration are likely to be familiar and recurrent phenomena that transform the terms in which identity needs to be understood.
>
> (ibid.)

Ultimately, Gilroy sees the idea of diaspora as unsettling entrenched assumptions about belonging and identity and constituting a site of cultural and political action that transforms existing cultural and political categories (Gilroy 1990/1991; Gilroy 1993a; Gilroy 1993b). Critics of diaspora see it as a non-progressive concept precisely because it is seen as harking back to some essential ethnicity or homeland (Anthias 1998; Brown 1998; Olwig 2000; Soysal 2000). However, for Avtar Brah, diaspora represents a critique of 'discourses of fixed origins, while taking account of "homing desire" which is not the same thing as desire for a "homeland"' (1996: 180; see also Fortier 2000: 17). It incorporates the conditions of displacement with desires to belong and the effects of these in reproducing new forms of identification.

Irish emigration has been theorised as an effect of the global labour market in a capitalist world economy (Mac Laughlin 1994b). Jim Mac Laughlin's world-systems analysis is based on the argument that emigration from Ireland became a significant option for economic survival as a result of a restructuring of the global economy in the nineteenth century with the emergence of Britain and North America as core of the capitalist world economy (ibid.). He suggests that processes of modernisation and class restructuring in Ireland, as well as the new global division of labour, led to the development of Ireland as a semiperiphery (i.e. including both core and periphery activities) in the second half of the nineteenth century. It became a 'global emigrant nursery' supplying Britain and North America with cheap labour (ibid.: 255–7). My focus is less on the economic factors affecting emigration and more on locating women's migration and the diaspora in politico-cultural re-workings of Irish belonging in the latter decades of the twentieth century. I investigate the ways in which the diaspora is incorporated within a cultural pro-globalism amongst some Irish politicians, commentators and business elites and their attempts to anchor a particularly Irish mode of 'the global'.

Globalisation is now a globalised term with multiple meanings, but most often understood as the compression of the entire world and the development of consciousness of the whole world as a single place[15] (Robertson 1992). Instead of portraying globalisation as an independent force, phenomenon or 'new reality' (Larner 1998: 601), my aim is to examine how globalisation and the global have come to have the discursive currency that they have in the late twentieth century (in Western liberal democracies at least). I am interested in the various discursive sites of the global and globalisation in the context of Ireland and the diaspora. Discourse is seen here not just as a form of rhetoric but 'a complex system of meaning that shapes institutions, practices, and identities in contradictory and disjunctive ways' (ibid.). Foucault treats discourse 'sometimes as the general domain of all statements, sometimes as an individualizable group of statements, and sometimes as a regulated practice that accounts for a number of statements' (1972: 80). All utterances have some effect but a particular identifiable group of utterances, for example those that articulate 'the diaspora', 'the Irish family' or 'the global', have some coherence and are invested with power. The global circulated in the late 1990s as an imagined location and an effect of discourses of globalisation and had constitutive power as a context, fantasy and as practice (Franklin *et al.* 2000). Robin Cohen argues that there is an 'elective affinity' between economic globalisation and diaspora, based on the importance of ethnic and cultural phenomena to the smooth operation of global markets (1995: 12). Inderpal Grewal and Caren Kaplan (1994) also identify an 'elective affinity' between diaspora and globalisation, but extend the relationship between them to political and cultural domains as well as economic. The synergies between diaspora and the overgeneralised global subject are seen as potentially supporting agendas of neo-liberal capital (Kaplan 1996). We are left then with the question of how to reconcile theoretical concerns with diaspora with the socio-political climate created by 'the global'. Avtar Brah offers one way forward when she argues that movement associated with discourses and practices of globalisation must be differentiated from 'diasporic journeys', which 'are essentially about settling down, about putting roots "elsewhere"' (1996: 182). I want to examine how these discourses and practices of globalisation, 'diasporic journeys' and the affinities and distinctions between them position Irish women who move and those who stay put.

The chapters that follow record and analyse the dynamics of gender and the Irish diaspora in the 1980s and 1990s. The 1980s represents the most recent period of large-scale out-migration from Ireland and the research on which this book is based took place in the mid-1990s. While these two decades represent different economic and political contexts in Ireland and for the Irish in England, taken together, they represent an important 'moment' in the emergence of Ireland as 'a global nation'.[16] The 1980s were marked by recession, mass unemployment and high out-migration in the Republic of Ireland while the 1990s saw Ireland becoming an economic success story based largely on foreign direct investment in electronic and information technology industries.[17] In England in the 1980s and early 1990s, the experiences of Irish migrants was affected by the IRA bombing campaign and an uneven and complex racialisation of Irishness. In the later 1990s, the IRA ceasefire, the Northern Ireland peace process and the circulation of Irishness in global consumer culture, while not superseding earlier constructions of Irishness, produced new sites and perceptions of Irish identity in England. Despite the social, political and cultural differences that mark these decades (already artificial periodisations), I argue here that official and popular discourses of migration in the 1980s prefigured the discourse of the diaspora in the 1990s and that continuities between these discourses can be tracked with regard to the figuring of Ireland as a 'global nation'.[18]

Although migration has marked Irish history for two centuries at least, 1980s migration was different. Those leaving were predominantly middle-class, fewer women were leaving than in previous periods of high out-migration and the Ireland they were leaving was being repositioned as 'modern' through notions of 'the global'. Return migration was also a feature of the 1980s, which intensified in the latter years of the 1990s.[19] Gender distinctions amongst migrants, so strongly drawn in the past in official, church and media discourses of migration, were less evident in the 1980s.

As intellectual skill replaces physical strength as a labour market requirement and reproduction is increasingly separated from sexed bodies, gender
difference may be less at stake in national discourses of migration. However,
gender did feature in feminist discourses of out-migration in the 1980s. By
then feminism had become 'an inescapable term of reference' (Abu-Lughod
1998: 3) following the visible activities of the Irish women's movement
since the 1970s and the public circulation of feminist discourses in response
to new Right agendas that made abortion and divorce constitutional issues
in the 1980s and 1990s. There emerged, therefore, the beginnings of an
analysis of migration as a gendered process that could be understood also
as a response to the social positioning of women within Irish society.
Although Traveller women were beginning to gain some recognition as rights
bearing Irish citizens, their mode of nomadic movement between Ireland and
England and vice-versa was not acknowledged within debates about migration[20] and, for the most part, remained outside Irish feminist debate and
activism (see Levine 2002 for evidence of some feminist engagement with
the politics of Traveller women's positions in Irish society). In the 1990s,
Irish Traveller women were beginning to obtain political visibility largely
through the expansion of multicultural initiatives in Ireland and in London,
but also via the work of the London Irish Women's Centre. The contradictory positioning of Traveller women forces us to rethink those categories
such as 'the individual', 'class, 'society' and 'citizenship' that lie at the heart
of modernity. The inadequacy of these categories as traditionally conceived
(Marshall 1994) is most poignantly articulated in the accounts of Traveller
women discussed in Chapter 3. While acknowledging the contested nature
of the categories 'women' and the 'Irish diaspora' and the many other categories that these categories reference, this book takes both of these categories
as its starting point. By embracing diaspora as a key category, I do not mean
to conflate migrancy and diaspora. Indeed, the immediacy of the migrant
experience, memories of and ongoing relationships to the country 'of origin'
mark *migrant belongings* out from *diasporic belongings*. Yet, these belongings overlap, as migrancy and diaspora are deeply interrelated categories.
This book locates migrancy in relation to diaspora and, by its focus on the
migrant generation of women, points to the many layers of temporality,
spatiality, mobility and memory that constitute the composite category of
diaspora and how these are gendered. In the next section I discuss the specific
geo-political context of this study in relation to the iconic sites and imagined contours of the Irish diaspora.

'The Irish Atlantic' and 'the Irish Sea'

In the popular imagination 'mass' Irish emigration is temporally located in
the mid- to late nineteenth century originating with the Great Famine, and
spatially identified with the United States of America, the destination of most
nineteenth-century migrants (Jackson 1963).[21] It is hard to emerge from the

shadow of the United States as the emblematic locus of the diaspora and the classic Irish migrant narrative of crossing the Atlantic and following the 'American Dream'. Despite the dominance of the US in the Irish diasporic imaginary, Britain has always been significant both as a destination for Irish migrants and as a kind of 'diasporic switching point' (Appadurai 1996). In the nineteenth century, the 'ports of Liverpool, Glasgow, [and] Plymouth were nodes through which the lines of communication of the worldwide diaspora flowed' (Akenson 1993: 192). The varying status of Britain as a transitional, seasonal or permanent destination, combined with the legacy of colonial relations[22] may have rendered it too contested a site to be emblematic of the Irish diaspora. Migrations across the Irish Sea to Britain, the most significant destination for Irish migrants in the twentieth century,[23] are perhaps too spatially, politically and temporally proximate to hold imaginative purchase.

Indeed, the proximities of Britain and Ireland extended into many spheres of life in the 1980s and 1990s. Noting the specific domains of sport and leisure, food, popular music and fashion, O'Tuathaigh suggested that Ireland and Britain constituted a single market for 'cultural consumption' and that the 'key markers of cultural differentiation' had been weakening since the 1970s (1991: 23). Garret Fitzgerald and Paul Gillespie point to the uniquely high level of human and family ties between Ireland and Britain (1996). Noting that there were nearly 9,000 trips a day across the Irish Sea in the 1990s, the long history of Irish migration to Britain and the impact of British television and British press, they suggested that Britain was 'familiar, even intimate' for most Irish people (ibid.). Attempts such as these to reframe relations with Britain along lines of everyday interaction and intercultural exchange gained some momentum in the 1990s as a result of the Northern Ireland Peace Process and President of Ireland, Mary Robinson's attempts to revise perceptions of Anglo-Irish relations. As part of this project, former president Robinson acknowledged the relative absence of attention in Ireland to the Irish in Britain who she suggested 'were the particular Irish that I had to be in touch with, whose identity and confidence I wanted to bolster' (quoted in O'Leary and Burke 1998: 192). Yet, complex negotiations of sameness and difference are at stake in the bolstering of Irish identity in Britain and the characterisation of relations between Britain and Ireland in terms of everyday interaction and exchange (see Chapters 5 and 6). For example, Ailbhe Smyth suggests that these interactions and exchanges are marked by 'euphemisms, elisions and evasions' (1994: 17), not least the evasion of Irish feminist politics within British feminism (ibid.: 24).

The exclusion of Britain from conventional understandings of the Irish diaspora tends to construct movement between the two countries as 'simply an internal rearrangement of bodies' within the same region (Walter 2001: 78). The 'common travel area' between Britain and Ireland which was bi-laterally agreed in 1952 and internationally acknowledged as the Common Travel Area (CTA) in the 1997 Treaty of Amsterdam (Meehan 2000), renders the act of migration between these countries unremarkable. Also, implicit identifications of British and Irish belonging with 'whiteness' render the specificity of Irish experiences less intelligible within frameworks of multi-culturalism[24] and anti-racism that repeatedly invoke a 'white'/'black' dichotomy (see Chapter 6). However, the geographic and cultural proximities between Ireland and England, as the accounts discussed in this book suggest, make the persistent distances all the harder to articulate and render the 'short passage to England' the 'most problematic act of relocation' (Brewster 1999: 126).[25]

The British destinations of Irish migrants in the 1980s were mainly London and the southeast of England, the headquarters of high technology industries, financial and information services sectors (Hickman and Walter 1997; King 1995; Owen 1995).[26] The extent of this migration was noted by the media in both Britain and Ireland which suggested that for many young Irish adults, 'London, not Dublin, [was] becoming their capital city' (Popham 1990: 22). The ongoing conflict in Northern Ireland marked Anglo-Irish relations in the 1980s in ways that reproduced numerous silences. The Prevention of Terrorism Act and issues of security governed much of the politics of the Irish in Britain, prefiguring the post-September 11 era, when suspicion attached to ethnicity became a mode of justifying the intensified policing of and discrimination against particular 'ethnic' groups. My focus in this book is on this proximate nexus of England (London and Luton in particular) and the Republic of Ireland as the most significant transnational context of the Irish diaspora in the late twentieth century. The book investigates the dynamics of diaspora and migration in the nexus of London/ Luton/Republic of Ireland and examines the extent to which England can still be identified, to paraphrase Ruth-Ann Harris (1994), as 'the nearest place that isn't home' for Irish women migrants in the 1990s. The 'Irish Sea', as much as that of the 'Irish Atlantic', offers a trope for thinking the mobility of people, cultural, socio-political, media and other flows which constitute Ireland and London, England, Britain in myriad and contested ways.

Researching women and the Irish diaspora – journeys and encounters

As noted already, this book draws on empirical research conducted in the Republic of Ireland, London and Luton in the mid-1990s. This research involved focus group discussions and interviews with Irish settled and Traveller women who stayed in Ireland and who migrated to London and Luton in the 1980s. The aim of the research was to investigate the ways in which Irish women were positioned and positioned themselves in relation to Irish belongings 'at home' and through migration at the end of the twentieth century. Three aspects of the study concern us here: first, the profile of the women who took part, how they came to contribute and some of the exclusions that this study perpetuates; second, my own geographical and personal locations in relation to the research process; and third, the nature and status of the data collected, how it is analysed and put to work in this book.

The group of women who contributed to this study was largely self-selecting based on responses to widespread advertising in national print media in Ireland and England, women's centres, lesbian networks, Travellers' centres, Irish centres in London and through word of mouth.[27] The largest response was to newspaper letters and notices in Ireland and Britain. These respondents were mainly urban-based and could broadly be defined as middle-class. In order to reach a wider cross-section of women, I targeted specific groups and eventually included a young single Irish mothers group in London, a group of women who frequented the same bar in Luton, Traveller women in Dublin, a group of women on a women's studies programme in Dublin, women on an adult literacy course in Dublin, a women's network in a semi-state organisation in Dublin and a group of rural women who were farmers, worked in the home and in local employment in a rural area in Ireland. Of course, lack of access to particular groups made it difficult to include some groups of Irish women such as homeless women and Traveller women living in London. The actual sample of women who took part in my study reflects modes and paths of access, which enabled me to include some women and not others. Those taking part in the study cannot be seen as representative of 'Irish women'; a representative sample would have been almost impossible in the circumstances. In any case, my aim was not motivated by the wish to 'represent', but more to open up questions of women, diaspora and Irish modernities in ways that, instead of taking these categories for granted, challenge their operation through the accounts of differently located women.

In the event, a total of 111 women took part in the study, 36 in London/Luton and 75 in the Republic of Ireland. The Republic of Ireland based cohort included 17 women who had migrated and returned and 16 Traveller women, 8 of whom had lived in Britain at some stage in their lives. Women from urban and rural backgrounds (even if now living in cities) were more or less equally represented in both national locations. Nine per cent of the women in Ireland and 3 per cent of those in London came from non-Catholic, mainly Protestant backgrounds. Forty-nine per cent of the England based cohort and 64 per cent of those based in Ireland identified themselves as Catholic. Many women felt uncomfortable about identifying in relation to class, some because it was a category they did not identify with, and others because they were conscious of a gap between what they perceived as their personal class position and that of their family background. All of the women looked 'white' and were from Christian backgrounds.

The same semi-structured question schedule was used for both group discussions and interviews. The schedule focused on four main areas: what it meant to identify as Irish; perceptions of the category 'Irish women'; the significance of migration in constituting Irish identity/belonging for women; and responses to images of Ireland (see Appendix 1). Participants were invited to discuss images and symbols of Irish identity as represented on a poster, which aimed to represent a diversity of images of Ireland[28] (see Appendix 2). The fieldwork which took place between 1993 and 1996 involved focus group discussions and individual interviews in the Republic of Ireland, London and Luton (see Appendices 3 and 4 for a profile of those taking part). All of the interviews and group discussions were tape recorded with the permission of participants. Some group discussions were with women who knew each other and were held in their workplace, recreation, education or support settings, while others involved bringing women together who did not know each other. On average, there was only a 60 per cent attendance rate for the latter groups (this attendance rate is boosted by the higher percentage turn-up rate in Ireland). It was necessary, therefore, to invite ten to twelve participants for each discussion. Group sizes ranged from two to fourteen. Those women who registered a reluctance to join a group discussion, or who were unable to make group meetings, were offered the option of an interview, which they all took up. Most interviews took place in the homes of the interviewees. Group discussions and interviews represent different methods of data production and occasion very different kinds of interaction. I am aware that more could be made of these 'genres' of data production and the ways in which identity is performatively produced via each method. My approach in this book is rather to organise the data thematically quoting as extensively as possible from the discussions and interviews. In most cases the interaction in group discussions is discussed as part of my analysis because the dynamics of group discussions offer yet another layer of data on the subject matter in hand.

The experience of organising and facilitating group discussions in London and in Ireland was very different. Women were less 'available' to participate in discussion groups in London than in Ireland where groups were easily organised at a few days' notice. Also, the Irish-based discussions included more humour and irony than those in London. In retrospect, there was probably less at stake in their discussions of Irish identity and belonging. Although migration was a significant factor in their self-presentations (see Chapter 4), their sense of dislocation was markedly less palpable than for those in London and Luton. Returned migrants in the Ireland-based cohort had already negotiated their return, a decision that some of the women in London continued to struggle with. Of course, the London-based discussions and interviews may have also been more difficult for me as they closely reflected my own negotiation of belonging in England at the time as well as my ambivalence about my migrant status and questions of return.

In order to analyse the discussions and interviews, transcription was necessary. Transcribing is always problematic and transcripts represent only one interpretation of oral narratives. Group discussions involve contributors speaking at the same time, laughter and other interferences with sound which make transcription a difficult task. There is also the matter of how oral speech is textually represented. For the purposes of this book, I decided to exclude hesitations, such as 'ems', which undermine the coherence of phrases or sentences and affect the readability of the exchange. Given the textual nature of the book format, I thought it was important to extend the courtesy of excluding those aspects of oral delivery that might interfere with readability while not interfering (as far as I could be aware) with the sense of what was being said. Those contributors who were interested in reading the transcripts were given the opportunity to read and amend the transcript. Amendments were made in only one case. All were assured that pseudonyms would be used when quoting from interviews or discussions.

During the fieldwork stage of this research, I lived in Lancaster in the northwest of England. The fieldwork, because it was located in Ireland, London and Luton, all some distance from Lancaster,[29] involved considerable travel. Lawrence Grossberg sees the travel metaphor as appropriate to ethnographic research in particular, noting that the '*ethnographer* leaves her home (the familiar) and travels to the other home (the strange), and then returns home to make sense of it (the strange) in her writing' (1989: 59, emphasis in original). Although my research was not ethnographical, it was marked by travel. My experience of the research journeys was different from that described by Grossberg. To do my fieldwork, I left Lancaster (a location in the northwest of England only somewhat familiar to me) and returned to two former 'homes': London, where I had lived for seven years, and Ireland, where I was born and grew up. Both of these places were rendered unfamiliar by these returns and by the research process and topic. I was travelling to former 'homes', taking a detour through memories of different pasts, which inevitably put my own present location and changing relationships to these 'homes' under question.

The experience of travel became significant pre- and post-conditions of my research encounters and involved constant processes of translation between places; between Lancaster and London, Lancaster and Dublin, Cork, Meath and other parts of Ireland and, of course, vice versa. Travel, in this context, like that of most migrants, was not a heroic, bourgeois, or recreational activity (Clifford 1992), but was organised within a dependent economy of exchange. Travel involves uncertainty as timetables and connections do not always go to plan. When conducted with limited material resources, travel often involves the goodwill and support of others, whether strangers in airports, or family and friends near points of departure and arrival. My research travel was an ambivalent activity that involved the negotiation of differently located selves via differentiated relationships to place and in encounters with other Irish women's selves.

It was not only the *locations* of London, Luton, Dublin/Ireland and Lancaster which dominated my experiences of the fieldwork, but the *journeys* by train, plane, tube and buses, as well as the train and bus stations and airports. The fieldwork was marked by departures and arrivals, moving and waiting, anticipation and reflection. Auge (1995) and Urry (2000) have described airports in particular as non-places of modernity, sites of mobility that symbolise the flows of global modernity. Although certainly nodes of movement, I think that these sites take on the fullness of place (even if liminal places). For example, they are structured by the practices of border policing which mark individuals and groups of travellers in particular ways. Also airports facilitate the juxtapositioning of selves; they are places where some travellers, perhaps migrants in particular, inhabit juxtaposed selves as they leave one place, anticipate their arrival in another and are differently positioned by the border guards of different states. They are also sites of reconnection with family and friends and are, thereby, imbued with memories of transnational life practices. James Clifford (1992) argues that 'getting there' becomes as significant an aspect of the research process as 'being there'. The varied experiences of 'getting there' during my fieldwork became sources of insight enabling comparison and translation between Irish, migrant, woman, researcher and many other selves, as I moved between different locations of memory and belonging. Travel produced constant reminders of the dislocations of the migrant and the work of migrants in re-producing diasporic belonging(s).

The journeys involved in conducting my research meant that I left behind a researcher self in Lancaster and remembered an earlier migrant self in London, and non-migrant and potential migrant selves in Ireland. They involved encounters with other Irish women who were differently located in relation to Ireland, England and migration. In Ireland, my Irish accent and knowledge of Ireland produced familiarity, while my formal overtures of gratitude for the time and input of participants were sometimes identified as acquired 'English' affectation. During the fieldwork in London, my shared migrant status represented points of recognition. However, my academic interest in Irish identity was sometimes greeted with scepticism based on many of the women's deeper investments in career trajectory or their impatience with the practice of 'thinking about' and reflecting on the category 'Irish women'. Another form of distance was produced by my living in Lancaster, a city outside the imagined locations of the Irish diaspora. My research encounters and journeys involved reflection on the many differently located and contradictory ways in which I had taken and continued to take up the position of 'Irish woman'. They reminded me that at that moment when I, or any one of the women who took part in the study, spoke as an 'Irish woman', our subjectivities were never fully saturated by that speaking position; there is always more (Ang 1994: 4).

My research journeys were imbued with memories of the many differently located 'Irish woman' selves that I had taken up. I inhabited the category 'Irish women' differently in different places and times in my life and my inhabitance of the category in any place and at any time was always marked by the traces of earlier and different modes of inhabiting this category. The opening up of these shifting processes through movement and migration challenges the modern tendency to universalise through categories and classification. Also, the undifferentiated celebration of flows and mobility that mark discourses of global modernity are undermined by attention to the lived experiences of diverse conditions and modes of travel. There is no doubt that I enjoyed and felt excited by my ability to move between places which was facilitated by technological and transport developments. The ability to inhabit numerous spaces within a short period of time produces a sense of 'mastery' of space via mobility. No doubt it is this sense of space 'mastery' that contributes to the celebration of mobilities as a new way of inhabiting the global despite the new marginalisations, stratifications and exclusions it produces.

My ability to move was also enabled by my looking 'white', while I was simultaneously rendered suspicious by the operation of the British Prevention of Terrorism Act. Although mobility can become a way of inhabiting, or of constructing 'home' in the world, it can also produce a heightened sense of dislocation. This is because movement itself, and the ability to be in different locations relatively quickly and repeatedly, reveals the instability of belongings rooted in place. Migration (and indeed non-migration) in the 1980s and 1990s cannot be understood outside of travel practices and the promise of multi-locatedness. The question is how the relative ease of mobilities affects migrant and non-migrant sensibility and belonging and re-works gendered belonging in conditions of global modernity. The following chapters take up this question from different locations and perspectives.

Theoretical development, data generation and analysis developed in this study 'simultaneously in a dialectical process' (Mason 1996: 141) so that it is impossible to identify the research as purely inductive or deductive. The process, from the beginning, involved a moving back and forth between theory, my research questions, women's accounts, analysis and personal reflections. At times, the many differences between individual accounts both within group discussions and in interviews, made it difficult to think beyond individual specificities. These differences also forced a constant problematising of the (re)production of the categories 'Irish', 'women' and 'diaspora' as 'natural'. While the focus of my analysis is on the productive work being done by these categories and their effects, qualified generalisations are made.

This study is not a phenomenological one that tries to illuminate the meanings of Irish identity and belonging as they seem to the contributors. Instead, it is concerned with the knowledges or 'regimes of truth' which accord salience to particular categories, classifications and productions of the self. The women's accounts are analysed in ways that identify the women as both subjects and objects of discourses in such a way that the 'regimes of truth' that position women, although important, are not all. While one has to be 'positioned somewhere in order to speak', even if that is to unposition oneself (Hall 1991: 51), the accounts point to these positionings, but also exceed them. Indeed, they point to the 'unexpected and contingent results of lived experience', which can never be 'inevitably contained by that which seeks to produce us as bound subjects' (Coombes and Brah 2000: 14). The focus is on how discourses and politics of gender, migration and diaspora are disciplinary in the sense of ordering and classifying, but are simultaneously productive and creative. The formation of selves and cultural representations are also understood in relation to social and economic institutions and practices. What is at stake then, in the analysis of women's own accounts, is the ways in which the national, migrant, classed and gendered formations 'operate between abstract structures and concrete specifics of everyday life' (Skeggs 1997: 8). The focus is on the dynamics of the criteria used for what is seen as the 'truth' of the matter in the accounts. How come certain things can and cannot be articulated? How are particular 'truths' authorised and accorded legitimacy by contributors to this study? What is produced or made possible in and through the accounts? How is experience 'cut . . . in certain ways, to distribute attractions and repulsions, passions and fears across it . . .' (Rose 1999a: 31)? The texts of the accounts are analysed, therefore, to identify the 'truths' that are discursively invoked to explain why things are seen/constructed in particular ways.

In the following chapters I examine changing formations of Irish modernity via practices of government such as political speeches and policy reports, but most importantly through what can and cannot be thought, said or done in the accounts of the women who took part in this study. I analyse selected sections of the women's accounts by considering the particular vocabularies, techniques and authorities that govern individual women's relations to their selves and shape the way they understand themselves and are understood by others (Rose 1996: 305). My assumption is that there is no preconstituted inner self to be communicated in the world; it comes into being through discourse and the recognition of others. Therefore, the self is not knowable outside of discourse and recognition. In the *Use of Pleasure*, Foucault considers how individuals attend to themselves in ways that recognise themselves as subjects of desire and seek to discover the 'truth of their being' (1985: 5). The question then is what kinds of relation to the self are necessary for the individual to recognise herself as a subject. I consider how certain languages of description, explanation and judgement come to acquire the value of 'truth' and the kinds of action and techniques that are made possible by these truths (Rose 1999a: 8). As noted already, this approach challenges any essential unified interiority of the subject prior to its expression in thought, conduct, emotion and action, which in turn cannot be understood outside of their relations to certain knowledges and expertise (Rose 1996).

The group discussions and interviews discussed in this book represent new empirical data and are important cultural constructions in themselves. They are necessarily mediated by my selection from the transcripts, my interpretations of these, my research questions and theoretical concerns. I am distanced from the accounts by my position as researcher, interpreter and writer. By representing the accounts within the framework of this book I 'take control' of a body of data that involved particular contexts of collection, recording, and transcribing and which could be read, interpreted and re-presented in many ways at different points in the process (and by different researchers). My relationship to the women's accounts is one of 'speaking nearby' (Trinh 1988) rather than assuming a 'knowing' relationship to them or that they are in any way transparent. My aim is not to tell you – the reader – about 'her'/'them' but in an exploratory way to keep the possibilities of what might be at stake open. Speaking 'about' suggests a possession of knowledge or pretending knowledge *of* something (Kaplan 1997: 201). E. Ann Kaplan, following Trinh, seeks

> a position that functions in the gap, namely, 'speaking nearby'. The phrase conveys an idea of a closeness but with a necessary distance, because of difference; a concept of 'approaching' rather than 'knowing' an Other.
>
> (1997: 201)

In the following chapters, I take excerpts from the many group discussions and interviews and give them an independent existence as texts that are brought together to produce readings of the kinds of selves that are available to and taken up by the women as well an account of how the category 'Irish women' (as inflected by migration/diaspora) is constituted in the late twentieth century. But what happens to women's 'experience' in this approach to analysis?

When experience is constructed as incontestable evidence, the discursive construction of experience and its contextualised conditions of production are ignored. Individuals do not *have* experience, instead, it is 'subjects who are constituted *through* experience' (Scott 1993: 401; emphasis added). Experience then cannot be the origin of explanation, 'nor the authoritative (because seen or felt) evidence that grounds what is known, but rather that which we seek to explain, that about which knowledge is produced' (ibid.). A further problem with this catch-all category of experience is its conflation of the 'lived' with those discursive 'regimes of truth' that govern the transmission of the 'lived' into discourse. The ontological level of 'lived' experience can be understood as discursive categories working through embodied living subjects who perceive them as 'realities' (Brah 1996). Although the subject may be the effect of discourses, institutions and practices, 'at any given moment, the subject-in-process experiences itself as the "I", and both consciously and unconsciously replays and resignifies positions in which it is located and invested' (ibid.: 125). If experiences are discursively constructed, how is this achieved? Discourses become effective to the extent that they attach themselves to a technology for their realisation. Technologies in this context are collections of forms of knowledge which operate via particular techniques which are 'oriented to produce certain political outcomes' (Rose 1999a: 52). For example, discourses of the national can operate as a 'metalanguage', which produce national loyalties and mask the operation of other axes of difference and power. Discourses of the nation offer meaning to myriad aspects of life lending a discursive power that imposes erasures and closures. This is evident in the repeated slippage in the women's accounts discussed in this book from 'Irish women' to 'Irish people'.

The experiences articulated in the women's accounts cannot be seen as 'a pre-given ontology that precedes its expression' (Felski 1995: 21). They are constructed through the institutional and discursive technologies of nation, migration, diaspora, 'race', class and gender amongst others and the relative abilities of these technologies (in different contexts) to produce certain kinds of selves. The women's experiences emerge out of multiple social positionings and the interplay between these positionings in the forma-tion of selves. The category 'experience' is not self-evident but is 'produced in the moment when an activity becomes framed as an event' that is, when it becomes identified as something one 'has' when one reflects on one's self or invokes memory narratives of the self (Berlant 1997: 288). The project is not then about 'revealing' women's 'true' experiences, but about identi-fying the politics of gender, nation and migration and the power dynamics that constitute and normalise particular categories of difference that then get produced as Irish women's 'experience'.

The book

This book takes the question of the relationships between women and the Irish diaspora and locates it in the context of late twentieth-century modernity. Chapter 1 locates the study in framework of Irish modernity(ies). It argues for a refocusing of debates on Irish modernity(ies) towards the practices and positionings of differently located Irish women. It also traces the ways in which the diaspora reproduces global Irish modernity at the end of the twentieth century. In Chapter 2, the gendered narratives of Irish modernity are investigated with reference to the technologies of domesticity, family, reputation, individualism and global citizenship. The changing constructions of the category 'Irish women' over the latter half of the twen-tieth century are traced through the accounts of women in Ireland and London. Although in previous work I have tried to integrate my discussion of Traveller and settled women's accounts, I decided that the specificities of the category 'Traveller women' and its lived effects required the kind of analysis and contextualisation made possible only by devoting a specific chapter to this topic. I am conscious that this decision potentially re-inscribes the category 'Traveller women' as intelligible only outside of the category 'Irish women', but I see it also as a means of interrogating the conditions of Irish modernity based on how Traveller women are positioned and posi-tion themselves within (and outside) Irish modernity. Chapter 3 compares the anti-nomadism that operates in relation to Traveller women with official celebrations of global mobilities. It identifies the ways in which technologies of nation, family, femininity, reputation, individualism and multiculture are operative in the production of the category 'Irish Traveller women' as the 'constitutive outside' of the category 'Irish women'.

In Chapter 4, the dynamics of migrant/non-migrant women's relationships are examined in relation to questions of home and belonging in global modernity. This chapter looks at how possibilities of living bi- and multi-nationally might lead to new techniques and practices of differentiation between migrant and non-migrant women. Chapter 5 considers the topic of women and the Irish diaspora from the perspectives of the migrant women in London. It focuses on how these women construct their migrant Irish belongings as the outcomes of their individual choices and through refusal of particular classed and generational sites and practices of diasporic Irishness in London. This chapter also considers how collective Irish belonging in London is 'lived' in the accounts of these 1980s women migrants. Chapter 6 investigates how 'whiteness' or looking 'white' might be constitutive of particular modes of Irish belonging. Racialised belonging is examined with reference to both country of origin and of settlement and the relationships between these countries in the women's accounts. Chapter 7 offers a reading of the trope of the 'global Irish family' which is promoted by the current President of Ireland, Mary McAleese. By way of conclusion, this chapter brings together the themes identified in each of the preceding chapters to argue that new modes of Irish cultural belonging are being held out to Irish women (settled and Traveller) in Ireland and the diaspora, not least through discourses of global nomadic citizenship and the globalisation of feminist politics. The chapters that make up this book do not unfold in a unified narrative of women and the Irish diaspora, but offer different 'takes' on this topic through the women's own accounts and their many different locations, positionings and perspectives. The book therefore offers a differentiated account of women and the Irish diaspora as shaped by the conditions of global modernity and differently located women's engagements with these conditions.

1 'Women', the diaspora and Irish modernity(ies)

Theories of modernity tend to assume that it is a 'culture neutral operation' in which reason, industrialisation and increased mobility transform all cultures (Taylor 2000: 365). In most of these theories 'development' takes place through modernisation and 'tradition' is displaced by urbanisation, industrialisation and the rise of scientific reason (ibid.). However, instead of displacing tradition, modernity produces it. This is because tradition only gains meaning as 'tradition' through discourses of modernisation and change (Gibbons 1996). Neither can tradition be understood as unchanged remnants of the past in the modern because, like modernity, tradition is continually changing and taking on new meanings and significance (Benjamin 1973; Gilroy 1993a; Felski 1995). Instead of being the opposite of modernity, tradition is integral to it and is unevenly transmitted from the past and reimagined in the present (Gilroy 1993a). Although described as linear, progressive and liberatory, modernity brings with it contradictory social, political and cultural effects, often characterised as the 'condition of modernity' (McCarthy, C. 2000). One effect of the progressive and modernising drive of modernity is its perceived threat to the familiar, which produces a sensibility of dislocation and ambiguity (Berman 1983).[1] Home and belonging are rendered unstable in the conditions of modernity (see Chapter 4), so that the displaced and ambiguous subjectivity associated with migrancy is often posited as emblematic of modern subjectivity (Chambers 1994; Rapport and Dawson 1998).

Practices and institutions of modernity such as industrialisation, urbanisation and state craft have different histories, conditions of emergence and effects in different parts of the world (and even in different parts of the same country) so that instead of speaking of modernity, it may be more accurate to speak of multiple modernities. For example, in different modern societies, traditions and religious practice persist in diverse configurations alongside modernising forces and are often sustained by these forces. The question is how these different constellations of practices and relations to time might be thought in ways that do not constitute some as 'belated' (Felski 2000). Rita Felski argues that 'women's access to specific forms of modern subjecthood is indeed 'belated' precisely because they are constituted as such via the distinctly modern notion of separate spheres which renders it difficult for women to participate in public life (ibid.: 26).

Sociological accounts of modernity tend to rely on male exemplary figures and practices that are based on an autonomous male individual 'free of familial and communal ties', while women are aligned with the domestic and with those aspects of tradition that the 'newly autonomous and self-defining subject must seek to transcend' (Felski 1995: 2). Yet, the relationship between the feminine and modern cannot be understood purely in terms of the positioning of women as belated, marginal or absent because women appear unevenly and in contradictory ways in the self-understanding of modernity (Felski 2000; Lowe and Lloyd 1997). For example, the figures and practices of 'the Irish mother' and 'Irish woman migrant' pervade twentieth-century Irish modernity and are exemplary of the contradictory interpellations and desires that have structured modern Irish subjectivities in the twentieth century. The focus here is less on filling the gaps and more on considering how the feminine and the positioning of women operate interrogatively in the discourses of Irish modernity(ies) (Wolff 2000: 47). The multiple, uneven and contradictory ways in which Irish women are constituted in the narratives of Irish modernity are examined alongside how their own narratives redefine it be revealing the multiple times, spaces and disavowed differences and similarities that mark it. Their narratives cast women's lives at the centre of the (ambivalent) discourses that constitute Irish modernity(ies).

The modern temporality of the 'new', which constantly reasserts itself against much of the evidence, is often figured in gendered terms. For example, the trope of the family figures a 'natural' division of gender and legitimates different notions of progress and the 'new' (McClintock 1993). While 'men come to represent the progressive agent of national modernity (forward-thrusting, potent and historic), embodying nationalism's progressive revolutionary principle of discontinuity', women become 'the atavistic and authentic "body" of national tradition (inert, backward-looking, and natural), embodying nationalism's conservative principle of continuity' (ibid.: 66). But gender does not always operate in such a clear-cut way as an organising metaphor for temporality in modernity. The 'Modern Girl' in Ireland in the 1920s and 1930s became a symbol of emancipation, progress and potential that challenged associations of Irish women with the rural, modesty and the home (Ryan 1998). Also, Irish feminists at the turn of the twentieth century and into the 1920s used modern narratives of progress to position women as agents of history and to challenge the meanings of categories of citizenship, equality, liberty and revolution (Ryan 1994; Valiulis 1995; Ward 1983).

Feminists, as Rita Felski argues, have represented themselves as liberatory agents of the 'new' in ways that affirm modern chronological ideas of development and linear notions of time and often use modern metaphors of revolution and evolution to describe processes of social change (1995: 147). However, in recent years, feminists have critiqued these metaphors as instating a 'male-centered lineage of political modernity' (ibid.: 148). By positioning themselves as liberatory agents of 'the new', feminists, as well as making visible their contribution to modernity, potentially reproduce it within its own terms. At the same time, feminist theory and feminist activism have identified the deeply contradictory rhetoric of modernity based on the complex experiences of women and how they are positioned in relation to 'the old' and 'the new', the 'traditional' and the 'modern'. Although theorists like Walter Benjamin (1973), Marshall Berman (1983), Ajun Appadurai (1996) and Paul Gilroy (1993a; 2000) have in different ways, at different times and in different contexts, elucidated the multi-temporality of modernity, feminists have revealed the ways in which those aspects of modernity that are often represented as the positive and liberatory have in fact contributed to the subordination and marginalisation of some women. For example, the focus of much feminist thought and action has been on women's access to the public sphere as a means of individual and collective liberation. Although access has increased for many women, it has brought with it new practices of gender/sexual regulation and subordination often in and through discourses of women's liberation. Feminism is, therefore, both caught up with the logic of modernity as a thrust towards the 'new' and liberatory, and central to revealing its multi-temporality and the operation of the 'new' and liberatory as a regulatory cultural ideal.

Although traditionally associated with the time-space of the nation, by the end of the twentieth century modernity was increasingly being located in the more fluid times-spaces of the global and represented by metaphors of 'liquidity' and 'scapes' of mobility (Bauman 2000; Appadurai 1996). As the global gains significance as a framework for social life, so social theorists argue that new forms of sociality are emerging based on flows and mobilities. This emphasis on flows and mobilities is one effect of the shift from an industrial to a post-industrial, informational world that is also characterised as 'multicultural' (Featherstone and Lash 1995; see Chapters 3 and 6). Globalisation, seen by some as modernisation theory in disguise, began in and emanates from the West and is identified by some as a theory of Westernisation (Pieterse 1995). Jan Nederveen Pieterse tries to get around the problem of Eurocentrism in discussions of modernity and the global by suggesting 'multiple *paths* to modernisation' (ibid.: 48).

The idea of global modernity acknowledges the extent to which 'the global' has become the imagined context of action. Also, the placing of global and modernity together emphasises what Giddens (1991) identifies as the inherently globalising properties of modernity. Roland Robertson traces the shift to a consciousness of the world as a single place and to discourses of globality that refigure subjective and cultural matters including notions of 'home', 'community' and 'locality' within the context of the global (1992 and 1995). The local or national is not seen as in opposition or as a counterpoint to the global but as inflected by a global consciousness, discourses of globality and practices of mobility. The shift towards analyses of modernity as global represents an attempt to account for greater access to and velocity of mobility in the West at least. I argue that global modernity was emerging as a dominant mode of modernity in Ireland and in some elements of the diaspora in the late twentieth century. The social imagining of time, space and history that marked the 'solid', territorialised modernity of mid-twentieth-century Ireland was being displaced, to some extent at least, by more fluid notions of sociality marked by deterritorialised relations and an increasing consciousness of the global. My main concern is to investigate, through the accounts of migrant and non-migrant women, how these practices and formations are gendered and the implications for feminist politics. However, it is necessary at this stage to locate the categories 'Irish women' and 'the Irish diaspora' within a framework of Irish modernity(ies). My aim in the following section is to identify the significance of domesticity, the 'Irish game of sexuality' and women's migration in reproducing Irish modernity and modern Irish women subjects. In order to achieve this I examine how the ideology of the Irish Catholic family and domesticity[2] has shaped Irish modernisation.

The Irish game of sexuality on 'controlled' and 'globalised' modernities

As noted in the introductory chapter, specific practices and technologies of the domestic, sexuality and migration produced 'regimes of truth' that constituted the category 'Irish women' in certain circumscribed ways.[3] A 'controlled modernity' (Wills 2001) developed in Ireland from the mid-nineteenth to the mid-twentieth century, which positioned Irish women as nurturing, asexual mothers firmly located in the realm of the home and the domestic. Rural Irish women's lives until the 1970s were associated with unremitting hard work, subordination to men on small farms and oppression by the Catholic Church so that emigration was seen as holding the promise of liberation from a sterile country (for an alternative view, see Bourke 1993).[4] With large numbers of young single women emigrating, the Catholic clergy identified emigration to British and US cities as threatening women's moral well being, religion and national identity (Ryan 2001).[5] By the end of the twentieth century, traces of this 'controlled modernity' remained, but a global Irish modernity was gaining ground and producing new icons and practices of Irish femininity. Public discourses of migration, at first glance, seemed less gendered than in the past. Young women as well as men were being constructed as mobile and career-oriented 'young (Irish) Europeans'. Global Irish modernity is gendered in less obvious ways than the 'controlled modernity' of early twentieth-century Ireland. Although some work has been done on questions of women and modernity, the gendering of the modern as global has received much less critical feminist attention. This chapter traces the gendered formations of Irish modernity in the twentieth century as a basis for discussion of how global Irish modernity is gendered in the women's accounts discussed in subsequent chapters.

The dominance of agriculture in the Irish economy until the 1970s reproduced an economic imperative to maintain the small farm 'regardless of the cost to individual family members' (Kennedy 2001: 5). Those practices central to the modernisation of Irish agriculture from the late nineteenth to mid-twentieth century such as postponed marriage, celibacy and migration were negotiated within families (Inglis 1998a). Ireland's economic 'progress' in this period can be seen as having increased familial obligation and communal loyalty rather than promoting individualism or self-expression (Miller 1993).[6] A bourgeois nation-building project based on rural oriented economic imperatives provided the impetus for the promotion and circulation of an asexual family-centred ideology of Irish society (McCullagh 1991; see also Kennedy 2001). This ideology naturalised social inequalities and helped to manage the tensions and injustices within and between families brought about by the inheritance system, the exploitation of family labour by parents and, perhaps most emotively, by emigration (McCullagh 1991). The stem family inheritance system, with one son inheriting the entire farm, meant that other family members, particularly single daughters, were forced to emigrate. Because emigration was 'an enforced requirement rather than a free choice' it was 'a potential source of resentment and tension' (McCullagh 1991: 206).[7] The government Commission on Emigration and other Population Problems, which reported in 1954, emphasised the lack of socio-economic infrastructure in rural Ireland to keep women there, but did not recommend changes to the stem family inheritance system.[8] The accounts of women taking part in this study testify to the intra-family tensions, classed and gendered selves that familial negotiations of migration continue to produce (see Chapter 4).

Modern notions of progress, hygiene and domesticity were integral to the bourgeois Irish stem family and, by the end of the nineteenth century, were promoted by both the Catholic and Protestant Churches, although a Catholic nationalist ideology predominated (Wills 2001). The 'domestication of Irish society', Clair Wills argues, was driven by social mobility and an alliance between Protestant middle-class and official Catholic nationalism around 'the need for the "purification" of lower-class culture' (ibid.: 44). Redefinitions of women's domesticity identified the status of wife and mother as modernisers (Abu-Lughod 1998). Based on notions of scientific management, the home became the 'orderly household of the modern nation' and the site where children were reared and trained as the future citizens (ibid.: 1998: 9). It was in the home that nation building and a politics of modernity came together to position women as the 'civilisers' of future generations. Bourgeois sexual norms were enforced by devaluing partnerships other than marriage and by policing women's reputations. The professionalisation of housewifery represented a means of drafting women into the project of raising citizens and reproducing bourgeois ideals, with women's public personas being interpreted by their effectiveness as housewives and mothers in the private sphere. Discourses of scientific domesticity, although confirming women's place in the home, also gave them 'a quasi-professional status' (ibid.: 12) paving the way into the professions of nursing and teaching for Irish women in Ireland and in the diaspora.

While the ideal of domesticity was encouraged across Europe (Beaumont 1999; Clear 2000; McClintock 1995), in Ireland the concomitant ideal of privacy, which is understood as constitutive of the modern bourgeois individual, was discouraged (Wills 2001). The disavowal in Ireland of modern individualism based on free choice of marriage partners, privacy in sexual practices, romance, pleasure and desire, was based on the perceived threat to the stem family system, social duty and the continuity of land settlement (ibid.). So the reproduction of a territorially rooted, land-obsessed Irish culture relied on an attempted suppression of individualism, companionate marriage and the overt expression of sexual desire. Companionate marriage, in which the individual can expose and work on a sense of individual self, is seen as central to the development of the liberal individual (Taylor 1989 in Wills 2001). Yet, as Wills notes, different sites of familial intimacy, such as intimacy between siblings and other familial relations (identified by Scheper Hughes in her controversial West Kerry study in the mid-1970s) may (albeit via different dynamics) also contribute to the development of the individual self.

Paul Gilroy suggests that 'there are two private spheres rather than one'; the space of sexual intimacy is identified as a profane privacy while the relationship between parents and children constitutes the other more 'wholesome' site of intimacy (2000: 189).[9] Of course one could add relationships between siblings as another 'wholesome' site of privacy and intimacy. Following Gilroy's argument with regard to black identity, these 'wholesome and profane privacies' can be seen as competing loci in which the meanings of Irish identity were established (ibid.). Indeed, it could be argued that the suppression of sexual privacy and privileging of 'wholesome' family privacies (variously represented as sibling or parent/child) has been central to the production of Irish uniqueness. The private sphere of sexual intimacy was suppressed by the construction of 'the Irish body . . . as worthless, endangering, and constantly threatened' (Herr 1990: 22).[10] The deployment of sexuality through the regulations and principles of the Catholic Church and state-sanctioned inheritance and legal systems established 'a sexual self which denied sex to itself' (Inglis 1997: 13). In Scheper Hughes' study, young people would not talk about 'sexual love or intimacy themes . . . romance or marriage stories', but instead tried to 'defuse or desexualize situations in which the sexes are proximate in contact' (1979: 125).[11] Yet, the extent of state and church efforts to regulate sexual practices and the censorship legislation of the 1920s and 1940s point to the impossibility of encouraging modernisation through domesticity while 'denying exploration of the pleasure of intimacy – sex, love and romance – which went along with it' (Wills 2001: 51).

The logic of practice does not always correspond to the logic of discourse (Inglis 1997: 16). The assumed docility of women subjects was not always forthcoming as the evidence of sexual behaviour in Ireland indicates. Some studies of women's migration suggest that the state and church 'controlled modernisation' of early to mid-twentieth-century Ireland, while attempting to prohibit a culture of sexual pleasure and romance, did not prevent it (see Callanan 2002; Lambert 2001; Ryan 2001 and 2002). Migration operated both as another regulating practice that helped eliminate evidence of non-marital sexual activity in the space of the Republic of Ireland and as a tactic in the Irish game of sexuality. Representations of 'respectable' Irish family-hood throughout the twentieth century would not have been sustainable without the migration of those rural and working-class women who became pregnant outside of marriage (Callanan 2002). Middle-class women in similar circumstances had more options in Ireland (ibid.). Many women whose sexual practices offended the ideal of the Irish respectable family migrated as a means of 'keeping up appearances' of propriety and family reputation (see Garrett 2000; Jackson 1963; Kennedy 1973; Lambert 2001; Neville 1995; Ryan 2002; Smyth 1992b).[12] Migration would appear to have operated both as a resource in concealing pregnancy and as a means of expanding sexual possibilities for many Irish women.

Marella Buckley argues that England has been central to Irish women's 'inner picture of the reproductive life-choices' (1997: 122). Most Irish women, she suggests, 'know that if they needed an abortion or a non-accusatory climate for childbirth or a relationship, one available option is to try to get to England to find it' (ibid.). This, Buckley argues, marks their potential and actual migrations as different from those of Irish men. Indeed, the prohibition on abortion in Ireland into the twenty-first century operates as a sign of Irish Catholic specificity in Europe and bears the burden of ensuring that a global modernity does not obliterate Irish uniqueness (Martin 2000). This was most evident during the 1992 Maastricht referendum campaign which invited the Irish people to ratify an EU treaty that involved greater political and fiscal integration. Although about 5,000 women were travelling to Britain for abortions annually at the time, the debate focused almost entirely on ensuring that greater integration in the EU would not threaten Ireland's position on abortion (for more detailed discussion, see Smyth 2000; Smyth 1992b; Martin 2000; and Taylor 1996).

Ireland's modernity until the 1970s at least was marked by the promotion of a non-individualistic domestic ideal, which had specific implications for constructions of Irish femininity.[13] Migration represented one of the routes through which individualism and the pleasures of sexual intimacy were pursued. Because migration was indirectly represented in terms of desire, autonomy, and sexual opportunity, Irish women migrants in the first half of the twentieth century were identified as a threat to a communally oriented Irish modernity. Church, state and media anxieties about women migrants' potential sexual behaviour effectively projected a pleasure-oriented Irish modernity onto the diaspora. Although family formation in Ireland was tightly controlled, it also unleashed a desire for individual freedom and sexual pleasure, which, although thwarted in Ireland, could be imagined or lived through the diaspora. However, there is some evidence that Irish migrant women's experiences were also dominated by the cult of domesticity and Catholic Church efforts in their countries of destination to prevent the development of individualism and the occupation of a sexual self (Callanan 2002; Lambert 2001; Lee 1990; Nash 1993a and 1997b).

The modernisation of farming and the increasing pervasiveness of media and consumer culture in the 1960s and 1970s led to an intensification of the ideology of domesticity and a spread of values of individualism (Beale 1986: 47). Hannon and Katsiaouni (1977) found open emotional relationships and modern patterns of decision-making in nearly one-third of the rural families studied in the 1970s with women holding high expectations of companionate marriage. A series of EU surveys conducted during the 1970s and 1980s noted the dominance of the 'traditional model of women in the home in Ireland', but also the increasingly favourable attitudes towards equality with men (Galligan 1997: 117).[14] With the expansion of a service-based economy, the number of women in the paid workforce rose by 170 per cent between 1971 and 1997.[15] In the 1980s, Irish modernity was marked by paradoxical relationships to questions of sexual morality, marriage and the family; while typical of 'liberal European patterns', there was also an 'adherence to traditional conservative values' (Whelan 1994: 214). Individualism and liberal economic discourses of the national challenged the ideology of the 'traditional Irish family', but did not undermine it. It re-circulated in New Right anti-abortion and anti-divorce campaigns in the 1980s and 1990s in which gender relations and women's bodies became the markers of Irish specificity and authenticity.

With the rise of individualism came a concomitant investment in the right to privacy within the marital relationship (see *McGee versus the Attorney General* 1973 on the private use of contraception).[16] Questions of privacy, sexual autonomy and equal rights emerged as publicly contested aspects of Irish femininity and the Irish family from the 1970s. The establishment of the Women's Movement in 1971 and accession to the European Economic Community in 1973 meant that issues of equality and rights to privacy in sexual matters received some public attention.[17] Perhaps most significant of all was the proliferation of broadcast, but also the print media in Ireland since the 1960s, which imaged sexuality in new ways and disseminated multiple narratives of gender and sexual relations. Two distinct if related trends emerged in the 1980s and 1990s with regard to the game of Irish sexuality. First, there was the identification and public punishment of women who were seen as transgressors and second, there was a proliferation of sites of sexuality as resources for the production of the Irish woman self. Some women in Ireland who became more open and public about their sexual practices, rather than 'keeping up appearances' were positioned as sexual transgressors (Inglis 2002). A number of women were institutionally brought to account for their 'transgressive' behaviour in the courts, public tribunals and the media in the 1980s and early 1990s (Inglis 2002; Smyth 1994). This practice of revealing and publicly shaming sexually transgressive women represented an attempt at reasserting Catholic Irish values against the perceived liberalisation of sexual norms. The humiliation of these women had the unintended consequence of exposing allegedly 'traditional' Irish values to public scrutiny. A detraditionalisation of the so-called 'Irish' values that regulated the lives of women was already under way so that the public humiliation of these women did not go uncontested in the media at least. By the mid-1990s, the public telling of stories of sexual practices, fantasies, abuses and desires was being encouraged rather than inhibited. These stories were re-presented as resources for the self and sexuality was increasingly deployed by individuals upon their own selves in order to transform themselves (Fraser 1999a: 20). While represented as a more liberal approach than the close control of sexuality in the past, sexuality continued to operate as a regulatory discourse and practice through which sexed and gendered selves were produced. These sexed selves were governed primarily through discourses of testimony, choice and freedom, rather than through silence, constraint and rules. Abortion remains the limit case that continues to mark the specificity of Irish belonging.

Discourses of 'the global' and practices of globalisation constituted the country as a fluid mobile site of global capitalism and culture in the 1990s.[18] By identifying globalisation as an inevitable force outside the control of national governments,[19] it became more difficult for politicians to reconcile the relationship between citizen loyalty and global capitalism. One response was to associate citizen loyalty with the facilitation of the global marketplace through worker flexibility within the space of the nation-state. Irish women's national belonging began to be framed by a discourse of duty to participate in the paid labour force rather than, or alongside maternity.[20] The patriotic was located in business and economic spheres of life marked by flexible relationships to the labour market for women perhaps even more so than for men (see Bauman 2000 and Berlant 1993).[21] Women's lives in the 1990s, as subsequent chapters demonstrate, are structured by the tensions between the promise of participation in the labour force on equal terms, their actual experiences of the workplace, and their continued positioning as the guardians of family life and the mediators of cultural continuity in Ireland and in the diaspora. Late twentieth-century modernity was also marked by new relationships to memory as a site of collective belonging and the diaspora became both a site of memory and gendered belonging. In the following section I identify some of the links between global modernity and discourses of Irishness as diasporic, which emerged in the 1990s.

Emigration and 'the Irish diaspora' in the 1990s

Global modernity can be seen as producing new kinds of cultural imagining, not least when it comes to migration (Gray 2003a and b). My aim here is to offer a brief overview of academic and official discourses of 1980s Irish migration and then consider the discourse of the diaspora as articulated by former President Robinson and by Fintan O'Toole in the *Irish Times* in the 1990s. I examine how the limits of diasporic belonging are tested in debates about voting rights for emigrants in the 1990s. I am interested in how these various and contradictory invocations of the diaspora in the Republic of Ireland at this time simultaneously inscribe and resist a globalising of Irish cultural imagining.

Migration, diaspora and the work of nation

When it came to the 1980s generation of Irish migrants, it was not possible to account for their journeys out of Ireland without reference to the globally mediated country that they were leaving and the global imaginings that structured their mobilities. Richard Kearney characterised this generation as

> a new generation which grew up in the Ireland of the sixties and seventies – a changing culture where television, cinema and popular music exercised a more formative influence than the traditional pieties of revivalist Ireland ... a new breed of urbanized and internationalized youth determined to wipe the slate clean, to start again from scratch.
>
> (1988: 185)

Migration is constructed here less in terms of national failure and exile than as symbolic of a globalised Irish citizenship marked by a cosmopolitan mobility.[22] Because, for the most part, they looked 'white' and spoke English, many corridors of geographic mobility were open to Irish migrants.[23] The high-flying migrant in the 1980s became a symbol of a new and confident country reversing the well-rehearsed narrative of migrants escaping backwardness and underdevelopment for a confident modernity abroad.

Famously, the Minister for Foreign Affairs, Mr Brian Lenihan, in an interview with *Newsweek* noted:

> I don't look on the type of emigration we have today as being in the same category as the terrible emigration of the last century. What we have now is a very literate emigrant who thinks nothing of coming to the United States and going back to Ireland and maybe on to Germany and back to Ireland again. The younger people in Ireland today are very much in that mode ... It [emigration] is not a defeat because the more Irish emigrants hone their skills and talents in another environment, the more they develop a work ethic in a country like Germany or the U.S.,

the better it can be applied in Ireland when they return. After all, we can't all live on a small island.

(in Whelan 1987)

Although primarily a celebration of Irish success through mobility and career choice, a defensive note is struck in the suggestion (which has been refuted based on demographic analysis – see Lee 1990) that 'we can't all live on a small island'. Youth was a much-celebrated aspect of 1980s Ireland, yet these young people were leaving the country. This was not to be the contradiction it seemed because these mobile and skilled young people became emblematic of the nation as global. Youth was diasporic, produced through migration, practices of labour flexibility and globalised narratives of career advancement and potential return. The Republic of Ireland was repositioned as young, European and 'out there' encapsulated by the Industrial Development Authority (IDA) slogan 'The Republic of Ireland: We're the Young Europeans'.[24] One member of the diaspora, well-known in the arts world in London, suggested that the 1980s generation of migrants 'consider themselves as what they truly are, namely, Europeans of Irish origin who have considerable talents and skills . . . to offer to create wealth which, in turn, should ensure a better society for all' (O Cathain 1989: 180). Progressive Democratic Party TD,[25] Michael McDowell,[26] suggested that 'in our new situation as part of the mainstream of Western European economic liberalism . . . "emigration" becomes "migration". Capital, labour and enterprise are mobile – and they are moving' (1989: 126–7). He went on to argue that 'our index of fairness . . . must come to terms with liberal market forces' which, he suggested, were being forced on Ireland by outside forces such as the European Union (McDowell 1989: 128; see also Heckler 1989: 162).

The neo-liberal ideologies of small government which dominated British and US politics in the 1980s contributed to a repositioning of the individual citizen in a global economic market and the new work of nationalism became the enabling of individualisation and global mobility of goods, finance and people in certain circumscribed contexts. Although the politico-economic approach adopted in the Republic of Ireland in this decade involved social-democratic elements it was also marked by the neo-liberal ideology[27] that circulated as part of the global 'ideoscape' (Appadurai 1996). By the late 1980s the route to national economic and social success was seen as through deeper European integration and internationalisation (O'Donnell 1999 in Kirby 2002). Minister Brian Lenihan's speech quoted above and the state-sponsored IDA 'young Europeans' slogan publicised Irish youth, individualism and mobility as global resources.[28] However, this celebration of mobility and migration did not go unchallenged and some members of the Catholic Church were at the forefront of contestation (see, for example, Casey 1989: 36). A discourse of migration as a form of social exclusion was articulated by Tríona Nic Giolla Choille, who argued that migration was the 'direct result of the failure of the social and economic policies of successive governments' (Nic Giolla Choille 1989: 52; see also Mac Laughlin 1994).[29]

Mary Robinson and the Irish diaspora

In the mid-1970s, the idea of a culturally diverse Irish nation in which the diaspora became the site of diversity emerged among intellectuals and academics and circulated in newspapers, pamphlets and periodicals (Böss 2002). A critique of Ireland based on the view that economic modernisation was 'the product of the Irish bourgeoisie acting in collusion with British and American capital, with the result that Ireland was kept in a state of economic and cultural dependency' was articulated in the pages of *The Crane Bag* and in the publications of the *Field Day* launched in 1980 (ibid.: 140).[30] Academic, Richard Kearney's notion of a non-territorial and post-nationalist Ireland often symbolised by the diaspora represented an attempt to bring global and local together in a new formulation of Irish belonging. His ideas on 'the fifth province'[31] and the diaspora were incorporated in the inaugural speech of President Robinson and set the tone of many of her subsequent speeches.

Although a diasporic impulse has been central to some nationalist traditions for centuries and the 1916 Proclamation refers to Ireland's friends 'at home and abroad',[32] the diaspora was most publicly embraced in the 1990s as a means of transnationalising the very meaning of the Irish nation. This strategy of embracing emigrants and their descendants was also adopted by many other 'emigrant countries' at the turn of the twentieth century to position the national as global (Smith 2001).[33] The idea of the nation as diasporic circulated in official and media discourses of Irish identity in the 1990s[34] (see, for example, Gillespie 1997 and 2000; Kearney 1988a, 1990 and 1997; O'Toole 1994 and 1997), but the term 'diaspora' is now most closely associated with former president of Ireland, Mary Robinson.[35]

In one of her many speeches on the diaspora, former President Robinson invoked the deterritorialised figure of the diaspora as a means of destabilising the territorialised politics of nationalisms in Northern Ireland.

> Irishness is not simply territorial. In fact Irishness as a concept seems to me at its strongest when it reaches out to everyone on this island and shows itself capable of honouring and listening to those whose sense of identity, and whose cultural values, may be more British than Irish. It can be strengthened again if we turn with open minds and hearts to the array of people outside Ireland for whom this island is a place of origin ... emigration is not just a chronicle of sorrow and regret. It is also a powerful story of contribution and adaptation ... *our relation with the diaspora beyond our shores is one which can instruct our society in the values of diversity, tolerance, and fair-mindedness* ... If we expect that the mirror held up to us by Irish communities abroad will show us a

single familiar identity, or a pure strain of Irishness, we will be disap-
pointed . . . we will miss the chance to have that dialogue with our own
diversity which this reflection offers us.

(Robinson 1995; emphasis added)

In this speech the diaspora is a trope that enables a radical inclusiveness
and that holds out the potential to incorporate British cultural values alongside Irish values. Mary Robinson posits the diaspora as a resource that can
harness qualities of adaptation to the 'new' and values that embrace difference, the unfamiliar and 'impure'. Such values are implicitly offered as
antidotes to the perception that values of purity, sameness and a refusal of
difference marked the conflict in Northern Ireland. This speech locates
diversity and difference first within the space of the island of Ireland which
is identified as incorporating those who identify as British as well as Irish
and second in the diaspora which is positively marked by its multiplicity,
impurity and difference.

As well as symbolising diversity, mobility and connection, the Irish diaspora also figures fixity and continuity. With the potential undermining of
cultural specificity through globalisation and Americanisation, concerns
about cultural continuity and uniqueness took on a new sense of urgency
in the 1990s (Laffan and O'Donnell 1998: 174). One way of making the
diaspora a marker of continuity is to locate it simultaneously in the past and
present; in memory and in remembering. In her speech at the Famine
commemoration ceremonies in Millstreet, Co. Cork, in 1997, former president Robinson noted that the event was

> a dignified commemoration of all those who died during the Great
> Famine of 1845–50 and . . . a tribute to those who succeeded in their
> terrible journey to the New World . . . The miserable epic of the Atlantic
> crossing in these years has been *told so often and well* that it hardly
> seems necessary to recount its dreadful details . . . In its way *the memory*
> of the emigrant steerage has long been held as an icon in Ireland's
> oppression . . . but we must also remember that most Irish emigrants
> made it safely to the other side during the famine years and initiated
> *the creation of a new, Irish, Diaspora.*

Commemoration represents an important site for the staging of cultural continuity at a time of rapid social change in Ireland. The narrative of the Great
Famine produces both victim and survivor identities. These narratives of
Irishness have been told so often that their repetition has itself become a tradition. But this is a 'determinedly nontraditional tradition' (Gilroy 2000: 131)
because it is not based on a simple repetition as the many Famine commem-
orative events in Ireland and the diaspora in the mid-1990s demonstrate.[36]
The repeated calling up of the Famine in many sites and contexts of
commemoration, including the above speech, forces us to rethink narratives

of Irishness as mutable and varied. But the act of commemoration in this speech locates memory in the present and emigration in the past so that by juxtaposing 'us now' and 'them' during and after the Famine, it channels the present through the past to produce strength in continuity and confidence in change as a modern and progressive 'new, Irish diaspora' is asserted.

Fintan O'Toole, like former president Mary Robinson, is an exponent of the diaspora as a reflection of the potential for a pluralist, mobile and progressive modern Ireland. However, in one *Irish Times* article written by O'Toole, the diaspora becomes the backward 'other' of the modern Irish nation. In this article he contrasted the St Patrick's Day parade in Dublin and in New York noting how 'exuberant, ironic and playful' the Dublin parade was indicating 'what a smart lot we are' (O'Toole 1998: 9). This is compared with the 'religious exclusivity, intolerance and smug, swaggering power' of the New York parade (ibid.). The active exclusion of the Irish Lesbian and Gay Organisation (ILGO) from the New York St Patrick's Day parade and the open inclusion of gays and lesbians in the parades in Ireland is identified as indicative of progressive modernisation in Ireland. He goes on to suggest that 'Irish state institutions' should 'push for a re-imagining of what is, after all, the world's largest display of Irish values and aspiration'. If this does not happen, he continues, 'shouldn't we [in Ireland] have the courage to dissociate ourselves from it?' (ibid.). It is 'our' global and progressive modernity that is compromised by this non-pluralist ritual of Irishness in New York. The deployment of the diaspora as a sign of 'what a smart lot we are' in Ireland points to the significance of the homeland/diaspora 'contact zone' in constituting 'modern Ireland'. As the Irish 'at home' embrace global modernity, notions of cultural stasis are identified with ethnic enclaves in the diaspora.

Because no culture can create itself anew all the time, modernity relies on the past and elements of tradition that 'acquire new meanings in new temporal frames' (Felski 2000: 70). Perhaps the appeal of the diaspora is that it accommodates the impulses towards cultural continuity and globalising of Irish culture simultaneously. Indeed, the complexity of Irish global positioning means that discourses of the nation/diaspora produce multiple and often contradictory readings and effects. For many in the Republic of Ireland, the abstract notion of a multi-located, multi-generational diaspora was an 'imagined community' too far and was largely dismissed in popular opinion as a banal aspect of Irish life (Byrne 1995; Lloyd 1999). Yet, this discursive intervention has impacted on the national public imagination and politics[37] as, for example, in the framing of US interventions in the peace process;[38] media representations of Irish people and culture; and the amendment to the Irish constitution following the Belfast/Good Friday Agreement which officially recognises the Irish 'living abroad'.[39] In 1998, the Taoiseach, Bertie Ahern, in a speech in Dublin Castle adopted President Robinson's invocation of the diaspora as symbolic of a culturally diverse Irish nation:

I believe that Irish culture is at its best when it is both inclusive and generous. There is no exclusive definition of what it means to be Irish, nor should there be. The diversity of heritage and traditions of the Irish people, and the special position of the Irish diaspora, will be specifically acknowledged in the changes to the Constitution provided for in the Good Friday Agreement.

(quoted in Böss 2002: 155)

The language and sentiment of the President's speeches are mimicked in this speech on Irish identity and culture in the late-1990s. As Böss notes the 'special position' once attached to the Catholic Church[40] was being transferred to the diaspora marking a political conversion to the 'idea of a plural nation' (ibid.: 156).

Diaspora as invoked in the Republic of Ireland reflects three of the key themes in diaspora studies. First, it opens up a space for re-imagining belonging and identity based on diversity, multiple affiliations and multi-located identifications, thereby heralding new political imaginaries (Appadurai 1996; Bhabha 1994; Brah 1996; Fortier 2000; Gilroy 1993a; Hall 1990). Second, the 'elective affinity' between diaspora and globalisation can result in complicity between diaspora and neo-liberal practices of globalisation (Cohen 1995; Grewal and Kaplan 1994; Kaplan 1996). Third, the emergence of diaspora as a new form of cultural nationalism based on an assumed 'ethnicity' or 'nation' in common, often through practices of commemoration, undermines the potential of diaspora for figuring multi-culture, multi-locatedness and diverse affiliations (Anthias 1998; Brown 1998; Olwig 2000; Soysal 2000).[41] Diaspora as discourse, trope and practice therefore needs to be investigated within specific, local, cultural and temporal contexts. Although the notion of diaspora potentially undoes the binaries of migrant/non-migrant, 'home'/'away', I argue that the empirical and 'lived' distinctions between migrant and non-migrant, notions of 'home' and 'away', the interaction of these binaries with categories of gender, class and generation in the diaspora need to be kept in play. Diaspora, as Avtar Brah (1996) suggests, offers a broad frame within which to examine the ways in which these categories and the 'lived' experiences of them are changing and impinge upon one another, often with unintended effects.

The limits of diasporic belonging

Although the discourse of diaspora can be seen as opening up the idea of the nation, citizenship rights impose official limits to Irish belonging as is evident in debates about votes for emigrants. With the exception of Ireland, all other EU countries have taken measures to ensure that their citizens abroad are enfranchised. In the 1980s and 1990s, Irish emigrant groups organised in Britain and the US to campaign for the right to vote in national elections.[42] A Private Members' Bill on voting rights for emigrants introduced to the

Dáil[43] in 1991 was defeated 66–62 mainly because of a combination of the alleged administrative and constitutional problems involved.[44] As the campaign gathered momentum, Coalition governments in 1992 provided for a review of this issue in their programmes for government. In December 1994, the government committed itself to providing for the election of three *Seanad* (Upper House) members by a newly established constituency of Irish emigrants. A consultation paper including the text of the constitutional amendment, which used the term 'non-resident citizens' rather than 'emigrant citizens', was issued in March 1996. The government decided against proceeding with the proposals due to the divergence of views expressed in responses and shifted the matter off the political agenda by referring it for the consideration of the All-Party Committee on the Constitution.[45]

Arguments against enfranchising emigrants ranged from the disproportionate influence they might have on the outcome of elections to their being out of touch with 'modern Ireland'. Although the proposal was to enfranchise only those resident outside of Ireland for less than 20 years, one article estimated that an extension of votes to emigrants would add about 400,000 voters thereby increasing the electorate by about 15 per cent (Moore 1994).[46] Another factor was the perception in Ireland that emigrants were Republican in their politics and would skew the political complexion of the electorate (ibid.). There was also considerable resistance to the idea of those who did not pay taxes in Ireland influencing taxation and social welfare arrangements. Senator and media commentator, Shane Ross, in the (Irish) *Sunday Independent* (12 December 1995: 15) expressed the view that '[e]migration is a *personal* tragedy for those hundreds of thousands of Irish families who have lost children, brothers, sisters and grandchildren. But it is not a *political* disaster' (emphasis added). The implication was that emigration was 'a family affair' rather than a state responsibility or political issue. An *Irish Times* editorial noted the discomfort produced by this question.

> The debate provided yet more evidence of the unease and passion, even the guilt with which emigration is discussed in this country. Some of the choicest hypocrisies are reserved for it. Lamented in many a speech, it has nonetheless been extolled as a safety valve protecting social stability; or lately as a necessary preparation for middle-class careers, as if involuntary emigration was a thing of the past.
>
> (*Irish Times*, 5 April 1996: 13)

A further argument against enfranchising emigrants was the construction of emigrants as 'out of touch' and having lost any 'authentic' relationship to Ireland. Senator Ross, in the *Seanad* debate on this topic, argued that emigrants 'would hold us hostage when they knew nothing about this country. This is utterly and totally barmy, it is crazy' (Representation of Emigrants Debate, *Seanad*, 3 April 1996: 2110). In a different vein, Senator Norris's contribution to the debate identified the diaspora in the US as living in a fantasy world.

I was in America last month and celebrated St. Patrick's Day in Denver
... it was interesting to see the interest focused on Ireland, some of it
highly amateur and inaccurate. I heard leprechauns talking for the first
time and I can inform the House that they spoke with Mexican accents.

(Representation of Emigrants Debate,
Seanad, 3 April 1996: 2114)

Members of the diaspora were not seen as credible citizens in this contribution because of their distorted and sentimental relationship to Ireland. One
letter to the *Irish Times* echoed Norris' remarks noting that '[a] sentimental
attachment to Ireland, expressed from a distance of many miles and years,
should be no qualification for participating in Irish government' (Ben
Hemmens 1996: 17). The Irish abroad, then, were officially represented as
ineligible for full citizenship because of their numerical potential to distort
Irish politics, their alleged ignorance of national issues, their fantastic images
of Ireland, their extreme politics and their sentimentality, all characteristics
that rob them of the 'reasonableness' and 'responsibility' that are seen as
central to full citizenship.

In contrast to these representations of emigrants as out of touch, backward and nostalgic, those supporting the campaign in the *Seanad*, such as
Senator Magner, pointed out that

We are merely talking about extending the right to vote in this country
to passport-holding citizens of the Irish State who happen to be domi-
ciled, permanently or semi-permanently, abroad. They are not only
emigrants, they are citizens.

(Representation of Emigrants Debate,
Seanad, 3 April 1996: 2039)

His contribution counters the logic of arguments which imply a non-
compatibility of the categories 'emigrant' and 'citizen', or which represent
emigrant status as a diminishing of citizen status. Senator Dardis' intervention
also questioned whether the category of citizen could be disaggregated into
individuals with different citizenship status, noting that 'the issue should be
that citizens are full citizens and there are not different categories of citizens;
it is irrelevant where they live' (Representation of Emigrants Debate, *Seanad*,
3 April 1996: 2103).

Representatives of the campaign for electoral representation for emigrants
in the US and Britain emphasised the potentially progressive and modernising
influence of emigrants on Ireland. Emigrants' connection with the modern
world and their origins in a modern Ireland come together to position
them as a modern resource to a modern country in much of the campaign
literature. Dave Reynolds, a leader of the British campaign, suggested
that like most Irish emigrants, he hoped to return and went on to assert that
being an emigrant did not mean that he was not sharing in 'modern Irish

life'. Instead of being distant, sentimental and out of touch, he suggested that emigrants were very much engaged with a developing and modernising Ireland.[47] He also emphasised the economic power of the Irish abroad who owned many businesses, investments and properties in Ireland, so that '[t]he modern Irish identity owes much of its recognition to emigrants and children of emigrants' (Reynolds 1995: 106). In response to the shelving of proposals for emigrant representation in the *Seanad*, one letter to the *Irish Post*[48] suggested that '[e]migrants appear destined to occupy only the St. Patrick's Day constituency, when government ministers jet all over the world to pay lip service to them' (Michael Hurley 2 November, 1996: 10).

The assumption that formal political equality and citizenship presupposes cultural identity in common (Stolcke 1995) is complicated in debates around votes for emigrants. The limitations of discourses of the Irish diaspora, which assume some recognisable strand of culture in common, are revealed in debates about votes for emigrants, which reproduce discourses of cultural differentiation between entitled resident citizens and less entitled 'non-resident citizens'. Discourses of the Irish diaspora in the 1990s constructed a global Irish belonging in common based largely on a history of emigration which facilitated some transnational political alliances, for example, in relation to Northern Ireland, but which were not seen as providing a basis for political claims making in relation to the southern state. The limits of political and cultural belonging in common between resident and non-resident citizens were tested in these debates as were the limits of the category 'citizen'. Discourses of political belonging in the Republic of Ireland differentiated between territorialised and de-territorialised cultures of Irishness, with territorialised cultural practices being the basis for and marker of political rights.

Conclusion

This chapter has located the question of women and the Irish diaspora in a context of changing formations of Irish modernity. It has identified the significance of categorization and classification as central aspects of modernity and the need to investigate the changing operation of social categories. It has also pointed to the gendered social, political and cultural effects of these changing conditions of modernity. These changing formations of modernity cannot be accounted for in a linear or progressive narrative because they are marked by multiple temporalities and spatialities and by changing (if not always more liberating) games of sexuality. The regulation of women's bodies via notions of the ideal Irish family emerges as a central marker of Irish modernity and one that is interrogated in my analysis of the women's accounts in the chapters that follow. By locating the categories 'women' and the 'diaspora' in a context of an emerging global Irish modernity, this chapter raised questions about how notions of 'home', authenticity, migration and belonging were being re-negotiated at the end of the twentieth century. These questions are taken up from a range of perspectives in the following chapters. In late twentieth-century Ireland, the diaspora emerged as a means of figuring the national as global, but also as a mode of 'living' Irish identity within a deterritorialising global modernity. In the solid, territorialised and 'controlled modernity' of mid-twentieth-century Ireland, women's sexuality and sexual practices were identified as a threat to be regulated with particular effects for how the category 'Irish women' was constructed and lived. In the following chapters I examine the operation of sexuality and gender in relation to the constitution of the category 'Irish women' within the more fluid global modernity of the late twentieth century. If diaspora operates as a trope of both global mobility and cultural continuity, I ask how this contradictory operation of diaspora reveals itself in women's lives. In Chapter 2, I turn specifically to the category 'Irish women' and locate this category within narratives of twentieth-century Irish modernity as inflected by migration.

2 'Keeping up appearances' and the contested category 'Irish women'

I suppose when I think of Irish women it's a mix. *I see my mother and I see strength* and ... My godmother ... she's artistic ... women like her who are just so individual and creative ... they found some way of expressing their own creativity ... then [another aunt] has spent years on Valium. I look at her and the fact that she's been on that medication for so many years and how limited her life was ... Some of my mother's neighbours, one in particular who's been a Charismatic, she's still very strongly Catholic, she's also an alcoholic, she's very embittered about the choices her children have made and ... she's staunchly campaigned against divorce and so on, and yet, she's very compassionate on an individual basis. And I see that side of Irish women being stolen in a sense ... *by keeping up these appearances* to be the defenders of this faith and the defenders of this family and not asking at what cost to themselves and to the families ... For me, it's the Irish women who have got up and campaigned and Irish feminists that I identify with most strongly and feel a huge degree of gratitude towards them ... I feel a certain ... frustration about the aspects of Irish identity that are so strongly allied with being Catholic and being Catholic Irish or nationalist Irish ... there's a lack of recognition that there are Irish feminists, that there are Irish atheists, that there are Irish Jews ... a wider range of people who are Irish ... and are so cut off ... in the last couple of years there's been more open debate and discussion ... it's changed ... in some ways, without any real depth to it ... and I've encountered a certain reluctance to talk about things, I get told 'that's all changed it's different now' and you're thinking 'it's the same as back then'. ... So I do find myself, when I'm there for a while, getting really angry and *wanting to leave in another way.*

(Maeve, interview, London)

In order for post-independence society in the south to appear Catholic and Irish, women could inhabit the category 'Irish women' only in certain permitted ways. Women's belongings in Ireland in the twentieth century were circumscribed by a Catholic nationalist ideology of the family that idealised rural life, domesticity, and mothers whose 'unmediated naturalness' linked them mimetically with the 'natural' existence of an Irish nation

(Coughlan 1991: 90). By the latter decades of the twentieth century, the symbolic figure of 'Mother Ireland' had faded as a nationalist symbol in the south and was 'decried by the agents of modernity as a residue of atavistic Victorian celticism' and romantic nationalism now past (Lloyd 1999: 94).[1] However, as noted in the previous chapter, the bodies of Irish women, and mothers in particular, were constituted anew as sites of contestation over the specificity of Irish identity and an 'authentic' national 'we' in debates about contraception, divorce and abortion.[2]

In Maeve's account above, the imperative to 'keep up appearances' robbed women of their diversity, creativity, vulnerability, compassion and potential. Alcohol, Valium and the Charismatic movement emerge in her account as the means by which some women were able to reproduce the appearance of faith and family as defining features of Irishness. 'Strength' identified with her mother also lines up with the gendered imperatives of Irishness as Catholic, stoical and family oriented. Maeve's account implies that these women's 'potential selves' are unrealised and thwarted by the gendered requirements of Irish belonging. Irish feminists in Maeve's account represent a threat to these 'regimes of truth' concerning Irish women's conduct. Like Irish Jews and atheists,[3] she suggests that feminists are not recognised as 'authentically' Irish. A further mode of (dis)engagement with the gendered imperatives of Irish modernity was to emigrate. Maeve's migrant perspective on events in Ireland is not welcome (during her return visits) because 'it's different now'. Her desire to leave suggests a kind of 'voting with her feet' in which migration becomes a means of claiming recognition not available to her in Ireland. Her migrancy, instead of being intelligible as a response to social constraint in Ireland or a desire for recognition, is identified in Ireland with an 'out of date' Irishness. Her return visits confirm her experience of exclusion and non-recognition and become re-stagings of her desire to leave. Maeve's challenging of 'appearances' makes her an unwelcome guest. She defines the work of 'keeping up appearances' as the responsibility of Irish women. But how is this achieved? How do the 'truths' of Irish identity become attached to women's behaviour and what struggles, promises and threats were involved in the reproduction of these 'appearances'? What relations of domination, subordination, allegiance and distinction were made possible by the gendered imperative to keep up appearances? In what ways has feminism intervened and with what effects?

In this chapter I consider the implications of what is seen as a shift from a church and state 'controlled' Irish modernity to a mass-mediated global Irish modernity for how migrant and non-migrant women occupy the category 'Irish women'. Clair Wills (2001) argues that the lives of Irish women in the first half of the twentieth century were structured in and through a 'controlled modernity' that offered them conditional citizenship based on a particular ideology of domesticity. My aim here is to investigate how the category 'Irish women' was inhabited, refused and performed in the 1990s and what this has to tell us about the production of the gendered Irish self at this time. If the nation's virtue and value were located in the domestic zone of the family until the 1960s at least, and especially in the domain of the Irish mother, where was the virtue of the nation located in the 1990s?

Irish femininities in the 1990s

Women from Catholic backgrounds who took part in my research repeatedly identified the category 'Irish women' with their own mothers, who for the most part were described as 'strong' women. Although their accounts suggest that Catholicism played a lesser role in their lives than in the lives of their mothers, there is no doubt that it continued to mark the category 'Irish women' with different effects for women who were brought up Catholic and those who were not. Catholicism and family come together as the key sites of Irish womanhood although mediated in most accounts through discourses of liberal individualism and in some accounts by discourses of feminism. My assumption in reading these accounts is that the Irish woman self has its own history (Rose 1996: 295) and is an aggregate of the very techniques (for example, of national identity or individualism) that seek to describe it, or make it intelligible. In most accounts, the category 'Irish women' is unintelligible outside of the interplay of Catholic Church and state regulation which produced a martyred relationship to the self which they identify with their mothers and refuse for themselves. This martyred figure is caricatured in Nora's (a single woman who worked as a senior civil servant) joke.

> 'How do three Irish women change a light bulb?' And the answer is 'Don't mind me I'm all right in the dark'. This is very true, just grin and bear it. It might be strong but it's endurance. And I think it's like the martyr, I've put up with it all. Irish women are strong in the sense that they have succeeded against the odds, but I don't think that they have asserted themselves.
>
> (Nora, interview, Ireland)

The motif of 'Mother Ireland' and the martyred Irish mother circulated in the 1990s as a figure of ridicule and irony. The Irish mother and through this figure the category 'Irish women' was characterised by a relation to the self that was established through a self-conscious endurance. This was not selflessness, but self 'for others', a martyred self[4] constituted by the injunction 'I've put up with it all'. The Irish woman was defined through her familial connection to her children and the domestic realm and represented as the antithesis of individual autonomy. This characterisation of the category 'Irish women' is familiar to Nora but refused by her.

The figure of this martyred Irish mother emerges in Kieran Keohane's essay on music and Irish migration. He identifies the existence of an 'Irish women's culture' that 'has historically been a culture of abandonment, inspired by loss and destitution, a culture of being left behind minding the house' (1997: 281). In a discussion of the mid-1990s two-album collection by Irish women musicians called *A Woman's Heart*, he suggests that they reinscribe the familiar trope of the 'Irish woman as long suffering victim of abandonment' (ibid.: 282). These albums, according to Keohane, represent a conservative desire to preserve the power which resides within this 'tradition' through 'an aestheticisation of Irish women's traditional power' and a 'conservation of the security offered by the familiar' (ibid.). This 'traditional power' is represented in popular and academic literature as arising from the Irish mother's emotional domination and manipulation of her sons who remain indebted to her for all she has done for them (ibid.). This phenomenon, described as 'Irish women's culture' and epitomised by martyred mother figures, comes to represent 'tradition', thereby reducing women to modernity's other and reproducing 'tradition' in the modern as feminine, but also by implying a singular mode of Irish femininity. Abandoned by men, left 'at home' minding the house, the figure of the Irish mother is represented in Keohane's account as embracing a manipulative domestic power that is reproduced by narratives of female victimhood.

Irish Catholic women were interpellated by the ideology of middle-class domesticity which offered one of the few modes of access to authority available to women (albeit largely symbolic) within the new state (Bourke 1993; Inglis 1998a; Wills 2001). For Tom Inglis this site of authority could not be sustained without the support of the Catholic priest.[5] He argues that the 'dependence of mothers on the Church for moral power within the home' helped to maintain a mutually supportive relationship between the mother and Church (1998a: 9). Although facilitating the initial phase of modernisation of Irish society, once the alliance was established between the Church and mother, Inglis argues that it helped to maintain Ireland as a conservative society and delayed its full modernisation until the second half of the twentieth century. The dependence of mothers on men, family and on extra-family institutions such as the Church restricted their own development and is seen as rendering them a conservative force (for alternative views see O'Hara 1997 and O'Connor 2000).[6] The question of how Irish mothers' practices constitute a particular kind of modernity requires more empirical support than Inglis can offer here. His thesis unifies and homogenises the category 'Irish mother' so that the universal 'Irish mother', like 'Mother Ireland', stands in for the diversity of Irish women. In Inglis' account of the Irish mother, power operates to produce the 'truth' of the Irish mother's position as one of freedom and authority in the home. Invited to see herself as having authority within the private sphere, she is bound up in national and church regimes of governmentality, which operate through the ideology of domesticity and her own aspirations. Given the regulation of women's reputations and behaviour and the location of the 'ideal Irish family' at the heart of the nation by the Constitution of the state, it seems misguided to identify women as the conservative force in the way of further modernisation. Indeed, as many of the accounts that follow suggest, survival and the attainment of self-respect and dignity were always at stake for women in a 'controlled modernity' in which women's lives were marked by economic insecurity and the constant threat of exclusion by stepping out of line. Nora's account in which she reflects on the joke about Irish women's martyrdom suggests that autonomy and self-expression have been impermissible relations to the Irish woman self. In many of the women's accounts of their mothers as emblematic of the category 'Irish women', their mothers are constructed less as victims than as resourceful in negotiating the limited permissible narratives of the self available to them.

These accounts emphasise the extent to which the Catholic Church regulated their mothers' lives.

> The image of Irish women to me, and I am looking at my mother's generation . . . a generation of extremely strong women, most of whom had six or more children and ran clubs and . . . various other things . . . and never complained . . . and never said anything about it . . . and they are definitely the people in that country who ran the whole show . . . and they never look for credit and they never get any . . . that is my image of the Irish woman . . . the fifties women.
>
> (Maura, group discussion 2, London)

There are resonances here with the early modern discourse of motherhood, which represents it as an unquestioned duty involving self-sacrifice and suffering (Kaplan 1992).[7] Sacrifice and capacity for hardship are central to Maura's construction of Irish women's strength. This is not an individualistic or self-directed strength, but one that is subordinated to bigger familial and national agendas. Indeed, Rosemary Sayigh argues that the term 'strong' is 'used positively in nationalist discourse to describe women who are active in the movement and who can bear hardship and loss' (1996: 162).[8]

Interestingly, emigrant women of their mothers' generation do not offer reference points for thinking about Irish women as 'strong' in these accounts. Yet, the strength of Irish women is invoked as a resource for continuity and community-building in the diaspora. For example, Hasia Diner's work on Irish migrant women in the US suggests that they brought a strength gained in rural Ireland to the work of 'civilising' the Irish immigrant community in the US through the family. This nationally gendered construction of 'strength' is less to do with physical or bodily strength than with becoming the 'core' of a family and community and keeping it together through constancy and endurance. The constancy of the mother represents the 'timeless' qualities of the national cause. It is women's bodies and minds that become the sites of self-sacrifice and moral regeneration central to the business of nation-building (Duara 1998) and to the project of 'ethnic' community-building and maintenance in the diaspora.

The accounts of women in this study suggest that the Irish mother, though often located outside of history in the timeless realm of tradition, is also firmly within history as a source of agency in the home and in their daughters' lives. Many of their relations with their mothers represent complex sites of creative strength and of (sometimes enabling) anger.

> When I think of being Irish and a woman . . . that again is a huge conflict . . . in terms of the ways that Irish women have been treated in Ireland and the ways it's written into the Constitution[9] . . . that's why I have no time for the church whatsoever . . . it makes me want to fume with anger . . . it affected my mother much more than me and all her existence was about being trampled.
>
> (Cath, interview, London)

Cath's relationship to the category 'Irish women' is marked by her witnessing of the effects of church and state regulation on her mother's life. The category 'Irish women' in the 1990s is produced in the differences between her own and her mother's generation of women. The 'trampling of her existence' by the state (in the Constitution) and Catholic Church suggests less a martyred self than the denial of any form of self. Irish womanhood in the 1990s is inhabited by Cath through conflict and anger about how her mother's life was regulated and the legacy of this regulation in her own life. In common with many accounts she articulates conflicted identifications with the category 'Irish women'.

In contrast to the undifferentiated representations of 'the Irish mother' in some of the sociological literature referred to above, the women's accounts discussed here locate Irish mothers in relation to regulation, repression and diverse forms of resistance which produce complex responses of anger and admiration in their daughters. By distancing themselves from the institutional imperatives that directed their mothers' lives, these accounts instantiate a possessive relationship to the Irish feminine self. Some suggest that they see themselves, in contrast to their mothers, as authors of their own fate. Yet these selves are marked by the legacy of the category 'Irish women' as represented by their mothers' lives.

> I think my mother really epitomises it (Irish womanhood) for me. She wouldn't necessarily be typical of 'the woman in the street', but I just think she also typifies one type of Irish woman, which I think is just great. She was able to actually conform to a certain amount around her, but still be her own person; and that she was able to kind of cut out her way through and enjoy it and be optimistic all the time and for me that's a relatively common role in women. And having said all that, at the same time, I get mad with that sometimes too because it tends to put other people first a lot of the time . . .
>
> (Nell, interview, Ireland)

All of the accounts articulate an ambivalent relationship towards the primarily relational self associated with their mothers. Of course, this is not a specifically Irish phenomenon, as the mother in many cultures 'symbolizes "the unfree woman" whom the daughter dreads becoming' (Rich 1977 in Lawler 2000: 103). There is always a tendency to produce a unified notion of the mother that cannot do justice to the diversity of subject positions that mothers occupy (Lawler 2000). However, in these accounts the figure of the mother is both unified and differentiated, as it is through her that narratives of martyrdom and self *for* others are both projected onto institutional regulation and rearticulated as narratives of strength and resistance thereby opening up a potentially more enabling legacy of Irish womanhood for themselves. This analysis is not an invitation to women to return to their own mothers to 'find new histories of their strength as women' (Steedman 1986: 16), but an opportunity to consider how the institutionalisation of maternity and 'the mother' as archetypical of Irish femininity produces particular relationships to femininity and their mothers in these women's accounts. Carolyn Steedman suggests that the silence of daughters about the burdens placed on them by their mothers may be a measure of the price they 'pay for survival' (ibid.: 17). Although these accounts suggest, to paraphrase Virginia Woolf (1928/1984: 72–3), a thinking back through their mothers, there is a silence about what is negotiated in the gap between how they see their mothers' lives and their own. Their feelings of anger, admiration or indebtedness are articulated in relation to the conditions that constrained their mothers' lives, rather than as aspects of their relationships with their mothers as mothers. Indeed, their mothers are not discussed as mothers, but as 'a generation', a 'type' or 'effect' of institutionalised domination.

However, not all of the women articulated a relationship to the category 'Irish women' via their own mothers in these terms. Hazel, who was brought up in care in Dublin articulates a different relationship to 'the Irish mother' as framed by discourses of 'the Irish family'. Her negative experience of family and state care are intelligible in her account through national cultural practices of 'keeping up appearances' of an ideal Irish family/mother.

> My mother is very rejecting with me, there is no doubt about it . . . And secrets in the family I will tell you, I could write a book on it . . . I think Ireland has been a very cruel country . . . has a very cruel history. If you read the comments of pro-lifers and anti-abortionists and anti-divorce, they are so cruel . . . on the basis of some abstract principal . . . but that's what they do in families. You see, that to me, is the collective expression of what happens in private families in Ireland, what happened in my family, what happened in the children's home I was in. I saw so much cruelty I could not begin to tell you. And I think that I will never recover sometimes . . . my mother had thirteen siblings.

Not one of them came to see me in all the time I was in care. Not one of them ... some of them lived less than two miles from where I was for ten years. But they were too fucking selfishly preoccupied with their own fucking guilt and shame.

(Hazel, interview, London)

Like Maeve's account at the beginning of this chapter, Hazel describes the ways in which compassion is suppressed by the desire to conform to appearances of 'the Irish family'. A daughter or niece in care was a sign of failed familism, a breach of social norms and a source of shame. Ideologies of the Irish family positioned Hazel and members of her family as incompetent citizens through technologies of guilt and shame. Whether identified in terms of strength, resistance, shame or guilt, the subtext of most accounts is a national Catholic 'we'. In Hazel's account, the ideology of the Irish family has the effect of producing secrecy, cruelty and unquestioning loyalty to abstract principals. It mediates her relationship with her mother and to Ireland as a place of belonging.

Although the regulation of Irish women is associated with the Catholic Church in all of the accounts, many women saw a Catholic sensibility as continuing to be a marker of Irishness. Catholicism was not rejected but embraced in some accounts as a habitual and familiar background in common with other 'Irish' people.

Being Irish is being Catholic, from a very young age ... the whole environment is Catholic ... I wouldn't particularly be dogmatically anything, but I feel very *culturally Catholic* ... it's my culture ... I am Catholic till the day I die ... and the chances are that when I'm dying, I'll scream for a priest ...'I'm sorry I'm a lesbian, anoint me with your oils'!

(Joan, group discussion 5, London)

Catholic dogma, although relegated to the past, re-emerges as that which is familiar and Irish and which will ultimately undermine or displace Joan's lesbian identity. Defiance of its dogma and rules does not overcome its banal cultural familiarity.[10] The identification with cultural aspects of Catholicism as 'familiar' and thereby markers of belonging is both self-conscious and non-reflexive. It is self-conscious insofar as Joan has to negotiate her identification with Catholicism and as lesbian. Yet the account does not consider how her identification of Catholicism as a central marker of Irish identity excludes those from non-Catholic backgrounds.

I'd be very much of an 'a la carte' Catholic, yet I don't think I can be called a Catholic ... It's not the institution of Catholicism but the ethos ... I'm *culturally Catholic*.

(Siobhan, interview, Ireland)

Cultural Catholicism is much more difficult to define than an institutional Church-based Catholicism which produces encyclicals, letters and statements. Cultural Catholicism is a sensibility, a sense of shared past (experiences of convent school educations, devout mothers). This 'Catholic' sensibility marks Irish identity as unique and perpetrates and sustains certain exclusions. The accounts of Protestant women reinforce the view that cultural Catholicism continues to reproduce 'authentic Irish belonging'. For Protestant women, a 'banal' Catholicism, but also an institutionalised Catholicism operated as repeated reminders of their outsiderness. Suzy's account locates her within Catholic-oriented state and citizenship practices that mark her as an outsider because she is Protestant.

> ... For me, approaching the divorce referendum (in 1986), both as a Church of Ireland lay reader which I am, and as somebody who's in love with somebody who's separated, and we want to spend the rest of our lives together, there were a whole load of issues I had to address ... I discovered that my country said No, because it was dictated to by a majority church ... the country took a different position to my church ...
>
> (Suzy, interview, Ireland)

Suzy's church and her individual life circumstances are simultaneously disregarded by the performative reproduction of a gendered Catholic Irish citizenship in this referendum. The referendum result[11] reinscribed the 'ideal Irish family' as the only legitimate site of intimate relationships in the Irish Constitution. The referendum is also interpreted in Suzy's account as anti-pluralist because the majority set the parameters of Irish belonging. The instability of Irish Protestant belonging in the southern state is described in Esta's account.

> I had a very different experience ... of growing up Church of Ireland in the South ... my grandmother who would have identified as kind of Northern Irish or British and yet, at the same time, whenever she was talking particularly about politics, I never really knew when she said 'we' or 'I' if she was talking about 'I' as 'Irish', you know, were 'we' Irish, or British, or Northern. And I think there is quite a bit of confusion herself because she lived in the South for about thirty or forty years. So it was not really until I started getting involved in the Women's Movement that I started really feeling that I was Irish and finding my Irish identity and then I emigrated ... in England and America ... when I was there ... I became much more Irish in myself as well ...
>
> (Esta, group discussion 7, Ireland)

The indeterminacy of national identification marks all of the Protestant women's accounts because Protestant belonging in Ireland is always produced in relation to a Catholic national 'order of things' which affects the 'conduct of conduct' in the most intimate practices of everyday life. Identification as Irish is made possible (and sense of Protestant Irish in-authenticity at least provisionally overcome) in Esta's account by the collective political agenda of the women's movement and the encounter with non-Irish others as an Irish migrant. Ironically, what are often identi-fied as 'postnationalist' identifications with feminism or 'ethnicity' become sites of possibility in Esta's account for inhabiting Irish national identity (see also the case of Traveller women in Chapter 3).

In accounting for the category 'Irish women', the legacies of this cate-gory as embodied by their mothers are articulated most explicitly in the accounts of women from Catholic backgrounds. For women from Protest-ant family backgrounds, the dominance of Catholic cultural norms and their influence on state policy legislation emerged as a more defining narrative of their relationships to the category 'Irish women'. While women from Catholic backgrounds felt overdetermined by the category 'Irish women', non-Catholic women articulated ambivalence in relation to their (ex)inclu-sion in this category. However, themes of respectability, reputation and constraint structure the Irish femininities articulated in all of the accounts. Although the Catholic Church monopoly in matters moral and sexual has been fragmented (Inglis 2000), the habitual cultural resonances of Catholi-cism continue to structure Catholic, Protestant and other Irish femininities. The category 'Irish women' in the 1990s is recast in most accounts as a rejection of Irish feminised practices of self-constraint and an embracing of a possessive relationship to the self. The category is seen now as less depen-dent on maternity, self-sacrifice and endurance than it was in the middle decades of the twentieth century. But does this shift from a self 'for others' to a possessive relation to the self fully account for how the category 'Irish women' is constructed and inhabited in the 1990s? Is the gendered imper-ative to 'keep up appearances' of women's self-constraint sexually and socially as a sign of social cohesion a thing of the past? How are notions of the Irish family (and mother) being reworked and with what effects for Irish women?

Feminists, women in paid work and 'women in the home'

In the 1980s and 1990s, new pressure groups emerged to defend family values. In the early 1990s, Nora Bennis became a vigorous campaigner against the introduction of abortion and divorce. After the X case in 1992, which shifted public opinion on abortion onto more sympathetic ground, Bennis was instrumental in establishing a group called 'Women Working in the Home'. She also established the National Party in 1996, the central aim of which was to protect the value of marriage based on the idea that the family is the 'real strength of Ireland as a nation'.[12] 'Women in the home' were identified by the new Right as the losers in this new 'liberal' Irish society and were repeatedly invoked as the moral defenders of faith and nation, unlike their allegedly individualistic career-oriented and feminist sisters. This polarised discursive positioning of Irish women was dramatically staged at an event in which Hillary Clinton addressed a group of publicly active Irish women in Dublin. This event took place very shortly after the Divorce Referendum in 1995, which passed an amendment to introduce divorce by a very tight margin.[13] Finola Bruton, the wife of the then Taoiseach, John Bruton, made a brief speech on family values when introducing Hillary Clinton.

> Now is the time to recognise that the notion of equality does not necessarily give a natural primacy to a professional career over the other choices a woman may make . . . There has been a certain tendency in the women's movement which seeks to exclude or marginalize men . . . there is already clear evidence of a growing number of young men alienated from society . . . we need to affirm that a loving married relationship between a man and a woman is a core value to be recognised, affirmed and supported . . . I believe Irish feminists now have the confidence to develop their thinking, so that it becomes truly inclusive: inclusive of women in the home; inclusive of children; inclusive of men . . .

A language of equality and inclusivity is invoked in this speech to pose Irish women's position as one framed by choice. The term 'equality' is used here to construct all choices as equivalent but choice is then circumscribed as 'the choice' between a heteronormative familial and socially cohesive society and an individualistic feminism that excludes women working in the home, men and children and that presents a threat to social cohesion. Women's careers and feminism are identified as threats to social solidarity. Despite the espoused equivalence of choice, this speech constitutes the heternormative family as having 'natural primacy' above all other choices available to women. This speech and the controversy that surrounded it got more media coverage than any women-related event since the election of Mary Robinson as President in 1990 (Cummins 1996). The media represented the event as a spat between women with 'feminists' being pitted against 'women in the home'.[14] The media coverage of the speech and the angry responses of some women present portrayed Bruton as speaking for the strong, silenced mothers of Ireland.[15] Feminists, in contrast, were portrayed as aggressive and as making a fuss. Feminism was identified as a threat to the Irish family, but also to the figure of the Irish mother who remained, for those on the right at least, symbolically central to the continuity and integrity of the Irish nation.

The 'Finola Bruton speech' arose as a point of reference for thinking about the category 'Irish women' in many of the discussions and interviews in Ireland.

I think of conflict when I think of Irish womanhood. It was well captured with Finola Bruton and Hillary Clinton and I think there has been a difficulty in the women's movement here in Ireland because it didn't attend to the large number of women who are engaged in agriculture ... They (women in the Women's Movement) can't enter into the consciousness of women who are happy and fulfilled running large farms or whatever it is that they are doing. So a big division has arisen ... women who want to work in the home or who are engaged in agriculture are coming to the fore and that's the voice that Finola Bruton is letting us hear. So the women's movement is not a united movement at the present.

(Hilda, interview, Ireland)

If the women had said nothing it would have died a death ... nobody would have noticed ... But there's no doubt she showed up the divisions between women in this country and I think the so-called feminists, we'll have to call them that for want of a better word, we're all feminist but ... it was feminists versus women in the home. They showed themselves up badly, they should have kept their mouth shut ... let her say her little piece or whatever ...

(Doreen, interview, Ireland)

Vestiges of 'the strong Irish mother' who does not make a fuss but 'gets on with it' are reproduced here as a template for Irish femininity. Feminist activists and women in paid work are conflated within the category 'feminists' who are seen as unashamedly courting media attention. This incident is a classic example of how the media utilised 'binary divisions to set up women against feminism' (Skeggs 1997; see also Douglas 1994). The concerns of feminists who spoke out against Bruton's speech were trivialised and represented as petty when compared with women who were getting on with the important matters of bringing up families. Indeed, as feminism becomes an increasingly malleable sign with multiple meanings in the media in particular, the statement 'we're all feminists but' in Doreen's account suggests a 'loony' fringe that takes it too far. Anger is projected onto other women rather than the inadequate child-care infrastructure and the lack of debate about the relative merits of different forms of gendered work. These accounts reproduce the media focus on relations *between women*. Women become the focus of struggles between neo-traditional and neo-liberal discourses of citizenship but in ways that identify 'the problem' as the choices that individual women make and that conceal the systematic gendered and classed constraints that mark the choices available to different groups of women.

In a context of EU and national equality policy and legislation that are labour market centred, the marginalisation of those outside of the labour market is inevitable.[16] However, the pitting of women in employment against 'women in the home' is far from inevitable and has emerged in Ireland as a result of the identification of some Irish mothers as 'women in the home' in the 1990s. Women are addressed as 'free' to construct themselves through paid work, work in the home, consumption, or activism, so that these become equivalent 'lifestyle' options. Yet they have different public valences and are appropriated in a variety of ways to advance conservative agendas through gendered notions of the national. The socio-economic contradictions between the demands and rewards of the labour market and the needs and rewards of the personal and familial are projected onto women. Neo-traditional appeals to a unified notion of the 'Irish mother' via the category 'women in the home', point to the continued valorisation of this figure in the reproduction of Irish femininities in the 1990s. The 'strong Catholic Irish mother' has not disappeared but is reproduced anew as a sign of Irish alterity in response to the processes of individualisation and globalisation.

The following account from Ída maps out the material grounds on which liberal individualism and ideals of family life come together in her lived experience.

> I'm at home all the time, I was working and then I got pregnant . . . then the other kids . . . at that stage, my life stopped, two years ago, no money can't go out, can't get anyone in because I can't afford it . . . one of them is sick a lot, that's all because you get stuck in rut and I'm saying roll on September until the youngest goes to playschool and my life begins again . . . I'm in the house all day . . . if I was working it was my money and it's that I want . . . the money for the family is his money . . . As an individual I want my money, my independence, I was brought up to rely on myself . . . It's a thing that I hate . . . that I have to ask him for money if I want to buy a pair of tights . . . it comes down to that . . . If I had money I would feel more in control . . . He mightn't think he is, but he makes you feel that you haven't got it.
>
> (Ída, group discussion 5, Ireland)

The intersections of gender relations in families with class, urban/rural and other social divisions affect access to 'choice' and lifestyle options. Although 'women in the home' are mainly represented as making a choice to devote themselves to bringing up the future citizens of the nation, in Ída's case this is less a choice than an enforced degrading and isolating experience brought about by particular family, social and economic circumstances. The ideological monopolising of 'women in the home' for New Right and nationalist agendas stifled debate about the economic and social differences that mark Irish women's lives. The return to the ideal Irish family is not an aberration but can be seen as part of the logic of liberal global modernity. The uncertainty and the 'unknown' of the global is made familiar through discourses of the family where, paradoxically, notions of choice and individualism are reproduced and naturalised at the same time as kin becomes a resource for social solidarity (see Chapter 7).

Feminism offers a site of resistance for Maeve at the beginning of this chapter and a site of Irish belonging for Esta who is from a Protestant background (see previous section). In Romy's account, feminism constitutes a moral relationship to the development of the nation through female kin.

> I see myself very much as the contemporary inheritor of my fore-mothers or my fore-sisters who campaigned on feminist basis, not least in opposition to the 1937 constitution . . . it is a *moral* conviction that I am part of this society, however difficult it is both for me and for my society.
>
> (Romy, interview, Ireland; emphasis added)

Women's activism as 'tradition' and 'moral conviction' effects a relationship of attachment and obligation to the nation through the feminist politics of women ancestors in Romy's account. Her feminism is constructed as an imperative rather than a choice. An inherited self is passed down through time and suggests 'a fixity to that self through a tie with the past which *seems* unalterable' and the opposite of the individual 'who is "free" to "choose"' (Lawler 2000: 59 emphasis in original). Romy's account articulates a deep implication in the modern Irish national project, albeit through a feminist counter-narrative of Irish modernity. However, her consciousness of feminist resistance as integral to Irish modernity is not reflected in most accounts. This may be because of the relative lack of integration of feminism into the mainstream national political apparatus (Galligan 1997; O'Connor 1998) and the selective public dissemination of feminist knowledges (Skeggs 1997): it is as if feminism is only permissible as an inherited (and therefore involuntary) politics rather than an individual choice.

Media representations of Finola Bruton's speech and the accounts discussed in this section identify the ways in which difference is 'set up' amongst women who come to be defined by what are constructed as their mutual differences. Women, as the guardians of the family and home, become the dumping ground for anxieties about individualisation (for example, this speech can be read as a response to the introduction of divorce by a tiny majority vote in the divorce referendum of 1995) and the perceived dilution of national uniqueness. Although much of this debate is framed by a discourse of equivalent choice between 'career' and work in the home, Ída's account exposes the promise of fulfilment to women in the home as circumscribed by other factors. This is not to suggest that the promise of autonomy and fulfilment in careers is fulfilled for women; indeed, there is much evidence that this is not the case. I have been concerned so far with the operation of the terms of difference within the category 'Irish women'. In the following section, I consider some of the ways in which the contradictory positionings of Irish women are articulated in relation to two Irish women public figures in the 1990s.

Icons of Irish femininity – negotiating contradictory legacies

Mary Robinson was President of Ireland at the time that this research was conducted and she emerged in all of the women's accounts as a positive figure that reconciled competing discourses of Irish womanhood. During the election campaign in 1990, Fianna Fáil Minister, Padráig Flynn, questioned Mary Robinson's commitment to and abilities as a 'wife and mother'.[17] However, the Irish public saw women as having a right to occupy public office without reference to their families, and her eventual election demonstrated that a social and cultural transformation had taken place since the 1960s (Smyth 1992a).

> Mary Robinson to me is like the true defining symbol of Ireland in the 1990s . . . she really did establish herself in people's minds as a symbol of the country that they were proud of and the fact that she's a woman, she's modern and progressive everyone is having to embrace things new in Ireland.
>
> (Nora, interview, Ireland)

> She's one of the few world leaders at the moment that does anything for me, and, for me, that says something about Ireland and how we've managed to hold on to something . . . All the issues that she's brought to awareness in Ireland, like HIV and funding lesbians and her respect for rural tradition and supporting women. She seems to have pulled together something that we would normally be ashamed of. And shame and Ireland go together, this balance of this tremendous poetic and literary tradition and this huge shame and she brings something very rich.
>
> (Joan, group discussion 5, London)

Former President Robinson is emblematic of all that is associated with being modern, Irish and a woman in these accounts. Although she is from the west of Ireland, Ailbhe Smyth suggests that Robinson occupied the urban 'without a trace of the parochial or provincial' (1992a). She publicly acknowledged women's community work in rural areas, towns and cities equally incorporating women in urban and rural parts of Ireland into imaginings of the modern nation. All those named as outsiders were renamed by President Robinson as part of the Ireland she represented. The shame of different forms of exclusion was partly undone by identifying individuals in marginalised groups as full Irish citizens.

The former President's public identification as an Irish woman and with women invited a collective identification as Irish women.

The day she was elected meant so much to me ... She was a woman and she was so good at it and it was like we stepped forward that day. Okay, we had disgraced ourselves on other moral issues and social issues but this was proof that ... women had gone out and elected her and we proved that we had moved away from old politics.

(Siobhan, interview, Ireland)

Although the difference in levels of electoral support for Mary Robinson between women and men was probably fairly slight, the president acknowledged women's vote in particular in her inaugural speech.[18] Precisely because the presidential election was seen as somewhat outside of the mainstream of Irish politics, Emily O'Reilly argues that the public felt able to 'make a statement about Ireland and its future without fear of upsetting the short-term political apple cart' (quoted in Smyth 1992a: 62–3). However, in these accounts she emerges as a redemptive figure whose presidency makes up for a past marked by the marginalisation of women. Her presence dignifies Irish womanhood in a way that holds out the promise of respected Irish citizenship, not just in Ireland, but globally.

She is extremely important to me because she has this international sense, she has a concern for what's happening in the total global community ... and a contributing of Irish wisdom to things like caring for people that she gives symbolic tribute to in a visit to Rwanda or places like that. She has a sense of the goodness of Irish culture, that it is not something that you have to leave aside in order to be a citizen of the modern world.

(Bride, interview, Ireland)

Because she simultaneously occupied the position of President of Ireland, mother, professor, international human rights commentator and lawyer, she embodied both the modernity *and* the 'timelessness' of the nation. As symbolic of the modern Irish nation, she reconciled the national tension between the desire to modernise *and* to conserve the 'truth' of the national regime, often as represented in the bodies of women (Duara 1998: 294). The claim to newness and change enables the nation to imagine itself and its people 'as the subjects or masters of their history' (Duara 1996: 159). Yet, the nation is always also understood in terms of its glorious ancient or eternal character. At the heart of modern discourse of progressive change and nation building is this continuous subject (unchanging essence) that is often endowed with an aura of authenticity and identified with women (Duara 1998: 293). Robinson's incorporation of secular individualism with notions of an ancient past and the collective good refigured Irish tradition for a modern global Ireland and helped resolve the tensions between individualisation and communality, producing 'new combinations of meaning' (Smyth 1992a). As noted in Chapter 1, her new or redefined Ireland was not about forgetting the past, but putting it to work differently in the present.

Former President Robinson's 'capable' public persona was achieved partly by keeping her 'private life' out of the public eye so that no obvious tensions emerged during her presidency between her public and family life. Like the 'strong Irish mother' she got on with it without complaining. Indeed, Michael Böss notes that she translates herself into a 'latter-day all-embracing Mother Ireland' by offering herself as a symbol of what she called in her inaugural speech 'this reconciling and healing Fifth Province' (2002: 153).[19] The figure of singer Sinead O'Connor was also discussed with some passion in many of the discussions and interviews. O'Connor consistently challenges taken-for-granted institutional practices of Irish women's citizenship by making public her own personal sufferings and controversial opinions. Her tearing up of a picture of the Pope on American television, her fight for custody of her child, her ordination as a priest and coming out as lesbian unsettled assumptions about gendered citizenship and identity. The 'contradictions of her identity' can be seen as unsettling 'the representational and political machinery of a dominant culture' (Berlant 1997: 224). Unlike Mary Robinson, who becomes a redemptive national figure in the women's accounts, Sinead O'Connor is represented as a figure of pathological Irish femininity.

> She is sort of an angry young woman sort of thing in my book. She is probably about the same age as myself, but she seems to have had a hard time and she seems to be very bitter about it . . . whenever I hear about her it's usually something controversial, or you know, she tore up the picture of the Pope . . . She has also got a child and I was just wondering . . . whether she has anything positive to tell him about Ireland. I sort of see her as somebody who has left Ireland . . . still calls herself Irish, but doesn't have anything good to say about it.
>
> (Molly, interview, London)

> When I was in Australia . . . I remember seeing Sinead O'Connor on the Australian news . . . and she was saying the Irish were in medieval times and everything and I felt like strangling her and everybody just said she's a very interesting girl (laughter) . . . She was putting us back in the past. It got to me.
>
> (Joannie, group discussion 8, Ireland)

In response to O'Connor's open expression of controversial views and feelings, many of the accounts assert values of stoicism and silence. By raising difficult and less palatable aspects of Irish culture on a world stage, O'Connor is breaking the gendered national rule of 'keeping up appearances'. Even in a context of celebrity culture and the proliferation of personal testimony in the media, Sinead O'Connor is seen in these accounts as making public that which must be dealt with in private. In this group discussion, Sinead O'Connor's experiences are constructed as personal pathology and distanced from her nationality.

You couldn't sit her down and have a logical argument with her. So she means nothing to me. I just think she is unbalanced (laughter). I don't think she's a balanced person . . . (Paula)

I think she has very strong reason behind what she says. It's from personal experience. (Rosie)

Why would you think she tore up her picture of the Pope? (Paula)

. . . I don't know really. I know as a child she was abused by her mother. And it must be extremely difficult for somebody to come to terms with and she's a survivor in the real sense of the word. And I think that needs to be listened to before . . . (Rosie)

But Rosie is she really a survivor? (Mairead)

Oh yes, oh yes. (Rosie)

I wouldn't see it as survival. I think I'd go along with Paula, to me she's someone with a hell of a lot of problems. We all have our problems that we all have to deal with ourselves. You know what I mean, in some kind of milder manner . . . I just kind of think a lot of people have suffered what she's suffered but we don't like . . . hear about it as much. I know she has a platform and she uses that, but I think she is unbalanced myself . . . (laughter) (Mairead)

(Group discussion 8, Ireland – continued)

Framed by a therapeutic discourse of pathology, classification, consolation and healing, this discussion produces both a distancing from and identification with Sinead O'Connor as emblematic of the monstrous, but also the courageous Irish woman. O'Connor's testimonies provoke an identification with stoicism and self-control in Mairead's contribution. She reverts to the 'strong Irish mother' narrative of getting on with it and adopting a 'milder manner'. The circulation of images and stories of Sinead O'Connor in global and the Irish media turns her into a 'spectacle of subjectivity' which is often suggestive of social change (Berlant 1997: 223). O'Connor's public testimonies stage spectacles of a 'true self'. Such 'spectacles of sincerity', often staged by O'Connor in media interviews are imbued with affect and emotive testimony and appear to reveal a 'truth' of the self. Yet O'Connor undoes this very performance of sincerity and revelation of 'the' inner self by taking up many and often contradictory selves. She picks and sheds her 'true self' as if choosing between selves. This constant choosing between selves, as Bauman (2000) argues, has come to signify freedom in consumer society. Perhaps, it is this contradiction between the media spectacle of sincerity and the construction of self as consumer choice that evokes the emotive response to the figure of Sinead O'Connor in these accounts.

The discussion above suggests both a freedom to choose between selves and a perception of Sinead O'Connor as being out of control of her self. An identification with a more communally oriented Irish modernity emerges in Mairead's account of Sinead O'Connor as letting down appearances. The vulnerability, uncertainty and multiplicity embodied in her performances of

Irish femininity potentially unsettle women's relationships to themselves as 'Irish women'. The repeated invocations of strength and survival, through their repetition in this discussion, can be read as staving off the hurt, vulnerability and uncertainty inscribed on women's bodies by the institutionalised and discursive reproduction of Irish femininities. If former President Robinson 'keeps up appearances' of Irish modernity on a global stage, Sinead O'Connor is seen as letting them down again. The 'game of concealment' continues albeit now in relation to how 'we appear' on a mediatised global rather than national or British/Irish stage.

Conclusion

In Maeve's account at the beginning of this chapter, there is a suggestion that women's lives in the late twentieth century were regulated by the imperative to 'keep up appearances' of a Catholic family-oriented Ireland so that 'appearances' became the regulating norm. The women she looks to as embodying the category 'Irish women' are assumed to occupy unrealised selves that were constrained by this imperative of appearances. Her account suggests that church and state constructions of Irishness involved prescribed performances of femininity with various effects for her godmother and women neighbours when she was growing up. As media spectacles take the place of church surveillance in a mass mediated world, disciplining power is achieved via enticement and seduction rather than the coercion of church and state (Bauman 2000). The possessive relation to the self articulated in many of the accounts involves a working on the self to make it free to 'choose' paths in life that are less defined and defining than those taken by their mothers. However, the production of a self that is 'free' to choose involves the self in different modes of self-regulation, not least through differentiation from their mothers.

Class, religious background, migrant and non-migrant status also affect access to choices in the production of the autonomous Irish feminine self. These women's self-positionings in relation to the 'Finola Bruton speech' and the figures of Mary Robinson and Sinead O'Connor point to the ways in which the legacies of their mothers' lives as emblematic of the category 'Irish women' continue to structure this category in the 1990s. Mary Robinson, who is seen as simultaneously occupying the position of public figure and mother, reconciles the contradictions inherent in the designation 'Irish woman' and reframes the past as informing a progressive present. Singer Sinead O'Connor, on the other hand, reveals the persistence of guilt and shame as still resonant aspects of Irish femininities. These contradictory figures of late twentieth-century Irish femininity are invoked in different ways in the women's accounts both to assert a modern Irish femininity and, paradoxically, to reinstate self-denial, stoicism and endurance as recognisable practices of Irish femininity. The panoptical society of church and state is replaced, to some extent at least, by a synoptical society of consumer citizens forced to choose from an infinite array of possibilities, so that any life decision gets framed as 'consumer choice' (Bauman 2000). But the legacy of the imperative to 'keep up appearances' through stoicism and self-control lingers as a marker of the category 'Irish women' and allied subjectivities.

Women have been constituted and constitute themselves as modern Irish subjects in ways that have been central to the construction of Irish specificity, notions of national community, national modernisation and global Irish modernity. The communally oriented project of Irish modernisation produced the woman migrant as emblematic of individualism, sexuality and desire – all those things that constituted the 'other' of Irish femininities. The Irish mother was identified as the primary reference for the shaping of the Irish feminine self in relation to the category 'Irish women' in the women's accounts. As the emblematic figure of communality and respectability she was located at the heart of Irish 'controlled modernity'. However, in film and television in the 1990s, the Irish mother was often a single parent, violated, abused and unsure of where she was going – a more sexualised maternal body was invoked as embodying 'the nation's suffering' (Meaney 1998: 250).[20] The proliferation of modalities of maternity and non-maternity and ways of 'doing' Irish womanhood undermined the appropriation of the mother as a sign of authenticity in the late twentieth century. Kaplan (1992) notes that a plethora of contradictory discourses of motherhood in the 1990s all had anxiety in common because childbirth and childcare were no longer viewed as automatically natural parts of the woman's lifecycle. Motherhood was marked by 'the questions' of whether or not to be, and how to become a mother, as a result of women's changing lifestyles and new reproductive technologies. Maternity in the 1990s, although frequently invoked as a stable sign of the authenticity of the nation,[21] was less sustainable as such a sign. The category 'Irish women' is constituted in the accounts discussed above via binaries of mothers/daughters, feminists/'women in the home', Catholic/ Protestant and the figures of Mary Robinson/Sinead O'Connor. Although articulated and presented above in relation to these binaries the discussion and the accounts themselves exceed these in ways that locate the category 'Irish women' firmly *within* history. The contradictory figurings of Irish femininities as the strong Irish Catholic mother closely allied to 'women the home', the feminist, or career woman, produced 'Irish women' as a category marked by conflict in the 1990s. This category was also produced through exclusions, most obviously perpetrated in the above accounts by a Church-based Catholicism in the middle decades of the twentieth century and a cultural Catholicism in the latter decades of the century. In the following chapter I consider the ways in which Irish Traveller women were constituted as outside of the category 'Irish women'. I also address the social construction of Traveller mobilities; the identification of migration within Traveller culture as part of a nomadic way of life; and the gendering of Traveller belonging not least through practices of multiculturalism.

3 'We haven't really got a set country'

Global mobilities and Irish Traveller women

I think that the Traveller women are a lot more able to cope than the settled women with family and children and all that. Because we're married so young and we take on so much responsibility at a young age. (Helen)

And that's good? (Breda)

It's good, yeah; I think it's good. (Helen)

It's good because . . . of the culture again that we're in. Probably the settled people think that we're fools . . . getting married so young. (Anne)

It's bad for women to get married young and have children too; you have to live your life too. (Deirdre)

But there's no unmarried mothers, very few unmarried mothers . . . (Helen)

And if there was, she'd get a lot of support, or would she? (Breda)

No, it's hard to know, she'd probably be an outcast. (Helen)

No, no, she'd be outcast in her own family anyway . . . she'll be put down as the worst, and then after a few years . . . there'll always be talk about her, what she did and what she didn't do. (Anne)

Whereas the man wouldn't get the same. (Breda)

No. (Anne)

And I think if the girl did get pregnant, the fella, if he was a Traveller, would be made marry her by his family . . . (Helen)

Is that to do with religion or culture or both? (Breda)

Both, both. (Anne)

There's a lot of restrictions on the women, like girls even growing up you weren't allowed to go to discos or go to the shops. (Helen)

I have a young one, sixteen, and I don't allow her to go to discos. (Anne)

If she was going out with boys and messing she wouldn't get respect, she wouldn't get married then, would you? You'd never get married. (Deirdre)

To me she'd have no respect, she'll just wait there and keep herself right until someone asks her to marry them, and then you know that she's decent, clean. We could be wrong, but it's our culture, but I mean we don't hold it against what other people do. (Anne)

We don't believe in divorce or abortion or any of these things. (Helen)

(Group discussion 3, Ireland)

In the 1990s, there were approximately 4,083 Traveller families, or about 22,000 Travellers in the Republic of Ireland, constituting 0.5 per cent of the total population (Pavee Point Fact Sheet 1997).[1] The population of Travellers in Northern Ireland was approximately 1,200 and about 15,000 lived in Britain. The literature by Irish Travellers[2] and by anthropologists, sociologists and geographers represents Travellers as a small indigenous group with a long shared history of nomadism, their own language,[3] customs and traditions. Membership of the Traveller community is claimed mainly on the basis of descent (at least one Traveller parent) and a commitment to values of nomadism (Okely 1994). Unlike gypsies and Travellers in Europe, who are not closely associated with nation of origin, Irish Travellers identify and are identified as Irish. With the exception of small groups living in the USA, Australia and other countries in Europe, Irish Travellers are mostly confined to Ireland and Britain and move between these countries frequently. This movement is understood as part of their nomadic way of life rather than as 'migration' or 'emigration'.

The boundaries of Traveller identity are strongly asserted against a sedentary population whose ways of life are often defined in opposition to Travellers' practices and values of nomadism. The terms 'settled' or sedentary, used to denote non-Traveller, do not mean non-movement, but involve those modes of movement (including migration) that are incorporated into the self-understanding of the nation-state and increasingly the global nation. Nomadism for Travellers is often described as a state of mind or approach to life. While noting that different Travelling families have different traditions of nomadism, Michael McDonagh points out that, '[j]ust as settled people remain settled even when they travel, Travellers remain Travellers even when they are not travelling' (2000: 34).

As noted in the previous chapter, the category 'Irish women' is repeatedly represented in relation to strength and capability. In the discussion that started this chapter, Helen claims these characteristics in greater abundance for Traveller women. The positions of Traveller women within families are accounted for as the basis of their 'particular culture'. As in the settled population, notions of respect and reputation attach particularly to women's bodies and practices. Consent for this gendered regulation is achieved in the above group discussion through a discourse of cultural survival. The 'strong Traveller woman' keeps family and community together. However, an internal space of difference emerges in Deirdre's suggestion that 'you have to live your life too'. This is in response to my rhetorical question about whether being married and having responsibility at a young age is a good thing. This intervention shifted the discussion into a dialogue about how 'settled people' might evaluate Traveller culture and provoked a justificatory discourse of cultural difference. The gendered conditions of group survival and the maintenance of markers of cultural distinctiveness are at stake in this discussion. Anne's contribution at the end of this quote posits 'our culture' within a liberal discourse of equivalence between cultures by noting that 'we don't hold it against what other people do'. By the 1990s, a liberal multicultural discourse of cultural 'diversity' and 'ethnicity' was gaining prominence in Traveller advocacy and policy contexts (see later discussion).

Although gypsy and Traveller nomadism has been part of European society since the fifth century at least (Mac Laughlin 1995), the advent of the nation-state meant that gypsies, tinkers and vagrants began to be marked out as a specific group and distinguished from the general population by their nomadism. As noted in Chapter 1, conceptions of the Irish 'national' in the 1990s were shifting away from notions of a territorialised national space towards more mobile notions of 'the people' figured by the global nation and the diaspora. My first aim in this chapter is to examine how Traveller nomadism is constituted in relation to the mobilities of global Irish modernity. I investigate the ways in which Irish Travellers have become objects of knowledge and management in twentieth-century Ireland and how this is manifested in discourses of the national as global. In the previous chapter, I examined changing representations of Irish femininities and the category 'Irish women' focusing on the accounts of settled women. My second aim here is to build on some of the arguments developed in Chapter 2 by focusing on the relationships between Traveller and settled feminini-ties. I ask how Traveller women are constituted and how they constitute themselves in relation to Traveller, national, multicultural and global belonging(s). What are the relationships between the categories 'Irish Traveller women' and 'Irish women'? In what ways does the ideology of domesticity operate to constitute women as Irish and/or Traveller? My third aim is to critically examine the multicultural as a mode of national belonging. As discussed in Chapter 1, the globalised Irish 'we' relies on an appropri-ation of some 'differences', for example those of the diaspora, as markers of Irish globality. Multiculturalism represents another way of figuring the national as global. The question then is: What happens to the positioning of Travellers within this refiguring of the national as global, mobile and multi-cultural? Finally, I consider the ways in which a nomadic relationship to England opens up new spaces of cultural belonging in the accounts of Traveller women.

Irish Traveller mobilities and national belonging

Mobility is constructed by particular regimes and practices of differentia-tion and regulation. For example, the extent of mobility was a key factor in legitimating the 'civilizing' project of colonialism in sixteenth-century Ireland (Helleiner 2000).[4] By the eighteenth century, some British descrip-tions of rural Irish life still referred pejoratively to the large numbers of itinerant hawkers, musicians, vagrants and beggars (Helleiner 1995).[5] The Anglo-Irish ascendancy in the early twentieth century, saw tinkers, along with the peasantry of the west of Ireland, as embodiments of tradition, community and the pre-colonial past (ibid.). As an alternative engagement with modernity, Traveller lifestyles were seen as revealing the processes of rationalisation inherent in the development of the nation state and the consequent loss of connection with nature, spirituality and authenticity. J. M. Synge, for example, saw tinkers/Travellers as transcending history and representing a purity, simplicity and life of plenitude that contrasted with the materialism of modern Europe (1966: 199). Traveller women in particular represented a sexual freedom and eroticism that contrasted with the repressed sexuality of post-Famine Ireland. Mobility, freedom and un-inhibited sexuality were celebrated against the disciplining practices of the modern Irish state.

It must be noted, however, that these depictions of Traveller women operated in ways that enabled a refiguring of Irish belonging for male Anglo-Irish writers at the time. Some Anglo-Irish men writers invoked notions of a 'universal, heterosexual, romantic attachment' in order to legitimate particular masculine belongings to the national community (Nash 1997a: 75). However, Jane Helleiner notes a relative lack of sexualised images of Irish Traveller women when compared with gypsies in the British context (1997: 279–80). The circulation of such sexualised depictions of Traveller women was curtailed, perhaps because they potentially undermined the 'gender specific systems of value' (Armstrong 1987: 124) that underpinned sociality in the new state in the south. As noted in Chapter 2, constructions of Irish femininity were closely allied with settled small farm family ways of life underpinned by the cult of domesticity. Traveller women were located outside of this Irish modernity in a liminal space of Traveller nomadism and non-domesticity. Anti-Traveller sentiment from the end of the nineteenth century was linked to the ideology of female domesticity based on settled women's domestic and mothering roles and the perceived need for their protection from the unpredictability of encounters with Travellers (Helleiner 1995).

Twentieth-century Ireland's push for modernity located nomadism and sedentarism in opposition to one another by regulating and channelling mobility into acceptable pathways that could be read within the narrative of the nation-state. Based on an analysis of parliamentary and local authority sources from the 1920s to the 1940s, Helleiner suggests that anti-Traveller rhetoric often centred on the protection of settled women from a masculinised Traveller population (2000). However, Aoife Bhreatnach argues that this was a discourse of only minor significance at the time. She suggests that anti-Traveller rhetoric in the press emerged most notably in the 1950s due to changes in settled people's relationships to public space as a result of slum clearance and the extension of garden suburbs (2002). These developments encouraged an intensification of the ideology of domesticity, often with negative effects for Travellers who were increasingly defined by a perceived lack of domesticity. The expansion of public housing, the development of better environmental conditions and cleaner surroundings produced negative social attitudes to Travellers who became more conspicuous and whose presence was seen as 'spoiling' these pleasant suburbs (ibid.). Another factor affecting increased attention to Travellers was the modernisation of farming and urbanisation of Irish society from the 1950s onwards which reduced the demand for traditional Traveller skills and crafts, with the result that many moved to urban areas and cities. This move to urban areas raised new official concerns regarding accommodation and social welfare and led to a series of government commissions and policy documents on Travellers in the second half of the twentieth century.

The settlement of Travellers policy pursued by the government in the 1960s[6] can be seen as a corollary to the overall modernisation plan initiated with the government's *Programme for Economic Expansion* in 1958.[7] This settlement policy undermined Traveller women's economic autonomy and their position as mothers by criminalising begging, encouraging domestication and recommending more social worker and teacher involvement with their children. The Travelling Review Body,[8] established in the early 1980s, moved away from an 'assimilation' focus towards 'integration', but the existence of Travellers was still identified as a 'problem' (Helleiner 2000).[9] A Task Force on the Travelling community, set up in 1993 to advise on developing a co-ordinated policy approach, included five Traveller members. Its report acknowledged that Travellers have a distinct ethnic identity and culture that should be valued.[10] Although seen primarily as a progressive move, some have questioned the wisdom of gypsies and Travellers' identifying primarily in relation to ethnicity. For example, Colin Clark and Alan Dearling (2000) note that discussion of gypsies and Travellers' 'ethnicity' is absent in the literature on 'race' and ethnicity, which does not construct Travellers as its subject. They refer, for example, to recent work by 'race' theorist, Michael Banton (1997: 163), in which he suggests that Travellers welcome hostility because it helps maintain the community and keeps Traveller children separate from settled society. Such an analysis fails to consider the conditions that produce a desire for cultural purity and problematically locates the impetus for discrimination *within* Traveller culture. Clark and Dearling argue for a focus on nomadism above or alongside ethnicity as a basis for challenging anti-nomadic legislation and practices.[11]

The *Report of the Task Force on the Travelling Community* (1995) was identified as a progressive intervention, which framed the position of Irish Travellers within a liberal multicultural discourse based on cultural recognition, ethnicity and inclusive citizenship.[12] Multiculturalism is one of the 'rationalities of politics' that underpins this report offering a cultural analysis of the difficulties and proposing remedies of 'ethnic' recognition and social inclusion. This 'progressive' analysis proceeds in the report through the call for a recognition of cultural/ethnic difference, but also through the 'responsibilisation' of the 'ethnic' Traveller community. This community is identified as 'free' to practise its culture, but simultaneously made responsible for the conduct of the community and the representation of Traveller culture as an 'acceptable' ethnic or cultural difference. The report also incorporated less liberal positions in an addendum in which four dissenting members argued that 'alternatives of the nomadic way of life should be considered' and suggested that Travellers' lifestyles were incompatible with late twentieth-century life in Ireland (*Report of the Task Force on the Travelling Community* 1995: 289–91). This addendum can be read as a projection of anxieties about the pace of change in Ireland onto the changing lives of Travellers, as the implications of social change are more easily grasped when the negative implications can be identified with a particular group.

This report, its addendum, and the responses to it, demonstrate that by the mid-1990s the interface between sedentarism and nomadism was perhaps more obviously unsettled than in the past. A range of discourses came together to destabilise the social evolutionary assumption that there is a one-way progression from nomadism to sedentarism (McVeigh 1997: 11).[13] Traveller identity in 1990s Ireland was produced in the conjunction of liberal discourses of inclusion, multiculturalism and discourses of 'dependency culture' that identified the moral and cultural characteristics of Travellers as the cause of their exclusion. Broad questions of how national space was to be occupied, the management of social change and shifting cultural norms were being negotiated in settled/Traveller encounters and in official documentation on the position of Travellers.

As well as making the diaspora a central motif of her presidency, Mary Robinson publicly acknowledged the lives of socially marginalised and excluded groups including Travellers. Her public naming of anti-Traveller racism, visits to halting sites and Traveller centres as well as her invitations to Travellers to visit Áras an Úachtaráin[14] focused public attention on Traveller culture and added legitimacy and credibility to their organisations. In her contribution to the 1995 *Report of the Task Force*, she located the position of Travellers within a discourse of Ireland as a multicultural nation.

> [T]hey want their culture recognised, they want their dignity respected, they want to be full citizens of this country. I think that is the most important thing – that there is a real space for the Travelling community, for their own culture, for their own self-development and self-expression, that we have space for them and that we value them.
>
> (President Mary Robinson, quoted in *Report of the Task Force on the Travelling Community* 1995)

The implied reader of the report is a member of the settled community who is invited to include and respect 'them' by creating cultural space for this 'different' group. Travellers become incorporated into the 'we' of the nation, at the same time as that 'we' emerges as the national collectivity that has to live with cultural diversity and by implication with 'them' (Travellers) (Ahmed 2000: 95). The 'we' includes those who are constituted as unmarked Irish national subjects in contrast with those marked 'ethnic' Traveller subjects who, by 'our' agency, may be included.

In the late 1990s and after my research for this book was conducted, discourses and technologies of equality gained currency as a means of recognising Traveller marginalisation and as a basis for Traveller social justice claims. Equality legislation,[15] which specifically named Travellers, came into operation and began to open up questions of Traveller access to public and social spaces of belonging with new implications for the constitution of the national 'we'. However, my focus here is on the positioning of Irish Traveller women in the mid-1990s and how the national 'we' is constituted in their accounts. I am also interested in the Irish modernity that emerges from their accounts of nomadic movement between Ireland and England (as well as within Ireland). In the following sections of this chapter, I analyse and discuss two group discussions with Traveller women at a Traveller education centre called Pavee Point in Dublin. The focus is on the workings of national belonging in relation to territory, mobilities, multiculturalism and the bodies and practices of Traveller women. The gender differentiations that are produced in the settled/Traveller encounter are examined in relation to shifts in the grammar of belonging and political claims making in the women's accounts.

Telling 'the difference' – the ideology of domesticity and Traveller women

In Irish feminist and sociology literature, the category 'Irish women' tends to be subsumed within homogenised notions of Irish society and assumptions about women's common experiences in Ireland. The agenda of Irish feminism has been remarkably untouched by the existence or concerns of Irish Traveller women (for an exception see Lentin 1999).[16] Indeed, Traveller women are equally invisible in the literature on Irish Travellers (for an exception see Crickley 1992 and 2001). Although Traveller women are perhaps more visible than Traveller men as representatives of the Travellers in Ireland, the specificities of Irish Traveller women's lives tend to be subsumed in a dominant narrative of Traveller exclusion and marginalisation. When considering how Traveller women frame their identities with specific reference to gender, it becomes evident that Traveller women's relationships to public space in Ireland are everywhere regulated through dress, sexuality and family.

Settled writers have identified a 'strict sexual morality and rigid adherence to family and marital relationships' and high fertility rates among Travellers (Mac Laughlin 1996: 51–2). Jim Mac Laughlin notes that in 1987, only 3.4 per cent of Traveller births were outside of marriage, which was one third of the national figure at the time (ibid.: 52).[17] As the discussion that began this chapter emphasised, the preservation of a particular form of family life is seen as important for the survival of Traveller culture, placing responsibility for its maintenance on the bodies and practices of Traveller women. The specificity of Traveller family life, like that of 'the Irish family' of the new state in the south, marks out the values and culture of Travellers from those of the settled community. The distinctiveness of Traveller culture in most of the women's accounts is identified with the ways in which nomadism and other cultural values are practiced in Traveller families and community life. This is contrasted with what is seen as a less community-oriented and more state-interventionist approach to family and culture in the settled community.

> People help each other, you don't see many homeless Travellers . . . there's always somebody who'll take them in. (Mary)
> Or there wouldn't be many adoptions. Now Trudder House[18] (where Traveller children were placed in residential cares and some were sexually abused by settled staff) shocked me. I only heard of Trudder House when I came here (Pavee Point Centre). I didn't know that Traveller children were sent away in care for settled people to look after them. (Rita)
> And yet they won't let the Travellers take them in themselves. If Travellers want to take them in they won't let Travellers look after them. (Mary)
> See they're looking at you in the trailer you see, and they're looking at you with five or six children and you're only getting the dole. And to a settled person, now God forbid that Anne died or something . . . you'll rush in and take Anne's children. I'm absolutely for these children, to leave them in their culture and that I'll look after them . . . Years ago Travellers were not that rich, but they're not that rich today either, but the most important thing was that their children got . . . love. And that was the most important thing of all, as long as they had enough to eat, a stitch of clothes on them . . . But the children are getting taken today off poor people who are drinkers and Travellers . . . and they're handed over to the settled, children ten or eleven years of age, handed over to the settled people, I call them country people[19] . . . And the poor children haven't a clue what they're going into, its like people getting brought from Africa and brought to Ireland . . . It's like your children being handed over to us, that would be very strange, for your children from a different culture, and everything completely different. (Rita)
> Living in a caravan on the road. (Anne)
> It's the same. (Rita)
>
> (Group discussion 3, Ireland)

As those who are mainly responsible for parenting and domestic work, Traveller women's domestic practices are subject to state and media surveillance and regulation. The tasks of keeping the community together and keeping state interference at bay fall primarily to Traveller women. State regulatory practices of child protection both deny cultural difference and threaten the integrity of Traveller culture by challenging the value of

Traveller community support and its survival. The transcultural gap is both acknowledged and traversed in Rita and Anne's invitation to me to imagine a child of mine being placed with a Traveller family. The point was made by the invitation. The implication was that this would be an 'unthinkable' policy for a state that assumes and privileges settled norms.

The construction of the nation-state through sedentarism, understood as controlled practices of mobility, produces a dichotomy between an 'Irish people' who engage in 'settled' 'mobilities' and Traveller people whose mobilities are seen as chaotic, indeterminate and threatening. Mobilities are differentiated in relation to particular regimes of power. While an infra-structure of global mobility is everywhere facilitated within the state, infrastructures that enable Traveller nomadism are increasingly inadequate and have little public legitimacy.[20] Such infrastructures of mobility fall outside of global capitalist exchanges, practices of global Irish citizenship and the high velocity movement that marks global modernity.

> Sure they won't even let the Travellers be at the side of the roads now, and yet when they put them into sites they're not building right sites for them ... You have no place to travel ... there's no laybys and if there is, there's big stones on the sides of the roads ... If they're going to put us into sites let them give us proper sites ... After all, our children have to go to school, we'd like showers, we'd like hot water, we'd like electricity, we'd like tarmac and we'd like a clean healthy place to live in ... You've no washing machine, you've miles to go to a wash house, maybe some Travellers don't have ... a car to bring them ... and this is the discrimination ...
>
> (Elsie, group discussion 4, Ireland)

Improved roadways, motorways and other spaces of 'settled' mobility are replacing the halting sites that facilitated Travellers' nomadism. In the 1990s, the responses of many settled people to the establishment of halting sites near them varied from anti-Traveller public protests, to the invoca-tion of planning laws that designated low density development and appeals to environmental factors. Middle-class residents often invoked liberal discourses of support for Travellers' rights while identifying other reasons such as those cited above for why a Travellers' site should not be located near them. The absence of an infrastructure for nomadism, and the discrim-inatory responses of the settled population mean that, in Elsie's words, 'you have no place to travel'.[21]

The positioning of Traveller women as objects of the settled gaze oper-ates in a range of sites from the domestic to mothering practices, from personal appearance to shopping. The socio-spatial modes of exclusion experienced by Traveller women extend to spaces of consumption including shops, streets, pubs and social centres where the presence of Travellers produces 'suspicion' and often criminalisation.[22] Everyday encounters in public space mean that the boundaries between settled and Traveller women are always in play.

> If we walk down that city, me and her together, we are followed around as if we had ten heads ... in case we'll rob or we'll steal and there's people following you up and down that shop, and you know that you're not going to do this, and they're following you and it's very irritating. (Rita)
>   Straight away they're there. (Helen)
>   Or 'Can I help you?' when you go in, they come straight to you. (Rita)
>   John was retiring or leaving here for a while ... so we went down to get him a card ... there was only one woman in the shop, and there was only two of us, and the shop wasn't that full ... she let a shout into the back, 'Deirdre, I need you out here'... We left the card and we walked right out. We didn't even say one word to her ... You'd think we were going to rob the whole shop because she got ashamed herself, but we still wouldn't take that card. That's what we get now. (Helen)
>   (Group discussion 3, Ireland)

Repeated reminders of the suspicion with which Travellers are held constrain their mobility in public places. Public spaces are designed and inhabited as if Travellers had no right to occupy them. Travellers experience 'oppressive policing by the state in the interests of all sedentary people, not because of what they do, but because of what they are [seen to be]. Their very existence threatens, undermines, "invades" sedentary identity' (McVeigh 1997). In the example of buying a card above, this femininised practice is regulated by suspicion and open surveillance of Helen and Rita who took up the position of consumer citizens as a form of resistance. By returning the accusatory gaze they drew attention to the surveillance and discrimination inherent in the encounter and asserted their consumer power to take their business elsewhere.

Gendered stereotypes of women and men were contrasted with actual experiences and, for some, the question of whether Traveller women could 'pass' as settled in order to gain access to public spaces was an important issue.

> There's no advantage of being an Irish Traveller in Ireland, and being an Irish woman Traveller is harder than being a man Traveller. (Caroline)
>   How? (Breda)
>   The women do the hard work, and years back, it was even harder, because men were nearly always gone. (Caroline)
>   ... I know that men have an easier time, but *with settled people looking in* I think that the woman have an easier time, in terms of dealing with settled people. I don't think they like the men Travellers at all.

I think they look at men as being aggressive as being *bold*. (Fran, emphasis added)

The life of the Traveller man in our own community is simple, easy. But looking from outside, settled people looking in at Travellers, settled people, I imagine would get on better with a Traveller woman than with a Traveller man. (Moyra)

Because? (Breda)

Because I think that nearly all the time it is Traveller women that's dealing with the subject of discrimination and it's always the women that's talking about it, it's hardly ever the men. (Moyra)

Ah no, there are some men as well. (Fran)

There are a good few men that press for rights and that, but the women, they have to live in places like that. (Elsie)

I dispute that, because I think myself a Traveller man would blend much more clear, better than a woman. A Traveller woman stands out I think. If there's a hundred country people a Traveller man would blend in much better than a woman would. (Holly)

I think that – my mother, if you think of filling in a form or something like that, she won't do it, but he'll get up off the chair and do that and he'll talk to you, but she won't, maybe all mothers are not the same but. (Fran)

Irish society as it is looks at Traveller man as being aggressive . . . (Moyra)

How do you think that settled people see Traveller women? (Breda)

I don't know. (Moyra)

Dirt, dirty smelly women (other members of the group saying no) yes, dirty smelly women with shawls and wide skirts. (Fran)

(Group discussion 4, Ireland)

To account for the position of Traveller women, this discussion takes a detour through the assumed gaze of settled people. The extent to which self-representation is framed in response to the voyeuristic and regulatory 'settled' gaze is alluded to by Fran's reference to 'settled people looking in'.[23] The bodies of Traveller men and women are read 'through the eyes of those *who are telling the difference*' (Ahmed 2000: 125; emphasis in original). It is suggested that Traveller women's ongoing contact with settled people and skills of interaction with precisely those institutions of society that exclude, regulate and marginalise them, render them more 'visible' than Traveller men. This contact is a site of both regulation and potential resistance. The marking of Traveller identity is gender differentiated in the discussion above based on the perceived aggressiveness of Traveller men and the assumed lack of domesticity, dirty bodies and old-fashioned attire of Traveller women. This is not surprising given women's 'contradictory association with dirt itself (moral, sexual and material) and with its removal' (Morley 2000: 70). Differences between 'settled' and 'Traveller' are marked by the perception of Traveller women as 'dirty'. Dirt operates as a means of arranging cultures (Palmer 1989 in Morley) through differentiated femininities which are defined in part 'by how women manage dirt' (Morley 2000: 78). Like all those perceived as dirty, Traveller women are denied membership in, and protection by, the institutions that embody the moral structures of society (McVeigh 1992: 44). The perceived danger of contamination by the presence of Travellers produces distanciating narratives that render Travellers 'strange', 'dirty' and distant from Irish settled culture despite their 'indigenous' status. However, withdrawal from those who are constituted as 'strange' even when close is 'to be touched by those bodies' (Ahmed 2000: 49); 'settled' citizens are 'touched' by Traveller (anti-)citizens despite persistent practices of distancing.

The structure of this gendered marking is contested as the discussion proceeds. Some saw Traveller men as 'blending in' or 'passing' as settled, while others suggested that perceptions of Traveller men as aggressive by the settled population make it impossible for men to pass. The assumption is that when Traveller men do pass it is an unintentional passing based on misrecognition. Of course, the very idea of passing highlights the slipperiness of identities and the fact that there is no prior Traveller or settled identities, as they are repeatedly constituted in such encounters. For these women, Traveller identity is not as fixed as it might appear, but is subject to ongoing encounters of recognition and misrecognition. Although there are limits to the movement between identification as Traveller and non-Traveller, there is some potential mobility here. The discussion above suggests that while Traveller men might 'pass' unintentionally, Traveller women are more closely identified as 'other' through the signifier of 'dirt' so that they cannot pass.

> We had a meeting up here the other day with a school, and all the school children came in . . . a whole group of children, well sixteen or seventeen and the whole meeting was over and one of the women said 'What did you expect to find when you came in to talk to Travellers?' 'We didn't expect them to be wearing jeans, we didn't expect their hair to be tidy, we expected their hands to be dirty', and this is 1996 . . .'We thought you'd be in long skirts', and what Traveller will you get with a big plaid skirt on them and a shawl and a pair of boots, anywhere? It's 1996 at the end of the day . . . (Moyra)
>
> I've noticed, I don't drink or go out, but if I did, for the seldom time I used to go, I'd go with Joe, and he'd get in and what would happen me, I'd be turned away from the door and I'd be dolled up, I wouldn't even open my mouth, I'd take the earrings out of my ears and tie up my hair . . . I'd be turned away like a dog and he'd be let in. And that's why I never, I never go out anywhere at all, because I know myself, I've tried it in Cork and I've tried it up here (Dublin) and nobody, I wouldn't get in. (Caroline)
>
> Isn't it terrible now? (Elsie)

You've got to take off your earrings, fix up your hair just to get in, like settled person. It is hard. (Fran)

... I went to the door of the place and he said no and so I turned and was walking away, and thought he's not letting anyone in, and a girl came with a skirt on her that was barely covering herself and he let her in, so I said 'Why are you letting her in'? and he said 'If she never had anything on her she's still better than what you'll ever be'. ... sighs ... and I said 'I'll never wear a skirt that short for to get in anywhere' and he said 'And if you wore it to your ears you still wouldn't get in' ... He still came out the better at the end of it, he still answered me. (Caroline)

(Group discussion 4, Ireland)

Respectable settled femininity is not desired in this discussion but is reluctantly performed in order to pass and thereby gain access to public venues and services. Traveller women, as Caroline's account suggests, are not allowed 'a possessive relationship to femininity', but use it tactically in order to attempt to gain access to public spaces (Skeggs 1997: 106). She has to put on a performance of the feminine that mimics or impersonates middle-class ideals of respectable settled femininity. Caroline's narrative of 'not passing' is only intelligible by being 'joined to [Irish] forms of social and national belonging' which constitute Irish Travellers as outside the national imagined community (Ahmed 1999: 94). This attempt at passing destabilises the idea that there is some 'natural' body, because the body can be read in any number of ways. Yet the encounter appears to establish the 'natural' female Traveller body as a fact when, despite her efforts, Caroline's body is read in these terms. Her attempts to project a bodily image that might be read as settled does not work and is completely undermined when the woman who looks 'settled' is admitted.

Caroline initially assumed that she had successfully passed, but that because the venue was full, they were not letting anyone else in. Her response to the bouncer implied that she thought the 'settled' woman was allowed in because of her sexualised clothing. She was disabused of this rationalisation when the bouncer asserted that what made the 'difference' was that she was settled. The potential to pass here cannot be understood as a transgressive act as in some recent theorising of subjectivity and identity (see Chapter 6). It is a tactic to occupy public space. Even if Caroline had passed as settled, Sara Ahmed argues that the relations of power that give rise to such a 'passing' encounter would be secured rather than unsettled. This is because 'passing' is 'implicated in the very discourse around tellable differences' (Ahmed 1999: 89). The question of who counts as settled women and Traveller women would be at stake but would not necessarily be re-negotiated in the encounter. Whether within the Traveller community or in the encounter with the settled population, Traveller women's bodies, domestic and childrearing practices are both under surveillance and markers of a 'difference' that is constructed as beyond assimilation. Their nomadic 'way of life' represents the constitutive outside of Irish modernisation and Irish global modernity.

Contested histories and multicultural belonging(s)

'History' and 'narratives of origin' represented important sites of contestation for Travellers in late twentieth-century Ireland.[24] This is partly because particular narratives of Travellers' origins have been asserted in official policy documents since the 1960s, often in ways that can be interpreted as denying claims to Traveller identity. Just as history was being reconstituted as a 'fluid *resource*' (Cronin 2000: 139; emphasis in original) in rearticulating notions of the national not least as diasporic in the 1990s, it also represented a legitimising discourse of origins and belonging for many excluded and marginalised groups. In the following discussion 'Travellerness' becomes a form of 'categorical purity' (Malkki 1992: 35) that authenticates claims to belong on specific terms. The narratives of origin constructed in the discussion can be seen as producing an alternative 'nationalist metaphysic' (ibid.: 36), as ancient origins, blood, and ethnicity based on a tradition of nomadism mark the 'impassible' boundaries of Traveller identity. Although not linked to territory or a sovereign state, Moyra's statement below, that Traveller identity is 'the same as an Irish person feeling Irish', suggests an equivalent moral claim on Traveller identity as that of national identity.

> And you know, what makes it worse as well is the fact that people think that you do come from the Famine, that you only went on the road for an easy life. And we learnt here[25] last week that we go back as far as the eleventh century we went back further we even went back to the 9th century. And I often wonder why Travellers feel so Traveller, so much of a Traveller, it can't come from that you've just been a Traveller from a few centuries ago, because no matter where you go, you'll always say you're a Traveller. You can't feel that much of a Traveller, if it wasn't inbred in you for centuries and centuries. (Elsie)
>   And when you say you feel a Traveller what is that feeling? (Breda)
>   It's gone into your blood. (Deirdre)
>   I think it's the same as an Irish person feeling Irish. (Moyra)
>   You wouldn't feel it comfortable on the road with a caravan all the time, would you? (Elsie)
>   I'm sure I wouldn't. (Breda)
>   No, but if you were going on holidays you'd like to go back to your home eventually. (Elsie)
>   Probably, yes. (Breda)
>   Well, a Traveller doesn't find it like that. (Elsie)
>   I think that it is just a pride, that you are different from the Irish person in Ireland. You are an ethnic group. It comes down to pride, I'm

> proud I'm a Traveller. And I wouldn't be a settled person for nothing.
> You can't be a settled person, because you're born a Traveller ...
> (Moyra)
>
> (Group discussion 4, Ireland)

Although Traveller identification is represented as 'the same as' and, therefore, 'as legitimate as' Irish national identity, 'the difference' is made evident in the above discussion by the difficulties I, as a 'settled' person, might have with a nomadic lifestyle and Moyra might have with being 'a settled person'. While the categories 'Traveller' and 'settled' may be constituted as equivalent, the implication is that there is little possibility of moving between them. The effects of exclusion, regulation and marginalisation produce a close identification with Traveller identity and lifestyle in ways that reproduce belonging through some of the essentialising and legitimising motifs of the national. In this discussion, a narrative is constructed that produces a moral claim to 'authentic' Irish Traveller identity based on continuity, descent and ethnic difference. Movement itself is identified as a form of being 'at home'. The naturalisation and authentication of Traveller identity through blood, breeding and ancient origins enable the articulation of Traveller claims on a sedentary state that has legitimated itself through similar grammars of belonging.

Although narratives of origin and ethnicity tend to reify Traveller identity they represent an aspect of Travellers' relationship to the settled population over which they can exercise some control. Issues of ethnicity and origin have become key sites on which official policy documents have been contested and policy shifts have been achieved. The group discussion above, although invoking Traveller belonging within the grammar of national belonging, by its shifting points of reference, demonstrates that there is no pure point of origin. Instead, history and collective memory are contested sites of identification and are central to political claims making at a time when 'cultural diversity' as opposed to 'cultural difference' has gained legitimacy within contemporary 'multicultural' narratives of the nation. Cultural diversity here is understood as assumptions of already constituted difference while cultural difference is taken to mean the sociopolitical processes in which differences are constituted and named (see later discussion).

Charles Taylor argues that when identity is invoked in modern politics, it is based on calls for recognition and that multiculturalism is about enabling cultural survival through recognition (Taylor 1994).[26] The discussion below reveals the ways in which 'history' is central to a multiculturalism understood in terms of the politics of recognition.

> Now, in the schools, if a child maybe comes in from Austria, and we're
> the settled people and Rita is the Traveller and she has been in the school
> maybe for 4 years, yet the settled people never learned that Rita made

tins, what a tent was like, or that her mother baked, yet the very minute she (the Austrian girl) walks in. (Anne)

They want to know about her. (Rita)

They're going looking for a book to show who she is, what her country is like, and the world map is got out and we're shown how far away. (Anne)

They used to do history when I was in school, and do you know what the history was? How many (children) my mother had each year, how many brothers and sisters have you got this year, every year, I had the same teacher for three years and the same thing, every year she would say, now how many sisters and brothers have you. (Mary)

I wouldn't answer her. (Anne)

(Group discussion 3, Ireland)

Culture and history are identified as sites of injustice through non/mis-recognition and therefore as necessary terrains of struggle for Travellers. Travellers are 'seen as a people without history in a *progressive, cumulative, purposeful or nationalist sense*' (Mac Laughlin 1999: 139, emphasis in original) and as outside the official national narrative reproduced in Irish national schools. Their travelling cultures are rendered valueless and feminised (ibid.). Rita and Anne's accounts suggest that the lives of Travellers have been excluded from the school curriculum as if they did not exist, are ridiculed as having no history, or are reduced to a story of excessive fertility.

Ambivalences and conflicts between Traveller and Irish identifications emerge because they are often represented as mutually exclusive. However, the discussion below, through the complex articulation of discourses of decolonising nationalism, human rights and multiculturalism reveals complex and sometimes contradictory positioning and identifications.

I don't even call myself Irish, I call myself a Traveller that's all. We have no really set place anyway. We haven't really got a set country. (Mary)

So you wouldn't call yourself an Irish Traveller? (Breda)

I was born in England and I was reared in Ireland. Now if I were made to stand up to the Irish Anthem, I wouldn't even do it. I like Irish music. (Mary)

I like when the politicians speak out about the North and things. I'll tell you the truth, I get very angry that the English are trying to claim it. (Rita)

And John Major, you get sick of him, he's trying . . . (Mary)

They're trying to hold on to something that they don't own themselves. The Irish didn't bring up the history of the famine and all that. (Helen)

And now the Irish do it themselves, that's what I can't understand. There's one woman on RTE, and you'll hear her saying 'Ah don't go back on history', but don't the English go back on history? They're bringing up King Billy and everything (laughter), marches with the Orange sashes and all that ... they should be allowed to wear them because that's their culture, you know, just like we'd like to be accepted in Ireland, I've nothing against the English in that line. But ... like ourselves, we're outcast, because in Ireland, we're dirty and roving from place to place. (Helen)

... It makes you feel that you wish you were never born. Or sometimes you get it in your head that you wish you weren't a Traveller, you're discriminated against that much. But then you come back to yourself and you'd say, well I am a Traveller. And I'm quite happy with who I am if I was accepted for who I am ... And what annoys me most of all, the people that has them [Travellers] so low and is putting them so low is their own Irish people again. It's like a family, Ireland is like a family, and it's just like a person with a big family turning down their own family for the sake of maybe first cousins or far out relations, turning their own family away. And that's what Ireland is doing ... (Anne)

(Group discussion 3, Ireland)

Questions of patriotism and identification with Irish identity arise and are negotiated here in complex ways. For example, performances of patriotism through singing the national anthem are refused, while Irish music is embraced as part of Traveller culture in Ireland (see Gaul 2000; Joyce and Farmer 2000). Although the views of Travellers have been absent in the political arena relating to the politics of Northern Ireland and Anglo-Irish relations, this discussion suggests an identification with nationalist territori-alised discourses of sovereignty and ownership, with the English being seen as 'trying to claim' part of Irish territory.[27] By refusing to invoke 'history', some southern politicians and media figures are ridiculed for weakening southern claims to the North and losing a sense of themselves. Ironically, this territorialised discourse of history is identified as critical to political positioning and is reworked as the discussion proceeds.

In the initial part of the discussion, history is invoked as central to political claims-making. This is followed by some backtracking when Unionists in the North, described as English, are identified as being overly concerned with commemorating history and identity. Then the parallels between Traveller concerns with culture and history are recognised and an equivalence is drawn between the position of Unionists and Travellers. Discourses of multiculturalism and diversity identify them both as minorities on the island of Ireland. Multicultural constructions of 'ethnicity' come to incorporate Unionist cultural identities in the North and Traveller nomadism as equivalent forms of diverse 'cultural expression'.[28] Multiculturalism offers 'a space' in which both Unionists and Travellers might inhabit the Irish nation. It involves the 'management of the consequences of difference' based on the assumption that the differences 'simply and already exist' (Ahmed

2000: 103; see also Fraser 2000). The different histories that mark the 'difference' and the socio-political processes that structure their locations in relation to the Irish nation are concealed. Multiculturalism, in this sense, celebrates cultural diversity while neutralising 'the differences that it apparently celebrates' (Ahmed 2000: 105) and the power dynamics in which differences are constituted as particular kinds of difference.

Although the national 'we' may be refigured as an inclusive multicultural 'we', the processes by which 'difference' is marked and the assumptions of sedentarism that render nomadism unacceptable and threatening remain largely in place. It is important to distinguish, as Bhabha (1994), Ahmed (2000) and others do, between notions of cultural *diversity* and cultural *difference*. Cultural *difference* as opposed to cultural *diversity*, for Bhabha, is not about the projection of some originary cultural tradition, but addresses the dynamic process by which cultural subjectivities are produced, a process that is marked by historical contingency and contradiction. If cultural diversity represents a space of regulatory surveillance, cultural difference represents that space/encounter in which regulatory surveillance fails (Rose 1995). Cultural difference then is understood in relation to the workings of regulatory surveillance and production of subjectivity focusing on the uneven and contradictory power relations that constitute 'difference'. Liberal multiculturalism, which is based on notions of cultural diversity, tends to assume pre-given contents of cultures as if they were lived unsullied by their historical and contemporary interactions and call on pure mythic memories of collective identity (Bhabha 1994: 34).

When the social is represented in terms of cultural diversity, encounters that place us at 'the edge of experience' or that confront us with difference which can never be fully represented are concealed (ibid.: 126). Cultural difference is homogenised and reified into a 'diversity' of apparently fixed differences. Internal differences among Travellers and settled people are erased and the ways in which ongoing encounters between these groups produce the changing identities of settled and Traveller are obscured. The ongoing social interaction and political struggle around the conditions of different mobilities and belongings are also erased. By calling for an acceptance and valuing of 'difference', those differences that cannot be reduced to 'cultural diversity' are concealed (Ahmed 2000: 95). The very notion of 'making space' for Travellers is premised on notions of cultural diversity and reproduces a similar kind of 'mastery' as attempts to make Travellers settle and assimilate. The settled 'we' asserts itself in a mode of master, or 'host' (ibid.: 190).

In Anne's account above, she articulates the effects of non-recognition and discrimination as producing a desire never to have been born, or not to be a Traveller. The *Report of the Task Force* in 1995 noted that because of the constant contact Traveller women have with state agencies and institutions, they 'can be left with the message that their problems can best be solved if they cease to be Travellers. This leaves Traveller women in an impossible and unenviable situation [of] effectively being blamed for being Travellers' (*Report of the Task Force* 1995: 272). The dynamic of simultaneous inclusion and exclusion described in Anne's formulation of the 'national' as a 'family' that excludes its Traveller members reveals the intimacy of the experience of non-recognition and consequent exclusion.[29] Whether through 'sympathetic incorporation' or 'unsympathetic repression', Robbie McVeigh argues that the aim of most institutions of the state and the settled community is to end the existence of Travellers as Travellers (1998: 158). Sedentary identity is secured then by the incorporation of Travellers (as Travellers and so 'different' from settled people) *and* the expulsion of Travellers (by rendering Travellers Other and abject).[30]

Inhabiting Irish identity as Traveller women in England

Travel across national borders to England is an integral part of the nomadic way of life of Travellers so that although movement to England has many parallels with the migration of settled people, it is experienced and accounted for differently by them. Nonetheless, settled writer, Gmelch (1975), identifies transnational nomadism for Travellers as emigration and argues that emigration can be a means of gaining anonymity outside of the 'small-scale society' of Ireland. Another settled writer, Mary O'Malley argues that the coming-and-going of Irish Travellers between Britain and Ireland is 'as old as the Travellers themselves' and so could hardly be called emigration (1991: 102). She suggests that Travellers' movement to Britain is often for 'a change of scene' and most return after two or three years in contrast with the economic reasons and often permanent nature of migration for most settled people (ibid.: 103). As a less easily identified minority in England, Traveller women suggest that they can inhabit public space in ways that would not be possible in Ireland. Many Irish writers and migrants have noted that their sense of Irish identity was intensified by migration. However, this experience takes on different dimensions for Travellers who find that they can inhabit Irish identity only when living in England.

On arrival in England in the 1970s, Travellers were able to 'move into flats or houses in large industrial cities such as Birmingham, Huddersfield, or Manchester and were able to pass as working-class Irish' (ibid.: 130). Passing as settled Irish is facilitated by the fact that their neighbours, often other immigrants, were unfamiliar with those signs that signal Traveller identity in Ireland (ibid.).

> When I was in England, I was four years in England, and all the time I was in England I was treated the same as the English settled people were. I went into posh hotels over there and all. (Áine)
>
> Is that right? You'd get in more places in England than you would in Ireland? (Mary)
>
> You're treated like dirt back in Ireland. (Caroline)

> You're treated like an Irish person in England, you're not classed as Traveller or gypsy or anything. (Moyra)
>
> I often heard them saying that you know the social workers over in England helps the Travellers a lot, families, I was never in England, but that's what I've heard. (Mary)
>
> ... Back here the children are called knackers, and yourself and all. But over in England when your children go to school they are just in with the rest. (Moyra)
>
> They're treated like ordinary kids. (Fran)
>
> Like I say you're treated more Irish in England than we get treated Irish here. (Moyra)
>
> (Group discussion 3, Ireland)

Although there is much evidence that Travellers in England experience discrimination in relation to housing, education and health, the perception in these group discussions is that there is less segregation and exclusion than in Ireland. New Age Travellers became the subject of moral panics in Britain in the 1990s leading to the passing of the Criminal Justice Act 1994 which restricted Travellers' movement and other liberties (McVeigh 1997). Also, British tabloids in the 1990s were depicting Irish Travellers as 'dirty, ignorant, malodorous, messy and thieving' (quoted in Mac Laughlin 1996: 60). By the end of the decade, the Home Secretary demonstrated the depth of anti-Traveller racism in an interview on a local radio station in which he suggested that there was too much tolerance and a need to 'crack down on them'.[31] Nonetheless, in a country in which postwar black immigrants represent the dominant 'other', Irish Travellers did not occupy the position of central 'out-group' status that they do in Ireland. Mary O'Malley argues that the designation 'Irish' or 'Paddy' in Britain was seen as affording Irish Travellers more status than identification as gypsies in England did (O'Malley 1991).

To be positioned as Irish in Britain meant inhabiting a cultural identity in ways that were not possible in Ireland. The persistent normalised everyday surveillance of Traveller life in Ireland was not replicated in England except in some Irish spaces such as Irish pubs and other businesses. Instead, Irish Travellers were subject to similar regulatory practices as other immigrants.

> I think in England, say Travellers, they're classed Irish, they're not classed Travellers ... I think there's a lot of discrimination against Travellers back here, but over there it is not as bad. Now I'm back here about a year. I was brought up in Manchester, I only lived here a year. (Helen)
>
> I lived in England about 3 or 4 years. I think that the English people are very nice, but it was the Irish again who had a pub or a hairdresser, and they'd put up a sign that wouldn't say Irish, but Travellers and it would be the Irish people again that would be over in England that

would be putting the Travellers down to the lowest of the low. I went out with an aunt of mine in Manchester, and here it was, 'No Travellers and No Dogs allowed'. (Rita) (laughter)

And it was an Irish pub? (Breda)

Ah, they are Irish because English people don't call the Irish Travellers Travellers, they call all people like that gypsies. And we were even speaking to some of the people who were in those pubs, who had those notices up and they were only temporary in England themselves in a country they weren't reared in and weren't born in. Probably Irish who would have been after going over say about 15 years ago and buying a place and buying a pub, and they'd have those notices up about their own Irish people. So they still put the Travellers out to the road. (Anne)

(Group discussion 3, Ireland)

Irish community, identity and belonging are lived so much through the exclusion of Travellers that these practices of exclusion and discrimination are transported in migration. The segregation between settled Irish and Irish Traveller migrants in London is evident from research reports and accounts of Irish Traveller life in London (see Lennon *et al.* 1988: 181–2; London Irish Women's Centre Report 1995; Southwark Travellers Women's Group Report 1992). These women's accounts suggest that access to Irish national belonging was opened up to them in England (with the exception of Irish migrant spaces in England) in ways that they could not imagine in Ireland. However, they noted that most did not stay in England because Ireland is 'home'. Annie's contribution to the above discussion notes the similar position of settled Irish migrants in England and Irish Travellers in England as often (being or seeing themselves as being) 'only temporary in England'. This 'temporary' relationship to England is seen as a shared status producing a similar relationship of belonging to the national space of England unlike the legitimised hierarchical relations of belonging of Irish settled and Traveller citizens to the national space of Ireland. Nonetheless, claims to Traveller identity are asserted in relation to the national space and polity of Ireland (in relation to the southern state at least) because even as that space and polity constitutes Travellers as anti-citizens, it remains the reference point for claims making and cultural identification. Claims to be recognised as Irish and therefore 'the same as' the settled population with equal citizenship rights are made alongside claims to 'difference' as Traveller and with specific citizenship needs.

Conclusion

The globalisation of the national and transnational 'order of things' has put identities and cultures in motion, normalising movement across ethno-, media and other scapes (Appadurai 1996). If the 'solid stage' of modernity reproduced a national classificatory order that allocated migrants, refugees and Travellers to 'liminal political spaces', then the more fluid boundaries and classifications identified with 'globalised' or 'liquid modernity' (Bauman 2000) might be seen to hold out more potential for Traveller belonging. However, as this chapter demonstrates, the conceptions of fluid boundaries that dominate discourses of the global are re-constituting boundaries rather than dissolving them. A degree of differentiation is required in relation to claims of a mobile modernity. The assertion that the mobile and indeterminate characterise current forms of sociality and that those who operate the levers of power are now beyond reach is a premature and obfuscatory one. It suggests too clean a shift in the structure of sociality, particularly when viewed through the accounts of Irish Traveller women. The stratification of mobilities in relation to velocity has turned the regulatory gaze more specifically on the quotidian mobilities of Irish Travellers. For example, the particular forms, paces and spaces of movement of Irish Travellers are marginalised by a mobile modernity that redefines boundaries via evaluations of movement in relation to speed and contributions to the global economy. Travellers' mobilities do not concur with or enhance global flows of capital, labour and goods and are subject to new and old techniques of control. Indeed, the ways in which Irish Traveller nomadism signifies within a global Irish modernity reveal the very specific meanings that attach to mobility in the contemporary Irish global/national 'order of things'. If global subjects are constituted through 'the promise of transcendent mobility, allowing them to move freely across time and space' (Stacey 2000: 141), the movement of Travellers is not transcendent because their movement is everywhere constrained by the development of a national infrastructure that facilitates only global flows in the local.

Another way in which the global increasingly affects the parameters of local belonging is through the global discourse of multiculturalism and human rights. These discourses legitimate cultural identity in ways that both underpin and undermine the nation-state as a site of political claims-making. In the global discourse of 'human rights', cultural identity and ethnicity are 'seen as variants of the universal core of humanness and selfhood' (Soysal 1997: 513).[32] Collective cultural identity has become an effective discourse of participation and means of mobilising resources. This mode of global belonging through the cultural has been taken up by Irish Travellers in ways that have produced new legitimated spaces of belonging, not least through the use of equality legislation. However, the women's discussions above point to the limitations of the spaces of the multicultural and equality. Their accounts suggest that Travellers are incorporated as representing an unassimilable and uninhabitable 'difference' and are then expelled as outside the national community (Ahmed 2000). Their identification as Irish and simultaneous exclusion from full citizenship produces both a disavowal of and desire for Irish belonging. Gender prescriptions for motherhood and assessments of respectability and reputation are integral to the operation of anti-Traveller racism. However, the circumscribed terms of Traveller/settled difference and the multicultural imperative to self-regulate Traveller identity tend to obscure gender and other differences and hierarchies amongst Travellers. The government of Travellers since the 1980s has been reshaped on the grounds of individual freedom and ethnic diversity so that practices of control and constraint are justified in a language of freedom, equality and cultural difference. Also, constraints on Traveller mobility are justified as a condition of the freedom and movement for settled people.

The close association between mobilities and consumption in a context of globalisation cannot be extended to the unassimilable other.[33] Nomadic Irish Traveller culture has not been appropriated for global consumer culture as Druid, Native American and Aboriginal cultures have in 'the West's bid to reinvent nature for itself within global culture' (Stacey 2000: 121). In a context where historical and material interests are hotly debated, it is harder to reduce Traveller cultures to signs of cultural difference or spectacle. The repeated positioning of Traveller culture as inadmissible and unassimilable difference makes it impossible to imagine the 'domestication' and commodification of Traveller cultures within global consumer culture. Also, the project of cultural survival positions Traveller culture less as a counter-modern or counter-global one than as a culture that is discontinuous with this global modernity. One young Traveller woman quoted in the media draws attention to how Traveller culture is seen as outside the modern:

> Some people think there is a contradiction between being a Traveller and being modern . . . Or that if we want to be modern we have to lose our Traveller identity . . . I am young, I am modern, I am a Traveller and I'm proud of it.
>
> (McDonald 2000)

The category 'Irish Traveller women' produces even more profound contradictions and elisions. The extent of exclusion and marginalisation of Irish Travellers makes it difficult to address the 'differences' within Traveller culture and among Traveller women themselves. The boundaries of the community are repeatedly constituted and reinforced in ways that reproduce a homogenising binary – settled/Traveller, making it difficult for Traveller differences and internal conflict to be articulated or publicly negotiated. The specific position of Traveller women was acknowledged by the 1995 *Report of the Task Force* which related their experience to that of 'Black and minority group women' who

> have extensively documented the interplay between, and contradictions of addressing, gender oppression and racism in their lives. This can involve these women in individual and collective choices between raising the issue of sexism within their own community and being in solidarity with their own community in resisting external oppression.
>
> (1995: 283)

Traveller women too are subject to the imperative to 'keep up appearances' of ethnic solidarity and reproduce the conditions of ethnic survival via prescribed familial performances of Traveller femininity. These femininities are not produced in the contrast between generations of women or in the tensions between a relation and possessive relation to the self articulated in many of the settled women's accounts in Chapter 2. Their selves are circumscribed by the feminine scripts available to them within Traveller communities and in settled/Traveller encounters. Although these women's selves are not constituted by the 'freedom to choose' to the same extent as in the accounts of settled women, this imperative represents an element of the workings of multiculturalism in which the 'choice' to identify as 'ethnic' simultaneously produces the responsibility to regulate that ethnicity. Deirdre's statement in the discussion that began this chapter – 'you have to have your own life too' – points towards a more possessive relationship to the self that is concealed by the multicultural tendency to collectivise Traveller identity. The discussion of women's accounts in this chapter points to how the development of Traveller/settled initiatives and women's groups through the Pavee Point Traveller Cultural Centre provides some new possibilities for public debate about the conditions of Irish Traveller women's belongings, but these are embryonic. Feminist politics and activism has to date developed around the concerns of settled Irish women in ways that constitute Traveller women as 'other'. Also, Traveller activism has been overdetermined by ethnicity in ways that have subordinated women's identifications as 'women'. In the following chapter, I return to the category 'Irish (settled) women' and how this category is reproduced in the negotiation of migration and staying put.

4 'The bright and the beautiful take off . . .'

Gendered negotiations of staying and going

A good friend of mine emigrated . . . she went straight from college to get a job because there weren't any here . . . We had a great row one night . . . about the issue of emigrants voting in elections here.[1] Now, I would be totally against that. The idea of someone living somewhere else, prescribing how I should live where I am . . . I'm sorry, I couldn't go along with that . . . She nearly went into orbit, she went berserk. Who did I think I was? What sort of an exclusive way was that to look on people? She was part of the diaspora, how could we possibly exclude her and hundreds and thousands of people like her who were driven out of their own homes? Jesus, the violins were out big time. I was really shocked that she should be so passionate about this. It was only then I realised, God, this isn't theoretical for her now at all, this is obviously a day-to-day frustration. (Lorna)

Did she feel forced out? Or was it just something that happened? (Eleanor)

She didn't go away looking for an adventure like some people quite like to. My younger brother emigrated to Germany and then to Saudi Arabia and didn't even look for a job here. He broke it gently to my mother, 'Goodbye I'm off now'. . . . She wouldn't have been in that category . . . so, if it came down to it, she didn't have a choice. (Lorna)

And she also wants to come back? (Mary)

Yes, she's always gone with the idea of coming back. (Lorna)

Why does she not come back, as a matter of interest? (Eleanor)

She can't get a job in the field that she wants one, that's it. (Lorna)

Because, I think it comes down to compromises really. Like, I never made a conscious decision not to leave Ireland. I did in fact want to leave Ireland just to travel . . . and experience different places and that, and it just so happens that I didn't . . . and I feel quite glad I didn't, because I really like it here [. . .] I want to stay in Ireland even though I could make more money abroad because, as far as I'm concerned, it's a better compromise to make, to have the life that I like here and to earn less money than going abroad . . . It just seems extremely single minded to me to always put your career, and always moving a step up, above coming home . . . Like she feels very bitter about the fact that she can't vote and that she doesn't have a hand in the country, but she's not prepared to compromise and come back here . . . [. . .] (Eleanor)

Being Irish is very important to her . . . she . . . always proclaims her Irishness . . . but does not want to be part of the ghetto Irish. (Lorna)

. . . she feels bitter about being cut off from her participation in Ireland and that, but there's a certain element of the feeling . . . I'm still here suffering along with the rest of the country so, I'm entitled to say that people outside the country have no say . . . There is a resentment that everyone who goes abroad is having a brilliant life and earning loads of money and it's always sunny abroad and as soon as you get out of Dublin it's sunny . . . You know, we're suffering here in the rain and we don't earn much money, what the hell are they worried about . . . (Eleanor)

One of the things that really pisses me off is this kind of strand that *the bright and the brilliant and the beautiful and the adventurous take off, you know . . . and all the boring daisies and common, ugly ones like ourselves stay here and keep the home fires burning* . . . that pisses me off big time . . . (Lorna, emphasis added)

You talk to people who have left and they're sorry for you . . . [. . .] (Eleanor)

Yea, like . . . how parochial of you . . . as if geography, you know, was going to change you from the inside out . . . give me one English Channel and suddenly I'm a new woman . . . (Lorna)

(Group discussion 1, Ireland)

The pervasiveness of mobility as a trope of global modernity forces us to pose the question of why 'particular people stay at home and . . . how, in a world of flux, forms of collective dwelling are sustained and reinvented' (Morley 2000: 13). One way of interpreting the above discussion is to see it as structured by dynamics of 'home' and 'anti-home', dwelling and movement within modernity and how these are re-worked by globalisation. Modernity is often characterised by 'a vocabulary of anti-home' that celebrates mobility, movement and boundary crossing while 'home' becomes a 'space of familiarity, dullness, stasis' (Felski 2000: 86). The impulse of longing is often seen as motivating modernity because it is marked by a desire for change (often through physical movement). On the other hand, 'home' and questions of 'rightful place' are also central to the dynamics of modernity. Globally mediated lives mean that staying in one place can produce similar experiences of 'displacement' to that of the migrant, so that all lives take on the characteristics of migrancy. However, I want to hold onto the specificities of migrant and non-migrant status and practices and to consider how they may be re-worked in the context of a global modernity that celebrates mobility. I am interested in how these practices (migrancy and staying-put) are themselves internally differentiated.

Many have argued that a kind of stability and uniformity was imposed on those who stayed in Ireland in the early decades of the twentieth century while Irish migrants became internationalised and modernised (Goldthorpe and Whelan 1992; Laffan and O'Donnell 1998; Walsh 1989). The Commission on Emigration and other Population Problems Reports 1948–54, acknowledged the circulation of the idea that 'emigration deprives the country of the best of its people' (1954: 139).[2] This identification of migration with personal initiative and modernisation implicitly positioned non-migrants as passive and lacking in initiative.[3] A counter-discourse of bourgeois Irish nationalism, which seems to have held less purchase, constructed out-migration as removing the 'weaker' element of the population, thus ensuring 'a stronger and more "manly" indigenous population' (Tovey and Share 2000: 117).[4] Thus, migrant and non-migrant constituencies were constructed in and through narratives of national loss or national strength in which the staying population were passive in opposition to migrant initiative, or strong and resilient in contrast with the feminised and less healthy migrant population. The migrant/non-migrant dichotomy worked to construct the national in particular ways and continued to do so at the end of the twentieth century. When high levels of out-migration returned in the 1980s, this new generation of migrants was appropriated into national narratives of modernisation through notions of 'the global'. Indeed, the increased valorisation of mobility and emergence of an official rhetoric of Ireland as a 'global nation' enabled a characterisation of migration as 'a beneficial experience for the best and brightest' (Corcoran 1998: 138) who, ironically, came to represent the country's progress since the 1950s.

In the discussion above the women's accounts frame their decisions to stay and relationships to belonging primarily within a discourse of choice that constitutes them as choosing individuals. Discourses of necessity and/or chance are also invoked in this discussion to account for migration, as for example, when Eleanor asks in relation to Lorna's friend: 'Did she feel forced out? Or was it just something that happened?' A further discourse of political exclusion is mobilised when Lorna identifies her migrant friend's resentment about her disenfranchisement. However, as the discussion progresses, there is a refusal to construct migration as exclusion or as a chance event. Instead, it is firmly located within a discourse of individual choice, reproducing the hegemonic construction of 1980s migration as a rational practice of career advancement (Mac Laughlin 1994a: 31). The conditions of Irish belonging are differentiated in the discussion through a discourse of choice between migration for career success and staying in Ireland to pursue an 'Irish' 'lifestyle'. Migrants, by lounging in the sunshine (in London!), earning high incomes and improving their career chances, are constructed as putting personal gain above lifestyle in Ireland and putting individual interest above national loyalty. Once gone, personal ambition and nostalgia ('rose-tinted glasses') constitute the migrant's desire to belong in Ireland as 'inauthentic'. Lorna defends her friend against 'inauthenticity' by asserting that she (her friend) is not part of an Irish migrant ghetto in London, implying the maintenance of an Ireland focused (and therefore authentic) Irishness.

Eleanor's account constructs staying and going via a cost/benefit analysis that identifies the costs of staying as 'suffering here in the rain', having fewer career prospects and paying higher taxes. But, on the positive side, staying represents a more 'authentic' relationship to the national collectivity when understood as choosing 'lifestyle in Ireland' over climbing the career ladder abroad. To leave would be to reject Ireland and its way of life in favour of economic advancement. Staying is framed by a discourse of choice that identifies it as just one modern response to global modernity – 'to have a life that I like here and to earn less money than going abroad . . .'. Despite the drive to reframe staying as agency in a discourse of choice, the discussion is haunted by representations of the migrant as 'the bright and beautiful' and the stayer as lacking the initiative to leave. One mode of countering the momentum that surrounds leaving is to reconstitute Ireland as a location of desire, a place that represents change, progress and resistance for women. Lorna's mocking of the 'new woman' produced by moving across the 'English Channel' (she may have meant to say the Irish Sea) suggests a distrust of (or frustration with) the narrative of migration as modernisation, particularly for women.

In this chapter, questions of staying and going are discussed in relation to the operation of choice as a technology of the self. I argue that longing *and* belonging in global modernity are constituted via a form of 'prescriptive individualism' (Strathern 1992: 152) that paradoxically offers no alternative other than to frame belonging through an individual narrative of choice. If Irish migration in the past was accounted for within 'an ideological frame which emphasized collectivity over individualism, patience over action, and fatalism over will' (Jacobson 1995: 14), I argue that by the late twentieth century, Irish migration was framed primarily by an ideology of individualism, action and will. In both cases, only particular kinds of migrant and non-migrant selves were permissible. Nonetheless, the discussion quoted at the beginning of this chapter points to the continued circulation in the 1990s of migration as a mode of changing the self – becoming a 'new woman'. This perception is examined in the following sections of this chapter, which consider the operation of choice as a 'truth' of the self in the women's accounts. These sections are structured by three broad question areas: First, how are staying subjects produced through discourses of choice? Second, what can and cannot be said about Irish migration in the 1980s and Irish women's migration in particular? Also, what can and cannot be said about staying? Third, how do opportunities for more frequent contact (actual and potential) than in the past affect migrant/non-migrant relations?

Resistance, choice, agency and staying put

The group discussion that began this chapter moved towards framing staying (albeit in opposition to migration) as an outcome of choice. This was a choice that represented an acceptance of Irish society as embodying values, a culture and way of life that, for the most part, these women stayers identified with. The homeland is constructed as an enriching place to be, a place that produces and affirms the self. But what are the options for those who find the cultural values and ways of life in Ireland non-affirming or excluding? For some, the response is to emigrate, but for others, staying becomes a political project of resistance and change. The figure of the migrant tends to have taken on the mantle of self-assertion, dissidence and independent thinking in ways that evacuate the radical from the homeland and from constructions of staying selves. Poet Mary Dorcey challenges this polarised interpretation of migrants and those who stay.

> There is a sense of wanting to assert a refusal to be banished . . . To be a queer who stays in Ireland and writes about it is to fly in the face of all our cultural expectations (which will accept any behaviour in foreign streets so long as it doesn't frighten Irish horses). We like to export our troublemakers, our dissidents, our critics. I have a dream of Ireland in which all the troublemakers have come home to roost. But for that to happen, some of us have to refuse to leave . . .
>
> (Dorcey 1995: 43)

It is difficult to articulate a relationship to staying or non-migrant status outside of its relation to migration. Migration is identified in the opening discussion with individual career ambitions, self-development and sexual freedom. In contrast, the staying self is produced as dutiful and willing to make career compromises in favour of an Irish lifestyle at 'home'. Narratives of staying as choosing futures and lifestyles have much in common with dominant narratives of migration. In spite of this framing of staying as choice, the staying self is implicitly produced in the discussion as a potentially un-realised self in relation to career and sexuality. In the enunciation of the staying self as agentic, Ireland itself is produced as a particular kind of place. While staying as a lifestyle choice constitutes Ireland as an authentic site of Irishness, narratives of staying as politicised resistance construct Ireland as a place of domination and exclusion. For example, in Romy's account below, staying is constructed in terms of feminist goals for social change in Ireland.

> When I initially became publicly identified with feminism and with the hard issues of feminism, it was put to me that if I did not care for the way that Ireland conducted itself in respect of these issues, I should . . . get out. And I took the view very very strongly that that's no way to behave, that if I have a complaint or an argument with my society, that I am entitled to engage with my society on those issues because, as the poet said 'I am of Ireland', my entire identity has to do with being Irish and being an inheritor of a very ambiguous political tradition, a very argued political tradition, and I see myself very much as a part of that . . .
>
> (Romy, interview, Ireland)

Romy assumes the 'burden' of liberty to choose and when confronted with the suggestion that she should 'get out', chooses to stay in the name of the project of liberation and freedom for Irish women. However, the individual choice to stay is authorised in her account via a collective 'tradition' of Irish feminist politics. Her choice is legitimated by a feminist identity that is further legitimated by her 'inherited' national identity.

A self that is free to choose to stay emerges in Bride's account below. This choice to stay is accounted for in relation to her particular contribution to Irish society.

> I choose to live in Ireland because I have a pioneering sense and I like to do new things and there's more of an opportunity of doing new things in Ireland, like the work that I'm doing (feminist theology) . . . while I lack the support, there are lots of people I can connect with via the Internet or whatever . . . I create the questions here that come up in other countries . . . At least if you're Irish and living in Ireland you can be real about what's happening in Ireland . . . if you're living in Ireland, to be Irish is something that you can't define because it's developing and changing, it's in process and what's happening today will be different tomorrow . . . But there are lots of people in Ireland as well who have a static notion of what it is to be Irish, as in the referenda debates (abortion and divorce), they have this kind of golden age that they want to hold on to. But for me to be Irish is to be developing all the time . . .
>
> (Bride, interview, Ireland)

Bride's account undoes the terms of the opposition between staying and migration by identifying different 'stayer' relations to Irish belonging and by framing staying as contributing to processes of change in Ireland. Bride's identification with a changing Ireland and active connection with individuals in other parts of the world challenges the construction of migration as an encounter with the 'new', with opportunity and change. New means of communication such as the Internet locate the stayer in a wider world than the national. The claims of the staying self to an 'authentic' Irish belonging in Bride's account are made on the basis of a familiarity with change and the immediacy of day-to-day experience in Ireland. Yet, her staying is facilitated by her Internet mediated global connections and later in her account she emphasises the significance of her ability to travel out of Ireland frequently. These accounts of staying are suggestive with regard to how modern selves are attached to a project of freedom and have come to live it in terms of Irish, queer or feminist identities (Rose 1999b: 262).

Although the choice to stay is variously justified as resistance, making a unique contribution to Irish society and as a lifestyle choice, the spectre of the migrant as a 'new woman' identified by Lorna at the beginning of this chapter haunts many of the narratives of staying. Staying is repeatedly constructed in relation to the desire to migrate or the promise of migration. It is frequently reflected on, therefore, through the imagined perceptions of migrants.

> I suppose they (migrants) would see me as successful and happy. Now, I often wonder do they see us as narrow in the sense of meaning, sort of settled? I'd hate to think that . . . and you're not sure whether that's a good or a bad thing in their eyes? (Kathleen)
> Yes. And would you see them as unsettled? (Breda)
> No, I wouldn't see them as unsettled, more adventurous maybe and maybe more courageous and lucky maybe to have a good chance. (Kathleen)
>
> (Interview, Ireland)

Those who stay struggle against valorised notions of the autonomous and actualised self achieved through travel and living elsewhere. It is assumed that staying represents constraint rather than choice in the eyes of those who go.

> I'm sure people come back here and think 'God, they haven't changed, nothing's changed a bit', 'God, she's still in the same place' and that kind of thing. I think they think 'How does she stay there?' *You're still sticking it out,* kind of attitude, which is kind of like *you're in a rut nearly*, which is close to saying, maybe a rut is too strong a word, but unchanged, but there's part of them trying to make sense of how do you still do that and they're studying and they're going on with other things and they're kind of wondering, 'what does she get out of life?'. . . someone who's never changed job although I've changed schools. I suppose they would know other things have happened to me [. . .] Maybe they see me as a bit unfree, a bit trapped maybe, or that I have set limits, maybe they see me as limiting myself, not branching out. The question 'How do you stay?' may not be negative or positive. They feel you're lucky that you can be contented and not *have to contend with this coming and going* . . . so there may be some of that, that you can be content. I've never heard them saying that 'You should leave' and 'why don't you come to England?' I've never heard them say that either . . . maybe limiting myself, maybe envious that I'm content to stay [. . .] I really don't know, maybe it's changeable, maybe people feel both things if I did ask people.
>
> (Siobhan, interview, Ireland; emphasis added)

A modern discourse of migration as a practice of self-development identifies staying as self-limiting, but also as enabling belonging through attachment to and investment in place, people and community. Home, in Siobhan's account, is implicitly constructed as a purified space of belonging in which the subject is too comfortable to question the limits or borders of her or his experience, indeed, where the subject is so at ease that she or he does not think.

(Ahmed 2000: 87)

Staying put, when conflated with static notions of 'home', is reduced to complacency and contentment. Ahmed suggests that this 'association of home with familiarity which allows strangeness to be associated with migration ... is problematic' because it occludes the strangeness and movement *within* homes (2000: 88). Instead, she posits homes as always involving 'encounters between those who stay, those who arrive and those who leave' (ibid.). Mobilities are also inhabited without physical movement when individual women, like Mary Dorcey, Romy and Bride quoted earlier, conjure up a place of their own that stands out from the circumstances in which they find themselves in order to resist 'settled' assumptions and norms. When understood as being on the inside and outside at the same time, mobility can emerge out of a refusal of the potential complacency of 'home' but can also be a mode of searching for 'home' as some of the accounts in Chapter 2 suggest.

Impermissible narratives of migration and belonging

If the boundaries between home and away, migration and staying put are reworked by the mobility of culture, people and finance and a discourse of choice, how does this affect what can be said about late twentieth-century Irish migration and women's migration in particular? The following discussion took place amongst a group of women undertaking a masters degree in women's studies in Dublin, most of whom had stayed and some of whom had migrated and returned. This excerpt focuses on what could and could not be said about women's migration. The suggestion is that migration can be a response to social conservatism, familial constraints and many other aspects of Irish life, but that such interpretations could not be openly articulated.

> There is an expectation of the people that are left behind that the people that go away have to be very successful ... *you can't admit that you went away for any other reason than to be successful, why else would you leave Ireland?* (emphasis added) Surely Ireland is so wonderful that you don't want to leave. The only reason you would go is to make your life better [. . .]you can't say you left Ireland because you couldn't get recognition, or you weren't happy. (Pauline)
>
> Why? What's wrong with that? (Martha)
>
> [. . .] people I suppose abroad, would wonder why you would ever want to leave such a place ... I mean why else would you leave, but to become successful? (Denyse)

But it is in here as well. You can't admit that Ireland is bad . . . we can't say there is anything wrong with Ireland . . . a friend of mine who is Australian, she lived here for two years . . . and she used to have people jumping down her throat at parties and discussions and everything because she dared to mention that Ireland wasn't, you know, paradise on earth . . . she had to get out . . . she lives in London now. The thing about Ireland is, you can't criticise Ireland, can't criticise the Irish, you know, in general. (Pauline)

. . . But apart from this whole idea of success, most of the people that I know who have left, have left for a specific reason that they are looking for anonymity. And if that's what is lurking here, if that is the problem for them, that everybody knows them . . . and what they are doing and what they are up to. (Jan)

[. . .] they have no sense of freedom to live their own lives . . . it's that idea that they leave here and head for a big city somewhere . . . and you could do as you please you know. Maybe you are gay or lesbian maybe, whatever, but you can actually live the life that you want to live without, you know, your aunt sending the parish priest around. (Pauline)

[. . .] Just one of the first things that pops into my mind is how many Irish lesbians I know who kind of almost feel that they had to go away to discover that part of themselves. And certainly relating to myself, it was as though, well, I wouldn't have had the words or the consciousness really or even support definitely here before I went. I found it was so much easier. And then I know the woman who was organising the lesbian disco in Dublin and she said that she could tell from the women coming in which ones had emigrated and come back, you know, the self-confidence that they brought back or different things about them. (Mo)

(Group discussion 7, Ireland)

If 'veiled suggestions of emigration – became a substitute for real communication' in earlier generations (Ryan 1990: 49), this discussion suggests that career advancement became a euphemism for the many factors motivating women's migration in the 1980s. Just as in the past, 1980s migration was surrounded by 'protective layers of ambiguity' (Lee 1989a: 375). The view that '[e]migrants must obviously be deluded, if not depraved, to desert God's own island' is rehearsed again (ibid.: 376), and the failure of the promise of happiness and recognition in Ireland, they suggest, is concealed by strategies of avoidance and silence. Ironically, migration offered a way of responding to this failed promise while not totally jeopardising claims to national belonging. To account for migration as a response to dissatisfaction with Ireland would be to locate oneself outside of the national 'we'. Although an act that can potentially be viewed as a rejection of the national community, this interpretation of migration is avoided by popular narratives of career advancement (and to some extent by a national 'tradition' of migration). Of course, the many who were leaving with limited education and few career prospects abroad were edited out of the narrative of career advancement (see Mac Laughlin 1997). However, the classed nature of 1980s Irish migration was often more evident in migrant destinations than in Ireland itself (see Chapter 5).

Although, one of the few permissible motivations/justifications for migration was career ambition, in the above discussion, many other motivations are alluded to. Migration is identified by Jan with the desire for anonymity based on the perception that the city allows 'new experiences of closeness and distance, freedom and danger' (Felski 2000: 65). The act of migration and the city of destination are seen as holding out the promise of anonymity, self-fulfilment and self-expression. The identification of Ireland with positive lifestyle choice in the opening discussion of this chapter is countered here by a construction of Ireland as a location of gendered surveillance and regulation. Pauline's account (and the group members' agreement with her) identifies the extent of this regulation by pointing to the imperative not to criticise Ireland or the Irish. Her Australian friend who transgressed the boundaries of silence 'had to get out'. As in many accounts, migration to London (and other migrant destinations) becomes a route to self-expression back in Ireland. Mo suggests that the constraints surrounding lesbian sexuality in Ireland are potentially overcome through migration. London is seen as a space in which a lesbian self can be inhabited and rehearsed so that it can be confidently inhabited on return (either to stay or when visiting). Because women's migration is represented here as shrouded in euphemism, there is an assumption that the migrant and the migrant narrative are never what they seem. There is a parallel here between the imperative to 'keep up appearances' of Irish femininity discussed in Chapter 2 and the imperative to 'keep up appearances' of an ideal national community in Ireland via prescribed narratives of migration. The perception that migrant narratives have to be fabricated casts doubt on the 'authenticity' of the migrant herself. What happens then when publicly legitimated narratives of migration are negotiated in the more intimate contexts of family and local community?

I take up the question of local and familial negotiations of migrancy and non-migrancy via the accounts below which focus on return visits to Ireland. In a group discussion in London, women identified some of the contradictory experiences of negotiating their migrant status in Ireland.

Yes, 'I can take or leave you', that is what people (in Ireland) don't like. (Maura)

 I think you are right, and you are going back (to London) too. (Bernie)

 That you are not dependent on home, and all that. (Maura)

 ... I think they are kind of curious as to how you can actually survive away from Ireland some of them; if they have not been away themselves ... They ask 'Do you like London?' And I say 'yes' and

they say 'But it's big' and I say 'Yes, I know that's why I like it'. . . .
They don't want to know . . . (Maura)

(Group discussion 2, London)

Unlike the group discussion at the beginning of the chapter in which Lorna's
friend is seen as demanding recognition in Ireland, these migrant women
suggest that it is their disconnectedness or their lack of demands on Irish
society that position them as outsiders on return visits. By appearing to have
no vested interest in 'home' and by their ability to 'come and go',
these women migrants' relationships to Ireland cannot be easily accessed.
They challenge the assumption that no one could want to leave or could
thrive elsewhere because they demonstrate that it is possible to 'survive
away from Ireland'. The accounts also suggest a fluid relationship to
belonging and lifestyle by their identification with *both* Ireland *and* the 'big
city'. The perceptions of migrants as unwilling to assume an expected dutiful
connection with 'home' is embraced by these women as both a mode of
resistance and as a form of liberation. But for other women migrants, the
perception in Ireland that they are now fully settled elsewhere is experienced
as rejection.

> Well, I think people tend not to make as big a fuss of you because they
> know you are only back for a weekend, or three or four days. And you
> are going away again and you know 'Oh, hi, how are you doing?',
> 'Welcome home', 'When are you going back?' sort of thing, which is
> fair enough, because your experiences are different to theirs and there
> is very little now to talk about . . . There is also some sort of envy
> because you are managing elsewhere . . . you are doing okay, thank you
> very much . . . there is a lot of that at home.
>
> (Hazel, interview, London)

It is difficult to negotiate geographically fractured family and friendship
relations during short return visits. Indeed, these accounts point to the limits
of multi-located belonging. The 'home' community is constructed in some
of them as unable/unwilling to extend the boundaries of belonging to include
migrant members – or at least to extend them on terms that these migrant
women see as incorporating their belonging in London. Return visits stage
an emotional encounter between migrants and those who stayed. In this
encounter, migrants find themselves positioned as outside the national
community (settled elsewhere) but harbouring a desire to return, and stayers
are seen as policing the (narrow) terms of belonging in Ireland. The conditions of leaving and returning and the multiple identifications and belongings
that mark Irish women's migrancy in the 1990s are present but remain
unspoken in these encounters. Indeed, the ambiguity that surrounds the
original leaving persists and is repeated in familial and friendship relations on return visits. Dynamics of longing and belonging are marked by

the legacy of the imperative to maintain perceptions of Ireland as 'God's own island'. Fixity and mobility, belonging and longing are negotiated in the tensions between national and global practices and imaginings. The bi-located belonging articulated in the migrant women's accounts produce an anxiety that compounds the ambiguities surrounding the migrant in the 'homeland'.

'Suspect' belongings – migrant relationships to the 'homeland'

Although recession meant that many *had* to leave to find employment in the 1980s, there is evidence that many left who already had work in Ireland.[5] This meant that perhaps for the first time in the history of Irish migration, more families and communities in Ireland had to address young Irish women's (and men's) active decisions to live and work outside of the country. These were the beneficiaries of a free education system; they were brought up in an Ireland that was represented by the southern state and media as 'modern', yet these young people were still embracing more desirable modernities in London, New York and elsewhere. Why was this 'new' modern Ireland not an attractive place for many young Irish people? Molly, who qualified as a doctor in Cork and is now living in London, noted:

> Some of my brothers felt that because I had a grant to be educated in Ireland that I had a sort of a duty to work there and that it was wrong of me to sort of take the free education and then leave with it . . . I think it was about a lot of people of the generation before me were forced to leave and sort of didn't like the fact that they had to leave and always wished they could come back. And they found it strange to think that somebody left and enjoyed it or, you know, that they could like somewhere more than Cork.
>
> (Molly, interview, London)

In Hazel's account, the migrant is seen as having to compensate for the rejection implied in the act of leaving by taking responsibility for the work of keeping in touch.

> But I remember going home at Christmas and I have a twin brother and . . . when I arrived, we hugged each other. And I said 'I have really missed you Gerry', and . . . he kind of pushed me away and he said you are the one that left . . . they make you feel guilty. I feel that they experience you as having rejected them . . . I experienced them as rejecting me; I am the one here on my own. They never support me ever. None of my family has come to visit me in this country. I am expected to do all the visiting even though I was the poor student . . .
>
> (Hazel, interview, London)

When interpreted as a rejection of the resources invested in her education in Molly's case and leaving family behind in Hazel's account, migration produces dynamics of distrust and suspicion between migrants and non-migrants. In many cases, these relationships are lived through innuendo, mis-recognitions and miscommunications. Visits to Ireland also meant a confrontation with the ways in which residence in England produces difference. The following contributions from Fionnuala in a group discussion in London suggest that she cannot inhabit Ireland as an insider anymore.

> One thing that really brought it home to me though for the last few years is when I go to Ireland, because I do go very frequently to see my family there. I will buy the English paper when I go out during the day and for a number of years I would always buy the *Irish Times* when I was in Ireland. I might buy the *Irish Times* now, but I will buy an English paper as well and I will also watch the English news, because to me, that is what is really happening now. (Fionnuala)
>
> So why is the English news different from the Irish news as a matter of interest? (Breda)
>
> Well, because there is obviously a different slant on English politics and, also because I am interested in the economic affairs of Britain which aren't reported in Ireland because they are not relevant. All that is important in Ireland is politics . . . when you turn on the news is just the North constantly. It seems to me, it's like 95 per cent of the news . . . but there are things happening in England that if you are a resident here you want to know about. (Fionnuala)
>
> . . . I certainly don't feel Irish when I am in our house because they all told me I am English. I mean they all say 'Oh your accent'. . . and, you know, when you are talking about going on holidays and stuff, and your lifestyle is so different to theirs anyway. And the last thing anybody would think was that you were Irish. So you don't consequently feel it. And everything you say is wrong. You know in terms of like. (Fionnuala)
>
> Everything you say is wrong. (Julia)
>
> (Group discussion 3, London)

It is impossible to return to a place that was once lived as home because 'the home is not exterior but interior to embodied subjects' (Ahmed 2000: 91). Ahmed suggests that return is inflected by failures of memory, as the migrant is not 'inhabited in the same way by that which appears familiar' (ibid.). Fionnuala articulates this inability to inhabit home like she used to by noting its many *unfamiliarities* and how her attempts to inhabit home differently are disallowed. Family members are estranged from one another and the once 'shared terrain of knowledge' (ibid.: 92) can no longer be assumed. These negotiations suggest a bigger agenda of 'political and personal struggles over the social regulation of "belonging"' (Brah 1996: 192), often articulated through gendered expectations of the 'dutiful' daughter. Attempts to re-inhabit the 'dutiful daughter' self by frequent return visits are unsuccessful when not recognised as such.

Fionnuala's interests, as a resident in London and manager in the private sector, are framed mainly by economic interests and not by events in Northern Ireland (which may well be seen as just as relevant to those living in England as in Ireland). England is identified with the economy, which is implicitly identified as a 'modern' concern while media in Ireland are seen as overly concerned with the political. Ambivalence about her position in the family as a migrant is reconciled via an identification with 'English' values above 'Irish' values. When identified as English by her family, Fionnuala's response is to identify with this designation and reject the Irishness that is denied her: 'they all told me I am English'. Yet, later in her account, Fionnuala expressed much regret and loss about her exclusion from family and community in Ireland.

While the migrant women's accounts emphasise a lack of recognition or understanding of their multi-located identifications, many of those who stayed felt unsure about how to interpret the expectations of migrants and the status of migrants in the family and community in Ireland.

> And strange misconceptions arise . . . I just find communication is difficult. You make promises 'Oh it doesn't matter we'll stay in touch', but it does matter . . . you do diverge . . . at a time in my life when I had a crisis . . . my friends, people that I should have been close to were in England and it has led to some misunderstandings and differences in family and that . . . She (her migrant sister) probably feels that 'I better . . . go home, maybe I'm supposed to or maybe they're all expecting me to'. We (family in Ireland) probably think 'No, she doesn't have to come at all, she has to travel from England'. So I think, unless it's discussed, a lot of family tensions arise about duty on both sides . . . 'Am I supposed to come home every time something happens?' Or, 'Are we supposed to go over to you?' or 'You don't have to come this Christmas', or, 'Will people be saying why didn't you come at Christmas?' We might be saying 'Here she is again at Christmas'. . . Nobody knows the rules or what games we're playing with in a way. There's a family home and people come to visit their parents, then when the parents die . . . where does she have to come to. And will she feel 'I have nowhere to go, so the others will have to take me in'. Or does she feel 'I have nowhere to go, that's great'. *You're stepping around people's feelings about how they feel about being emigrants.* I think it is a reality that *these people* are coming home and they don't know the country they're staying in and they don't know the family they're staying with . . . I remember being over in London . . . and realising this is Eileen's home now . . . and you have to consider that too (emphasis added). But it isn't discussed actually . . . in Ireland for all our talk we might not be the greatest of communicators . . . Emigrants might feel

quite defensive . . . they may be crying at the airport, but they may be absolutely thrilled to be getting away from the claustrophobia of it, they may be very very glad . . .

(Siobhan, interview, Dublin)

The gendered 'doing' of family and friendship are at stake in Siobhan's account of migrant belonging. She suggests that the only link to belonging 'at home' for migrants is through parents and the family home.[6] Yet, 'these people', her migrant friends and sister, are coming back to a home and family they no longer know well in her view, so that it becomes impossible for them to occupy the position of dutiful selves. They perform dutiful selves by returning at Christmas, but are not 'there' when they 'should' be. Their dutiful return visits reveal the fact that all dutiful actions are untrustworthy because the motivation for duty is always externally-defined expectations. Discourses of choice, lifestyle and career produce an autonomous migrant self, apparently unburdened by day-to-day family obligations. Claims to the category 'Irish women', at least when constituted in terms of duty and obligation (see Chapter 2), are undermined by perceptions of migrant women's inadequate performances of familial duty. In a review of studies of migration, David Morley suggests that migrants

> understand themselves to be morally obliged to make regular return visits, as they negotiate the respective claims of their 'home and away' identities, and continually refashion their identities as they travel through time and space.

(Morley 2000: 53)

However, the ways in which these moral obligations and 'home and away' identities are articulated and lived are culturally, racially, gender, class, geographically and time specific. Gender identity as it is constituted through national/cultural identity is at stake in how these obligations are taken up (or not) by Irish women migrants and in evaluations of the extent to which they are met by kin and community in Ireland. Legacies of concealment around emigration interact with the globalised conditions of late twentieth-century migration to produce sometimes fraught relations between migrants and non-migrants in these accounts.

Despite Ireland's history of emigration, Siobhan's account above suggests that there are no rules for migrant/non-migrant relations and relationships to family 'at home'. This lack of norms/rules becomes all the more acute in an era of faster and cheaper communication and transport. The ability to keep in regular contact produces a sense of closeness but also a heightened disappointment when migrants are not physically present at times of crisis. Siobhan's account is marked by a gap between performances of duty and communication and the assumed motivations behind these performances. The migrant/non-migrant relationship in her account is marked by distrust and unarticulated mutual expectations.

In Romy's account below, migrant relationships to places in Dublin city are discussed.

> It was in the air . . . and Christmas in Grafton Street in the 80s became absolutely horrible in a sense because what happened was that, instead of just ordinary Christmas euphoria . . . young professional people who were abroad came back for Christmas, hysterical, up to 90 as you can imagine and the place was just *infected with this absolute hysteria* . . . it was absolute hysteria (emphasis added). That was very symptomatic of the 80s, that people were away and they'd come back for these sort of ritual coming backs. I really didn't want to be part of that at all . . . (Romy)
>
> What kinds of things did that bring up? (Breda)
>
> At the time, when I was noticing that, in a sense, I felt sorry for the young people that they had to experience those kinds of violent emotions. Young people experience violent emotions, but one hopes that they're more positive . . . than being about: 'Who am I?' and 'Where am I?'. . . There was a nostalgia, you know, 'you were in my class at college and here we are both in The Bailey' (a pub off Grafton Street in Dublin), or something. 'Here we are on *neutral turf*, because you're in America and I'm in England and now it's Christmas, we're on shared territory' and it's all very hysterical . . . Because *I live here*, there was a sense that here were visitors and yet, my heart went out to them . . . those particular young people seem to me to be people *who have no place* (emphasis added). Unlike earlier generations of emigrants, they haven't actually put down roots where they went, but because they weren't here anymore, they were coming and going simultaneously, there was hysteria built into that. And it was very very uncomfortable . . . (Romy)
>
> (Interview, Dublin)

The construction of 1980s migrants as a 'sojourning' class 'living bi-nationally, and with "suspect" allegiances vis-à-vis the nation-state' emerges in different ways in these accounts (Mitchell 2001: 170). The perceived placelessness of this generation of migrants as a result of mobility undoes traditional assumptions of an isomorphic relationship between place and belonging. Unmoored from the governable spaces of the state and family and their norms concerning the 'conduct of conduct', these returned 'visitors' transgress the rules for occupying local spaces. The witnessing of their return rituals is identified as uncomfortable for those who 'live here'. Rituals of 'coming back' are seen as 'infecting' Romy's home city with a kind of 'hysteria' represented by questions of: 'Who am I? And Where am I?' Seen as having 'no place' of their own, these returning migrants turn Dublin into a 'neutral turf' for the celebration of migration and migrant connections with Ireland. Dublin is divested of its fullness of meaning to those who live there.

The return migrants' 'hysterical' temporary presences are partly reconciled in Romy's account through pity for their simultaneous 'coming and going'. The mobility of migrants is represented here, as in Siobhan's account earlier, as their loss rather than gain. In contrast with the discussion quoted at the beginning of this chapter in which the migrant is seen as pitying those who stayed, in this account it is the stayer, Romy, who pities these mobile visitors, who, unlike her, 'have no place' and are hysterically 'coming and going'.

The accounts discussed so far point to the highly charged social relations between migrants and non-migrants and the shifting parameters of these relations in contexts of global mobility producing unstable migrant and non-migrant selves. An 'authentic' Irish self by virtue of staying in Ireland was more easily assumed by earlier generations whose migrant peers put down roots in their countries of destination, thereby occupying the status of *emigrants*, gone from the space of Ireland and firmly located elsewhere. The boundaries between 'home' and 'away' were more easily maintained and appeared more clear-cut. In the 1980s and 1990s, London, New York and other Irish migrant destinations could be occupied as extensions of Ireland because many migrants moved back and forth, as did some of their friends and family. In Romy's account this generation is constructed as mobile and rootless, thereby troubling assumptions of 'us' and 'them', 'home' and 'away' because 'they' (migrants) make claims on 'our' spaces of belonging in Ireland in 'inappropriate' ways. 'Normal' life in Dublin is disrupted by conversations asserting the relative excitement of life in America and England. Dublin is turned into a 'neutral' space – a meeting ground in which memories of a past Ireland are shared and experiences elsewhere are exchanged. Home becomes a place to reconnect with other migrants (and non-migrants although they do not feature in Romy's account) while ' "abroad" is the place [of] . . . peak experience and real development' (Rojek and Urry 1997: 16). Irish migrants are seen as moving, like Bauman's (1993) vagabonds and tourists through 'other peoples' spaces' in ways that are seen as separating 'physical closeness from moral proximity' (ibid.: 10). Because she lives in Dublin, Romy's relationship to the city is rooted to the place in a way that produces a morally responsible relationship to the city. This moral proximity to Dublin is not shared by these temporary and mobile migrants who are 'home' for Christmas, but will soon be gone again.

As Ireland becomes a node in global flows of people, culture, capital, finance and so on, migration can no longer be understood as a linear trajectory that involves settlement in another country, but a practice that (for many) involves circuits of movement between places (see Gray 2003b). Therefore, the lives of those who stay are also marked by these mobilities. Although there is some de-differentiation between migration and staying put in global modernity, this does not go all the way down. The above accounts produce forms of re-differentiation which evoke anxious relationships between staying and migrant subjects. Increased contact between migrants and non-migrants intensifies mutual expectations and exposes the silences. However, these remain unarticulated as the legacies of denial, subterfuge and euphemism that surround Irish migration imbue these relations with ambiguity and mutual suspicion. The impermissibility of certain narratives of migration alongside the increased frequency of contact between migrants and non-migrants may account for the emotional tone of some of these accounts.

Conclusion

Kerby Miller, in a discussion of the rhetoric in Ireland surrounding Irish emigration between 1856 and 1921, refers to the work of anthropologist Robin Fox in Tory Island off the north coast of Ireland in 1978. Fox suggested that 'although a child who does not migrate is "lazy", one who does is "disloyal"' (Miller 1993: 285). Commenting on these findings, Miller suggests that while encouraging migration, parents did not want migrants to be motivated by 'hedonistic ambition' but only by 'familial obligations to relatives at home or already abroad' (ibid.). '[I]t was "a shame" to migrate, but also "a shame" to remain at home' – what Miller characterised as 'Paddy's Paradox' or 'Caitlin's conundrum' (ibid.: 286). Migration when 'undertaken in a proper "dutiful" spirit promised to mitigate all conflicts and resolve all contradictions (ibid.). Miller's characterisation of the dilemmas, subterfuge and concealment surrounding Irish migration enables us to make some observations about how the women's accounts above construct Irish migration in the 1980s. By then individual ambition rather than family loyalty had become the acceptable narrative of migration. However, the willingness of individual migrants to keep to the permitted narrative of emigration as career advancement can be interpreted as a form of family (and national) loyalty. This narrative also concealed a range of motivations and enabled the community and families to resolve the contradictions of continued emigration through a discourse of choice and globalised notions of career trajectories. The absence of opportunity in Ireland, the social discontent that many migrant women experienced and tensions within families were subsumed to a repetitive and acceptable narrative of individual achievement though a migration characterised in terms of privileged mobility rather than obligation, sacrifice or collective exile. A regime of the self emerges in the accounts discussed in this chapter in which these women's lives are understood not in terms of collective exile or fate but in terms of their ability to makes choices to actualise their selves. Irish women's migration is de-classed and de-gendered by the only permissible narrative of late twentieth-century migration as personal career advancement. It is clear from the discussions and interviews that women migrants and stayers in the 1990s are constituted and constitute themselves as 'not merely "free to choose", but *obliged to be free*, to understand and enact their lives in terms of choice' (Rose 1999a: 87; emphasis in original). The decision to migrate, or to stay, is identified as an attribute of 'the choosing person, an expression of personality and as reflecting back upon the person who made the decision' (ibid.). Ironically, the migrant choosing self can only be publicly articulated as making one choice in migrating, that is the choice to improve her career chances.

Vocabularies of 'home' and 'anti-home', belonging and longing are re-worked in the accounts discussed in this chapter. My interpretation and analysis of the women's accounts suggests that belonging is both subsumed to longing and posed more starkly against longing. The women's accounts are structured by discourses of choice, which privilege the impulse of longing. Choice is the site on which staying and going are negotiated. Longing, framed by a discourse of choice, is not only identified with phys-ical movement but also with staying put. It is choice rather than physical movement that is the essence of these women's individuality (Strathern 1992). As Anne Cronin argues, 'the expression and enactment of choice (and the capacity to choose) is framed as a duty to the self' and brings the self into being (2000: 149). Longing as defined by choice comes to represent the 'potential and discursive drive of the individual' (ibid.). Longing may be interpreted in Cronin's terms as a 'search for the "space of pure voluntarity" which ... is paradoxically articulated as *compulsory individuality*' (ibid.: 160; emphasis in original). As Rose argues, citizens increasingly fulfil their political obligations to the nation 'not when they are bound in relations of dependency and obligation, but when they seek to *fulfil* themselves as free individuals' (Rose 1999a: 166). Individuals are linked to society by shaping their lifestyles according to socially sanctioned modes. But it is the 'freedom' to be loyal to nation and family and to choose the kind of individual one wants to be that represent points of tension in these accounts. Duty and obligation are reworked through the 'freedom to choose', the ability to move and to 'keep in touch'. The dominant motif for both stayers and migrants is that of the choosing self who bears responsibility for her choices (or perceived choices). Choice is abstracted in these discourses from the modes of regulation and power relations that mark them.

The lived experiences of migration and staying put as articulated in the accounts are also marked by political discourses of Irish migration past and present and the ways in which regimes of gender and class interact with these discourses. Career advancement, although a popularly sanctioned narra-tive of migration, is mapped more easily onto middle-class work identities. Although the norms of migrant–non-migrant relations may be less clearly defined than in the past, gender identity continues to define the parameters of 'dutiful' familial relations. In spite of the collapse of migrant and non-migrant narratives of the self into a dominant narrative of choice, different potential narratives of the self are available to migrant and non-migrant Irish women. The legacy of migration/movement as modern and progressive for women in particular tends to reproduce migrancy as a paradigmatic site of choice and potential individual liberation. This is encapsulated by Lorna's ironic statement in the discussion quoted at the beginning of the chapter – 'give me one English Channel and suddenly I'm a new woman'. Although conceptually, migration and staying cannot be understood separately because moving is always a movement to, and staying put is always the recognition of the potential to move, it is evident from the accounts discussed here that these practices have specific material consequences in women's lives.

If impulses of belonging and longing, rootedness and movement are simultaneously integral to the logic of modernity, what happens to notions of longing and belonging in conditions of global modernity? Arjun Appadurai sees 'new conversations between those who move and those who stay' as necessary for the production of the 'diasporic public spheres' which are central features of global modernity (1996: 22). But the accounts discussed in this chapter suggest that such conversations involve a much more fundamental opening up of questions of family and community as central practices of gendered belonging. If journeys of modernity are underwritten as Morley suggests, by 'the "maternal" reassurance of the possibility of return and stability' (2000: 47), the stories of return in this chapter have the opposite effect. The 'motherland' does not provide security and integrity but displacement and an inability to inhabit a previously familiar national 'home'. The migrant is not always 'recognised' as belonging in the same way. This negotiation of 'home' is primarily in the context of family relations and in some cases local community. Although the migrant self is partly inhabited in response to non-acceptance as full members of the national community on return visits, in most accounts there continues to be an identification with Ireland (albeit alongside London or Luton) as a central locus of Irish identity. New, but not necessarily more mobile subjectivities are formed in the spaces of contact that are now enabled by processes (albeit uneven) of globalisation. Some of the accounts suggest that these processes produce even deeper experiences of displacement and reinscribe gendered familial obligations as markers of (un)belonging. Indeed, as one discussion in Chapter 6 suggests, for some, their migrant lives are haunted by the fear of being seen as 'different' from and less Irish than their peers in Ireland. Although migrancy, through an Irish tradition of emigration, may represent a claim on Irish belonging, this is a contested claim when it is articulated (in a context of more frequent return visits) as a relation of belonging in and to 'the homeland'. Migrancy, as the multi-local status it takes on in conditions of global modernity, produces new contradictions and tensions in the interstices between nation, transnation, multi-culture and the global. A tension emerges then between the individual who is obliged to be free to choose and the kinds of recognition available to her. To choose to belong in Ireland and London is one thing, but recognition as belonging in either or both is the point at which the choosing self meets specific constructions of collective belonging (see Chapters 5 and 6). In the following chapter I develop these themes of gendered transnational relations by examining the ways in which this generation of migrant women carved out spaces of Irish belonging in London.

5 'Are we here or are we there?'

Migrant Irish identity in 1990s London

I feel . . . a sort of a love–hate . . . coming to an Irish centre with the music and all the books and little shamrocks . . . (Bernie)

Yes, and the *Céad Míle Fáilte* on everything . . . tacky . . . It's like the Eurovision . . . absolutely hilarious. I don't know if you have ever seen this film, *Flight of the Doves. . .* It was sort of cringingly Irish. That is what I feel about Irish centres. (Brigid)

The Kennedy Hall (London Irish Centre, Camden), Oh God, you just immediately think of those three pictures, you know, Elvis, the Pope and Kennedy up on the wall and I just cringe. (Bernie)

You still see articles in the newspaper. They had one, last Saturday or Sunday, of a pub-crawl through Dublin. And I am just going, 'Well, you know, Dublin is more the International Monetary Centre and all that . . .' Surely there is somebody somewhere who can adapt and adopt a new image of Ireland other than this turf and cattle and sheep and, you know. (Brigid)

Yes, I am always trying to portray the well-educated race . . . I am always shouting statistics about what percentage of Second Level go to Third Level (education) and . . . what a skilful race we are and how we have got such a good chemical industry and pharmaceutical industry and all those other industries apart from Kerrygold butter . . . It's very European, like Scotland. (Bernie)

. . . if you move to England and immerse yourself in Irish culture why not stay at home? That is the attitude I have. I do think a smattering of it is not a bad thing, because you have to keep in touch and, as you said, certainly, I do look at Irish papers and I always read the Irish bits in the English papers first, you know, they catch your eye. But I don't want to be drowned in Irish culture when I am away somewhere else, because there is too much else going on. (Brigid)

(Group discussion 2, London)

In the discussion above, which took place in the Hammersmith Irish Centre, these 1980s women migrants define themselves against what they see as 'excessively' Irish, sentimental and old-fashioned images and activities of Irish centres in London. The Catholic and American iconic images which they suggest decorate the walls of the London Irish Centre in Camden are seen as representing a sentimental and kitsch Irishness. The portraits of Elvis, the Pope and John F. Kennedy identify a 1960s Catholic, 'white' masculine and American Irishness. Elvis and John F. Kennedy, icons of 'White Trash' in the US (Sweeney 1997), also represent liberated images of the body, sexual expressiveness and popular success. Elvis the 'poor white, country boy' comes of age in the urban slums where his young working-class body epitomises a threat to the disciplinary power of the dominant order (ibid.: 256). His 1960s media persona represented sexual liberation and release, even if by the 1970s his bodily demeanour represented addiction, excessiveness and resistance (ibid.). The image of Kennedy, an icon of 1960s US modernity, glamour and Irish-American identity, heralds the end of the promise of modernity. His mass-mediated death is identified with a loss of the modern belief in progress and 'the American Dream'. In contrast with the other two images, the picture of the Pope instates a Catholic labelling of the body as in need of sexual containment and marks Irishness as Catholic. All three of these images point to different sites and practices of patriarchy in the reproduction of Irish identity in the diaspora. They can be read (by their location in the US and Rome) as representing the contradictory and often conflicting impulses of sexual release, manual labour, economic and political success, religious identification and repression that mark the diaspora. They can also be read (by their US/Rome references) as signifying a longing for diasporic Irish cultural belonging that is insulated from an English context, or indeed, 'a refusal of incorporation' in England (Lloyd 1999: 92). But, more than anything, the above discussion identifies these images as kitsch.

Kitsch is significant to communities that have experienced displacement and migration because it is 'the articulation of the simultaneous desire for, and impossibility of restoring and maintaining, connection' (Lloyd 1999: 92).

> The word 'kitsch' . . . is often seen as synonymous with sentimentality . . . grounded in a conservative longing for past traditions and aesthetic conventions . . . catering to an infantile desire to flee from the complexities of reality into a predictable fantasy world of immediate and unobstructed gratification.
>
> (Felski 1995: 118)

The idea of being 'out of touch' and living in a 'fantasy world' is highlighted as a sign of displacement and diasporic Irishness in London in the above discussion. These relatively new migrants read practices and representations of Irish identity in these Centres as 'kitsch' because they suggest a longing for an imagined organic relationship with a culture that is only available in London in the form of recreation (Lloyd 1999). Although represented as anti-modern and old-fashioned these technologically reproduced images are of course artefacts of Western modernity.

The group discussion identifies high educational attainment, industrialisation and the International Financial Centre in Dublin as more appropriate signifiers of contemporary Ireland and Irish identity.[1] Yet these women have left this 'modern' Ireland. In the discussion, the International Financial Centre in Dublin marks Ireland as a European and global site (see Clohessy 1994).[2] The International Financial Centre metonymically signifies 1990s Ireland as a global space, just as the London Irish Centre stands in for a 'static' version of the Irish community in London. Each of them represents the exercise of power over place/environment, one producing globality in the time-space of the national and the other producing ethnic community in a national space, but also in a diasporic context as the London Irish Centre references other Irish Centres and the wider US-based diaspora in particular. Together these 'centres' represent different temporal/spatial nodes in the 1990s Irish global ethno- and financescapes (Appadurai 1996). This part of the discussion ends with Brigid's injunction that part of the migrant condition in the 1990s is that you have to 'keep in touch' with Ireland while also taking part in London life. For these new migrants, self-definition is predicated on ongoing connection with a changing Ireland *and* a mapping of Irish individuality onto London in ways that resist ghettoised collective formations of Irishness. The discussion asserts a modern European/global Irish identity that is portable through migration, but is also marked by displacement produced by English media stereotypes of Ireland and Irish culture and what are seen as 'excessive' performances of diasporic Irishness in London. In order to occupy the subject position of the 'modern Irish global or European citizen', a distancing from stereotypes of Irishness and a disavowal of involuntary migration, past and present, has to take place.

In the 1980s, most Irish women migrants to England settled in the southeast of England and mainly in London. The centralisation of financial and corporate headquarters in a few 'global cities' in the 1980s meant that these cities, of which London was one, became central nodes in an international 'elite' labour market.[3] Middle-class professionals were in demand by the multinational corporations of these cities and many left Ireland because their career paths and personal aspirations required international experience (Hanlon 1991). Less well-educated Irish migrants were also in demand to fill vacancies in the many support services required and many were leaving Ireland with few qualifications (Mac Laughlin 1997). In the 1991 British Census, 45.4 per cent of young Irish women (19–29) were represented in managerial and professional occupations compared to 26.5 per cent of all women in Britain (Hickman and Walter 1997). When non-health occupations are considered, thereby editing out the large numbers of Irish women in nursing, 29.7 per cent of Irish-born women were in this managerial/professional category so that fewer young Irish women migrants were entering low-paid, unskilled casual work than in the past (ibid.). How did this shift in the class profile of Irish women in London impact on their cultural and migrant identities? This chapter focuses on how 1980s women migrants lived

Irish identity in London and how this might be inflected by changes in class profile; increased opportunities for contact with Ireland and the construction of London as multicultural in the 1980s and 1990s.

Class, generation, 'homeland' and Irish identity in London

The women who took part in the above discussion looked to Ireland to identify what they considered 'authentic' modern Irish identity. The practices of earlier generations of migrants in Irish centres in London were identified as out-moded, inauthentic, 'too Irish' and excessive. They imply that such ethnic or cultural excessiveness is only possible in the diaspora. But, what is at stake in such strongly articulated disavowals of some Irish cultural sites and practices in London? How do class, generation and 'white' ethnicity mark out gendered terms of Irish belonging in London in the 1990s? In the following discussion, Julie, a social worker, who worked in an Irish centre in London for a year after she arrived, distances herself from what she identifies as the 'excessively Irish' environment she encountered there.

> ... But in some ways the Irish Centre experience put me off because it was almost *more Irish than the Irish themselves*. I actually found it repulsive. And I found it embarrassing because ... you had to slam on the country and western or the real 'come all ye' stuff ... we never did this at home, you know, we just didn't.
>
> (Julie, group discussion 3, London;
> emphasis added)

The phrase 'more Irish than the Irish themselves' signals the break of migration, which separates migrants from 'the Irish themselves'[4] still located in Ireland, and suggests the reproduction of an identity 'out of place'. The invocation of country and western music and nostalgic ballads as signs of Irish cultural excessiveness conceals their origin in modernity as a response to urbanisation and social change. This representation of the Irish centre also elides the modern practices of welfare advice and advocacy undertaken there. This aspect of the Irish centre activities would involve openly articulating Irish differences in London within discourses of class and ethnicity. The pattern of Irish migration to England to occupy working-class positions in the English labour force as 'navvies', domestic servants, factory workers and so on tends to mark the Irish presence in England as working-class. This class marking of the Irish was reinforced by stereotypes, which identified Irish immigrants (until recently at least) with drinking alcohol, Catholicism and ghettoised cultural practices. The maintenance of middle-class Irish identity is therefore threatened by classed stereotypes of Irish ethnicity in England. An anxiety about class positioning marks some of the accounts discussed on p. 109. For example, Julie's account suggests that her class identity is threatened by what she perceives as 'excessive' performances of Irish identity by her Irish colleague.

> I work alongside a woman who is fifty-six and she is from Crumlin (Dublin). She is one of thirteen and she came, over thirty odd years ago . . . and she is more Irish than the Irish themselves, sort of thing . . . and I think, please Jesus don't let them think I am, I mean we are from very different backgrounds anyway I have got to say . . . And there is an Irish shop up the road . . . and, bloody hell, you have only got to get your barmbrack . . . Calvita cheese and brown bread . . . And I get really mortified and . . . that's when I remember that I am very Irish, but very different from this other woman . . . On St Patrick's day she would bring in the shamrocks . . . and I think, *but we never did this at home, you know, we just didn't* . . . Because I don't feel that need, I don't wear my heart on a sleeve in that respect because I am comfortable, so *comfortable with who I am and why I am here* (emphasis added) . . . But then I have spoken to one woman . . . and she said, 'but your (1980s) generation is so well educated'. And she said . . .'We want to proclaim that we are Irish and we are proud of it and that all this anti-Irish racism has not ground us down over the years'. And it's like a siege mentality. If there is enough of us gathered together in one place and we all establish the fact that we are Irish, get our shillelaghs out and shamrocks. And that's how they sort of combat this thing. It's a strategy that people of that generation use. And, I have said it to her before, that that is the difference between you and me, because not only are we from different generations but we actually come from a different Ireland.
>
> (Julie, group discussion 3, London)

Although Irish women may face greater pressures than men to adapt to English society, (Lennon *et al.* 1988), there is also the impulse to avoid assimilation because of the imperative to maintain Irish identity, particularly within their families (Lambert 2001: 102). Arriving from a country that constructed a post-colonial identity in opposition to perceptions of English identity, assimilation in England was seen by many of the women in Lambert's study as selling out (ibid.). My own research suggests that this injunction against assimilation in England continues to operate. However, Irish cultural maintenance in 1990s London was recast by increased contact with Ireland, multiculturalism and contestation over forms of 'ethnic' Irishness in London. Julie (a social worker in London) reads her colleague's public performances of Irishness as 'excessive' because they are displayed without consideration of how they might be interpreted. This performance of 'excessive' Irishness unsettles Julie's contained, privatised and 'discerning' performance of Irish identity and potentially marks her through her Irish 'ethnicity' as working-class. Julie's relationship to Irish culture must be policed in order to keep up an appearance of 'respectability' against stereotypes of working-class Irishness. This is achieved by taking control of her migrancy. She is not an involuntary migrant – 'I am comfortable with who I am and why I am here'. By occupying a migrant self who is 'free to choose', Julie locates migrancy in a discourse of choice in which Ireland and London become equivalent 'chosen' places within the global space of individual mobility. Yet the conditions for the reproduction of a class-differentiated Irish identity are very different in these places.

The 1950s generation of migrants is seen as caught between harking back to the old country and its traditions and defending these traditions within the new culture which can never become 'home' (Hughes 1992: 10). Eamonn Hughes suggests that these traditions, while apparently offering a stable source of identity, betray their upholders because they trap them, as Julie's account suggests, between cultures and times. So the social and cultural effects of migration, in contrast with constructions of migration as modernisation, are identified in terms of reified 'tradition' in contrast with a 'living culture' 'at home' (ibid.). Julie repeatedly identifies some migrant Irish practices as 'inauthentic' with the assertion 'we never did this at home'. Yet the practices of Irish home-making in England through rituals of food, commemoration and celebrating St Patrick's Day compose a 'living Irish culture' in London. The dichotomous representation of 'tradition' in London and 'living culture' in Ireland is impossible to sustain when cultural practices and formations are considered in a diasporic/globalised context. Paul Gilroy (1993a) argues that 'tradition' and change co-exist in the movements of people and cultures across national borders. Gilroy's formulation of 'tradition' as 'the changing same' incorporates dynamics of continuity and discontinuity. It offers ways of interpreting 'excessive' formations of Irish identity[5] as aspects of diasporic living that produce *new* modes of identification and belonging. The disavowal of Irish centres and 'kitsch' symbols of Irishness in London, such as shamrock, are part of the ongoing processes of negotiating tensions between multi-temporal and multi-located practices of Irish identity. Cultural traditions circulate therefore in ways that do not have to congeal and get trapped between locations and times.

Yet the construction of Irishness abroad as excessive is pervasive in these women's accounts. Excess, as Gael Sweeney reminds us, means 'out of control' (1997: 255). It operates within logics of visibility and invisibility, the classy and the unclassy, the appropriate and inappropriate, the respectable and unrespectable, the culturally correct and culturally incorrect. 'Excessive' performances of Irish culture are constructed as grotesque, terrifying and unsettling to some new migrants who wish to take up those spaces of neutrality offered by middle-class identity and unmarked 'whiteness' (see Chapter 6). However, it is not just previous generations of migrants who, through their diasporic practices of Irishness, are essentialised and stigmatised in these accounts, but particular groups of 1980s migrants as well. The group discussion continues below with Julie and Fionnuala (a housing manager) identifying certain migrants as 'other' to their own cosmopolitan, well-educated and well-travelled migrancy.

> . . . We (members of this group) probably come from, you know, Dublin, east coast, and we have all obviously travelled before we came to London. I travelled as a student around Europe and went to America as well. So our experience would be completely different to somebody say who came straight from Tipperary and got off the ferry, but you know. (Julie)
>
> I also think the fact that you are educated is quite different because you assimilate experiences in a different way. You know, and it's not, I think, as difficult to actually accept an alternative lifestyle. You are more open when you are educated. Even travelling helps. (Fionnuala)
>
> And I think that age group as well are very much stuck in like earning the fare home and it's whatever, it's sixty-nine pounds at it's best to get home. (Julie)
>
> I know, any weekend you feel like it. (Fionnuala)
>
> (Group discussion 3, London)

Fionnuala and Julie constitute themselves as global Irish citizens via discourses of mobility and class which confer social sophistication. Their kind of migrancy is differentiated from rural and working-class migrancy. The latter is identified with an earlier less mobile phase of industrial and territorialised modernity symbolised by their arrival by ferry. Mobility and cosmopolitanism mark out a 'modern' Irish migrancy that is middle-class. It is working-class and 1950s migrants who are positioned as out of time and relatively static in these accounts. Young, educated migrants, on the other hand, occupy the position of global Irish citizenship recognisable by geographic mobility and adaptability. Earlier generations of migrants and rural or poor migrants in the present become emblematic of a 'solid' and out of date industrial modernity (Bauman 2000). The accounts discussed so far identify late twentieth-century Irish women's presence in London through constructions of Irish generational and class difference based on access to mobility, cultural adaptability and public/private negotiations of Irish identity.

Irish migrant femininities in London

In this section, I probe the question of how migrant Irish femininity is negotiated in London. I ask what happens to the category 'Irish women' in the context of settlement in London. In Molly's (a medical doctor) account, Irish clubs in London are identified with a specific kind of 'Irish woman'.

> I think people's perception of an Irish woman in London is that you're sort of involved with a lot of Irish clubs. And you belong to, you go to

a lot of Irish functions, and I don't do that. So from that point of view I would say *I am more of a woman from Ireland rather than an Irish woman* (emphasis added).

(Molly, interview, London)

Because they are seen as constituting 'Irish women' as domestic, familial and community-building subjects, Irish clubs and centres are refused as sites of modern Irish femininity. Indeed, the designation 'Irish woman' forecloses the many modes and possibilities of inhabiting migrant Irish femininity in Molly's account. She identifies herself as a woman *from* Ireland through a discourse of national origins rather than through gendered Irish ethnic community practices in London. The act of migration enables her to identify herself in relation to movement 'from' Ireland rather than with any apparently stable category such as 'Irish woman'. In nearly all of these accounts, their class and urban backgrounds *in* Ireland represent firmer grounds of identification than sites and practices of Irishness in London, which were seen as homogenising Irish culture as masculine, working-class and Catholic (see later sections). Joan, a housing support worker in London, embraces a differentiated Irish identity through her unique individuality.

I have a certain resistance to being homogenised with the Irish abroad . . . I'm not a *céilí* goer, I'm not an Irish pub goer, we don't spend a lot of time in pubs, a lot of this may be to do with our sexuality, because if we go out it may be to a gay venue, but that's not always true because we have a mix of friends. But I don't feel the same kind of Irishness that can be represented as . . . gather[ing] around centres or activities, be it bingo or *céilís* . . . there is almost a forced community around it here . . . it feels like I'm Irish, because I'm Irish, because I'm me, and that it doesn't have any great tags to it. It's not because I gather around Irish activities or because I have any huge amount of Irish contacts . . .

(Joan, group discussion 5, London)

The 'tags' of collective Irish identity in London are refused in favour of a more individualistic assertion – 'I'm me'. Irish ethnic spaces in London reproduce homogenous heteronormative Irish communities. It is only since the mid-1990s that discursive and physical spaces of Irish lesbian belonging in London and indeed within the category 'Irish abroad' or the diaspora have emerged (Luibheid 1999 and 2000; Maguire 1997; O'Carroll and Collins 1995; Smyth 1995). Until the 1970s, there were no centres or organisations which addressed issues specific to Irish women.[6] The aim of the London Irish Women's Centre[7] (established in the mid-1980s) was to promote diversity amongst Irish women, to recognise and enable the articulation of Irish feminist and lesbian subjectivities and to offer a site where women could identify as both Irish and feminist without their cultural credentials being challenged (London Irish Women's Centre 1993; Curtis *et al.* 1987; O'Brien and Power 1997). At the London Irish Women's Conference in 1987, the Irish Lesbian Group discussed the blatant discrimination they experienced within the Irish community, an example of which was the refusal by the England-based paper, the *Irish Post,* to print the words 'Irish lesbian'. The conference noted that many Irish lesbians were forced to shed their Irish identity and to find support in the English Women's Movement.[8] This centre was pivotal in facilitating dialogue between women identifying as heterosexual, bisexual and lesbian, different generations of Irish women, women in Ireland and in London, and between Traveller women and settled women and women of all ages and abilities. However, feminist challenges to practices of Irishness in London reveal the difficulties of challenging the heteronormativity of mainstream Irish community organisations and activities in London.

> I've experienced being made to feel that I'm *outside of a recognised Irish identity* even in London by Irish people and groups. And it's ... around feminist issues where that's been interpreted as an attack on the Irish culture or Irish community ... I've felt it as a lack of recognition that here am I, an Irish woman, and this is my experience, and these are my concerns ... and then being accused of attacking an Irish identity, of being anti-Irish ... *Being an Irish feminist is wrong, it's something evil and destructive, it's an attack on basic values of the Irish culture.* For me to be an Irish feminist is it ... the Irishness without it for me is oppressive and I find it very insular ... I've had women who have said things like, when I've raised an objection to something ... 'As an Irish person and as a woman this is what I feel' and it is in the vein of saying this is what every other Irish woman would obviously feel so therefore, what does that make me? It's not Irishness it's something else, it's *something I've picked up from over here*, or it's not recognised as something coming from myself, or from my own experience, and certainly very threatening ... (Maeve; emphasis added)
>
> So when you think of Irish women what images come to mind? (Breda)
>
> The London Irish Women's Centre. I tend to think politically about Irish women because it gives me a feeling of strength ... it's an empowering feeling to know that those women are out there and have been out there individually fighting. Because ... the other side of Irish women is the awful oppression and the pain of their lives. (Maeve)
>
> (Interview, London)

In migration, women are positioned all the more anxiously as markers of continuity and emblematic of a cohesive and recognisable ethnicity.

Imperatives of 'respectability', family, and ethnic reputation follow from this positioning. Irish women's bodies are ritually ethnicised as they circulate within predefined Irish cultural spaces of the family, the Catholic Church and cultural centres (Fortier 2000). Those women/feminists who refuse the gaze and disciplinary narratives of the ethnic community are potentially de-ethnicised and de-nationalised. Maeve's account identifies how the category 'Irish women' is naturalised and 'Irish feminist' denaturalised, rendered artificial and something that must have been 'picked up' in England. It is only through feminism and the London Irish Women's Centre that she can inhabit Irish identity in London.

Fionnuala refuses to identify publicly as Irish in London and sees the private space of an 'Irish family' as the only site of Irish identification available to her. Because she sees an Irish future as only available to her through an Irish partner or return to Ireland, she constructs her present in terms of Anglicisation.

> Well, I am definitely Irish yes, because I am a product of Ireland in my formative years, so I wouldn't say I was Irish, I would say my attitudes are very cosmopolitan. And as the years go by, I will become more Anglicised whether I like it or not. I think we all will, but some more than others. And it's highly unlikely I will ever meet an Irish partner unless something extraordinary happens. So, therefore, you know, I won't have Irish children. So, I don't see like an Irish future stretching ahead. I would never be able to get a job in Ireland doing what I do. So therefore, I don't focus on that because that would be a waste of time as well. So, but, I mean it's regretful, I mean I still try and preserve a certain amount of one's identity. I don't know why. (Fionnuala)
>
> You don't know why? (Breda)
>
> I don't know why, yes. I suppose it's because we all want to have an identity. But I am coming to realise that I don't really have one now because I am neither one thing nor the other like. (Fionnuala)
>
> (Group discussion 3, London)

Like Molly's earlier account, Fionnuala identifies as a woman from Ireland rather than identifying with the category 'Irish woman'. Although Anglicisation offers a potential modality of integration, as Homi Bhabha reminds us, 'to be anglicized is *emphatically* not to be English' (1987: 200; emphasis in original). In other words, despite her mimicry of Englishness, Fionnuala still occupies a version of otherness in England. She may become almost English, but can never 'be English'. As a 'product of Ireland' and through her Anglicisation in London, she finds that she cannot fully identify as either Irish or English. Yet Irish belonging is repeatedly and anxiously negotiated in her account within and through notions of the familial and return to Ireland. The potential for Irish belonging therefore is located in potential future events such as meeting an Irish partner, but is refused as a focus of concern in the present. Much later in the discussion Fionnuala characterises the complex sense of cut off and separation produced by the short distance between London and Ireland.

> I came here for a job and if I had found the same opportunities in Ireland that I found here I would . . . probably have been happier in the long run. Because the practicalities that I have encountered over the last few years with my mothers' failing health. My brothers who have young children and their marriages have split up. I can see where I could have been of assistance. And I am not around. And you know, when you have a crisis in your family, as I have had and you are a long way, well, *you're not a long way away, but you're not there*. And you have got to tell people in your work here that you have got to go away. And they are not quite as understanding as they would be in an Irish situation . . . because they don't understand our position. When I think of all of that . . .
>
> (Fionnuala; emphasis added)

The phrase 'you're not a long way away, but you're not there' encapsulates the complex relationship between distance and migration. On the one hand, you're not a long way away, so how can there be any difficulty in 'being there' for family and friends in Ireland (see Chapter 4). Yet, in order to get 'there' at times of 'crisis in your family' involves negotiating a different culture of family and work in London. The idea that she might have been happier if she had stayed in Ireland powerfully contradicts her account of pragmatic adaptation to life in London through Anglicisation (and her uncomfortable visits to Ireland discussed in Chapter 4). While in many ways migration represents one attempt at disarticulating the many dimensions of women's lives that line up with the 'impacted social space' of the family (Sedgwick 1994: 6), the family re-emerges in migrancy as the site of national and gender displacement. Although some accounts identify the struggle to inhabit Irish spaces in London outside of heteronormative narratives and practices of Irish ethnic belonging, a few like Fionnuala identified difficulties with occupying an Irish self outside of an 'Irish family' situation in London. So in all of the accounts Irish femininities are produced in the gap between the invitation to occupy the position of the 'choosing self' and recognisable Irish identities in London. These accounts identify the ways in which women who identify as single, career oriented, lesbian, or feminist, find themselves outside of a 'recognisable' Irish identity in London. For Fionnuala, this may be reconciled by Anglicisation in the present or becoming part of an 'Irish family' in the future, but for others it means refusing or resisting sites and practices of 'recognisable' Irishness and thereby being positioned as 'other within' in most Irish contexts in London. In many accounts, Irish migrant women's selves are produced in efforts to bridge this gap but also in attempts to pursue the quest for simultaneous belonging in Ireland and in London as discussed in the following section.

Women's transnational lives – hybrid or divided selves?

Global modernity holds out the promise of multi-located belonging. But the expectation of making and maintaining 'homes' in many places can present its own difficulties (see Chapter 4). Also, the potential for multi-located belonging is unevenly available. As noted in Chapter 4, late twentieth-century migration can necessitate the occupation of different (and perhaps conflicting) selves in one's country of origin and of destination. Helen, a journalist, differentiates in her account between Irish and English migration and suggests that Irish migration produces a particular sense of displacement.

> I feel like quite happy here in one sense. Sometimes I think I am kidding myself about how accepted I am . . . I think that it is a unique situation that we always have to think about it. It's like – *are we here or are we there*? English people, I really envy them the fact that they don't have to think about it. If they choose to emigrate it's a very big radical step that they do it for a particular reason . . . it just isn't the same thing about emigrating and then spending ten years trying to decide whether to go back or not . . . and they accept that they will end up here (England) most of them . . . they have the history of empire behind them. So if they emigrate, they don't see themselves as emigrating, they are going to another part of England . . . that might be 10 thousand miles away, but they are going to create some colony there.
>
> (Helen, group discussion 2, London; emphasis added)

English migration is identified with empire and the recreation of the English 'homeland' around the world[9] while the more banal and spontaneous nature of Irish migration means, in Helen's account, that settlement is never achieved. Her account suggests a distrust of her own perception of belonging in England and a discomfort with the idea of belonging in both places. The short migrant journey between Ireland and London produces a re-evaluation of self, location and belonging framed by Helen's question 'are we here or are we there?' Her Irish migrancy in London is characterised by the impossibility of 'inhabit[ing] fully the present or present space' (Ahmed 2000: 92). Helen's migrant self is one that is always on guard against feeling 'at home' in England. Her migration involves negotiating the uneasy and politically fraught positioning of the Irish in England, but also a difficulty with settling down that she attributes to a specifically Irish mode of migrancy. This uneasiness is repeated in Joan's account, which constructs living in London as a potential threat to her identification with Irish culture and identity.

> *I feel very alien here*, I feel it to be an extremely alien culture and I find the whole thing extremely negative on the one hand, and on the other hand, I feel *I've got an enormous lot out of it* . . . it was only a

couple of years ago that I began to call myself an emigrant because it . . . set me apart from the culture here in a way. I'm not bloody English . . . I feel very separate from the whole society structure here . . .

(Joan, group discussion 5, London; emphasis added)

Identification is a process that incorporates ambivalence. To identify as 'emigrant' is to render Ireland her point of identification and simultaneously to acknowledge her absence from that place. Emigrant status also guards against assimilation. It signifies more than a reinstating of a relationship to the 'homeland' because it is associated with exile and oppression (Miller 1985). Joan's proximity to the English 'other' in London arguably produces an even sharper sense of Irish specificity. Yet the benefits of living in London are also acknowledged as Joan suggests that she could never have embraced her career ambitions so openly in Ireland, where she felt prohibited from inhabiting an ambitious self.

If Helen and Joan's accounts suggest an inability to create 'home' in migrancy because of how they are positioned in England, Cath, who worked as a social worker in London at the time of the research, can only account for her presence in London in relation to occupying two selves simultaneously.

It is very much *a schism of your spirit and everything else when you come over here* because, you definitely do feel pulled, and you feel that very much, emotionally I think, it wreaks havoc with you. I can see where some people, just can't deal with it and don't know what to do. I mean you've got to make some decisions and if you don't . . . you could lead a completely different life over here to the one you were living at home. You could hide so much, and people at home would never know you and people over there would never know the you over here, the one you slip into like me going home and *being a daughter*. But for you, that would be so soul destroying in the long term. I've struggled against that, but I used to feel like it was *two lives*. I worked hard with my mother and father . . . to get them to see what my life was like over here and to keep saying to them come over . . . my parents haven't come over, but my sisters have and my brother has . . . They can feed back to my parents where I live and make a connection because I think a division and the tearing is just heart wrenching you know. Its all about religion and culture . . .

(Cath, interview, London; emphasis added)

Although migration holds out the possibility of occupying another self and 'hiding' this new self from family in Ireland, Cath suggests a need to integrate the selves associated with Ireland and London. Her account suggests that her gender identity in Ireland is overdetermined by the role of 'daughter', which in turn produces a gendered dislocation in migration. She attempts to recover the familiar status of daughter by attempting to maintain contact and connection with her family in Ireland. Her attempts to simultaneously occupy the daughter self and independent migrant self produce the sense of an irresolvable schism. Later Cath notes, with regard to the possibility of returning to Ireland, that her family there might not accept her London lifestyle (including living with her boyfriend). This schism is therefore also about the translating of gender and sexual politics across national contexts marked, as she notes in her account, by different religions and cultures. Nonetheless, she works at resolving this disjuncture by repeated attempts to achieve family recognition of her adult migrant woman self. Because neither her 'daughter' self nor her 'adult woman migrant' self are recognised by her parents in Ireland, there is a suggestion of anxiety that she might somehow disappear from their memories.

Many of these accounts suggest that the emotional work of bridging divisions produced through religion and culture is onerous. Maura, who worked as a personal assistant, had the following to say:

> But I have had all my crew, all my family over here one by one or in pairs . . . they have all been over here. They have all been over here this year so far and they were all over last year at various stages, yes. And for me, that is very important, because I want them to see what I am doing here, what sort of life I live, so that when I go home, I can talk about them and *they know exactly what I am talking about*, that there isn't *this gulf thing* and that has been very important for me. And that has worked very well and they are all coming back again next year . . . and they have met all the people I live with . . . But, no, *I love my independence here, and I wouldn't ever have achieved that at home*, no way, I don't think. (Maura; emphasis added)
>
>   What would have stopped you? (Breda)
>
>   Well, the *total autonomy*. The being *anonymous* in this town has been great for me because I have had to do things. (Maura; emphasis added)
>
> (Group discussion 2, London)

Although London represents autonomy and anonymity unavailable to Maura in Ireland, technologies of communication produce a desire to make her life in London knowable to family in Ireland. New technologies enable frequent contact,[10] which in turn heightens expectations of integration and involvement in one another's lives (see Chapter 4). As in Cath's account, Maura describes the work of creating and sustaining connection, but her aim is to keep contact while also maintaining independence and anonymity. The desire to bridge the religious, cultural and historical differences that mark their experience of migration to London permeate these accounts. But these women's migration and attempts to produce transnational connection are also tied up with the perceived impossibility of inhabiting autonomous, independent or ambitious selves in Ireland and the obstacles to translating between gender regimes in England and Ireland.

In one group discussion, women who attended a drop-in service for young lone Irish mothers in London were less inclined to preserve a sense of belonging in both Ireland and London. Like many of the earlier generation of women migrants who participated in Sharon Lambert's study, some of these women felt that their presence in England was about upholding the reputations of families in Ireland (2001: 23/71). Ireland was identified less as a home than a place where their right to a future or cultural belonging was contested or unrecognised. Ger's account identified the material experiences that structures her belonging in London and Ireland.[11]

> There was no future in Ireland. Sure when I was growing up, I knew no future. The jobs were here. You can survive on less, the cost of living is less, but you're totally isolated, no family support (in London). There's always someone to turn to there, but you wouldn't have the same opportunities for training in Ireland or the nurseries.
>
> (Ger, group discussion 1, London)

At the time of the discussion, Ger was using a specifically Irish-oriented service for support in overcoming the loneliness and isolation of being a lone Irish parent in London. In contrast with the confident and educated Ireland represented in many accounts, Ger identifies migration as a mode of social exclusion from Ireland. As a working-class girl growing up in Ireland, the path of migration lay before her as the only way of ensuring a future for herself. Although not pre-destined, migration is marked in Ger's account more by necessity than choice. Her account constructs migration as holding out the promise of individual self-development through access to training and the labour market in London. Migration also offered her recognition in ways that her life as a single parent in Ireland did not. The sense of having no future in Ireland meant having to imagine her future somewhere else from a young age. London becomes 'her liberator, or at least a benign nurse' (Buckley 1997: 121).

Karen, another woman taking part in this discussion, describes bringing her black partner to Ireland and contrasts the potential experience of bringing up a black-Irish child in Ireland and in London.

> When I was pregnant and we went home, people came to the house to see him (her partner). They (her parents) were more worried about what will the neighbours think. They were not thinking about me, or my child, but what the neighbours would think. They had no awareness. In London people know about different cultures ... and there's more privacy, people aren't looking in your windows ...
>
> (Karen, group discussion 1, London)

Later Karen describes London as 'a place to be', implying that Ireland is a place where she could not exist (at least as she wanted to). A multicultural London provides spaces of black-Irish identity (public and private) that were not available to her in an Ireland preoccupied with the racialised maintenance of family reputation. The lives of most of the women who took part in this group discussion were structured by the exclusions they experienced in Ireland, a sense of isolation and loneliness in London, but also by the availability of social welfare support and a more accessible British adult education system. The gendered and classed dynamics of migration and migrant status produce, in many accounts, a transnationally negotiated, but conflicted self. Migration, in these accounts, is a transnational practice that is marked by both choice and constraint but also by an imperative to bridge the gaps between national spaces and gendered practices of belonging. The chosen path of autonomy, anonymity and privacy in the city is countered in many accounts by a longing to make this anonymous self known/ knowable to family and friends in Ireland. The promise of potentially achieving continuity of the self by bridging the gaps between nations and between adult migrant and daughterly selves is all the more enticing in conditions of relatively cheap mobility and communication. Yet the gendered political and cultural contexts of cultural and religious differences both within and between England and Ireland reproduce these gaps. These accounts are testimony to the limits of the notion of 'home' or belonging as multi-located and remind us of the ways in which notions of 'home' are constituted in and through gendered socio-cultural and historical-political dynamics.

'Peg' communities and multicultural London

The discussion so far suggests that Irish migrant and 'ethnic' communities in London are at best reluctantly embraced as points of identification and belonging for this 1980s generation of Irish migrant women. Nonetheless, it is unclear from these accounts whether a particular formation of Irish community can be identified with 1980s migrants to London. There is considerable evidence that this generation of women migrants have been instrumental in producing new spaces of Irish belonging in London via initiatives such as the London Irish Women's Centre. These initiatives can be located within the project of developing a 'multicultural' London; a local political project that facilitated the articulation of new kinds of 'ethnic' and gendered Irish belonging in London. Multicultural policies and initiatives were facilitated by the Greater London Council in the 1980s and facilitated a new 'mainstreaming' of Irish ethnicity within the multicultural, in contrast with the more 'ghettoised' Catholic Church and Irish centre oriented cultural activities of previous generations of Irish immigrants. The 1980s generation of migrants (with some exceptions) did not establish physical clubs and centres, but set up 'networks' facilitated by telephone contact and the relatively easy reproduction and circulation of newsletters. Jenny, who worked in education, describes her access to Irish culture through membership of the London Irish Network.[12]

> I do go . . . to quite a few Irish things through the London Irish Network . . . I went to a very good music session. It was an Irish group called *Sin É*. But in their publicity they say they mix songs, African, Asian and Irish. So they were using some African drums and things. And they had an Asian musician as well . . . so there is a lot of that kind of thing in London. And that interests me . . .
>
> (Jenny, interview, London)

Networks, according to Zygmunt Bauman, involve a 'sharing of intimacies' and produce communities 'as fragile and short lived as scattered and wandering emotions, shifting erratically from one target to another' (2001: 37). They are 'peg' communities, 'a momentary gathering around a nail on which many solitary individuals hang their solitary individual fears' (ibid.). It is possible to characterise the London Irish Network (LIN) and the more ostentatious London Irish Society (LIS) which were established by 1980s migrants, as 'peg' communities.[13]

LIN was formed for Irish people who wanted to expand their 'range of social activities'. The London Irish Society (LIS), which gained a higher public profile, held an inaugural ball in September 1987 at the London Hilton and organised Christmas and St Patrick's Day parties to raise money for Irish charities in England. In the first copy of its newsletter *Ballyhoo!*, the LIS announced a commitment, not only to the disadvantaged Irish in London, but also to Ireland. The expressed aim of the society was to develop 'projects which will, to coin a phrase "put something back into Ireland"'. While wanting to 'put something back into Ireland', this group of Irish migrants also saw themselves as contributing significantly to English society: 'One of the beliefs of the society [is] that the Irish in London have something valuable to contribute to sport, culture and the arts in Britain and should not be too inward-looking in this' (Letter from the LIS Committee, *Ballyhoo!* 1988: 3). Politics and work are noticeably absent from this list. The focus on consumption and the leisure pursuits of sports, culture and the arts challenges over-determined constructions of Irish men migrants as construction workers and women as domestic workers or nurses. Although many 1980s migrants worked in construction and low-skilled employment, this network (aimed at middle-class migrants) represented new migrants as middle class and successful. Anxieties about the danger of getting 'too inward looking' or self-regarding can be identified in some of the rhetoric of the LIS newsletter.

> The purpose of the [Sense of Ireland] Festival[14] is not to lend added weight to the paraphrase 'nothing fascinates the Irish as much as the Irish'; the activities are of such diversity that they will likely appeal as

much to other nationalities as to Irish people. It is an international cultural event that happens to be focusing on Irish culture.

(Collins 1988)

The London Irish Society interpellates a 1980s middle-class constituency of Irish migrants who want to avoid the 'ghettoisation' of earlier generations. At a time when world music, dance and literature were celebrated within a global marketplace, Irish culture can be slotted in with the rest, constituting it simultaneously within frames of equivalence and diversity. Ireland became a place that these migrants left in order to progress their careers, but which equipped them with the skills and 'cultural capital' to participate in an international economic, social and cultural context.[15] Irish cultural activities in London became both reference points for identification while also maintaining identifications with Ireland. These networks by definition reproduced 'peg' communities for mainly young, middle-class, single migrants in the 1980s and 1990s.

For this generation of migrants, relations of belonging in London were also framed through a discourse of multiculturalism.

> I ring up . . . maybe public services . . . there may be an Irish accent at the other end of the phone . . . counsellors who have got English accents with Irish surnames, so it feels quite comfortable in that way . . . Kilburn is in Brent . . . The County Kilburn! . . . there is a very nice theatre called the Tricycle in Kilburn and they do quite a lot of Irish plays . . .
>
> (Jenny, interview, London)

Discourses of multiculturalism identify the Irish as a minority ethnic group with ethnically specific claims on public services. The notion of 'County Kilburn',[16] although an ironic reference, identifies a 'depth' of Irish belonging in this part of north London that is ever-changing and marking out new spaces, such as the Tricycle Theatre (which stages many Irish cultural productions). Jenny frames her presence in Brent (Kilburn is in the borough of Brent) in a tradition of Irish settlement, which is evident in the Irish accents and surnames of workers in the council offices. The evident integration of the Irish in Kilburn and Jenny's identification with Irishness in Brent mean that the subject, Jenny, and the space of Brent 'leak into each other, *inhabit each other*' (Ahmed, 2000: 89; emphasis in the original).

In a reading of Kilburn High Road, Doreen Massey identifies an Irish presence by the names of the newspapers on sale, posters, IRA graffiti, notices of an Irish play at the Tricycle Theatre, and an Irish band in one of the local venues, but notes an equal number of indicators of an Indian presence (1994: 153–4). For Massey, it is a place of many identities and incorporates a globalised sense of place. She uses the idea of 'power geometry' to account for the varied experiences of such places as some residents are more mobile than others. Some can initiate the flows of cultural images and people, while others may feel trapped by the globalised forces that constitute such hybrid places.[17] Traces of Irish presences in Kilburn High Road need to be differentiated as they reference differently located Irish identity formations in London. The Tricycle Theatre, for example, represents a differently classed and generational site of Irish identity than the National Ballroom, yet each is inflected by the Irishness signified by the other. The power geometry of Irish presences in London is constituted through struggles between sites and practices of Irish identity, between Irish migrants and other ethnic groups, not least the English. It is impossible to assume an *a priori* ordering of power relations, as the power geometry identified by Massey is the outcome of ongoing struggles over representation and resources (Smith 2001: 15).

Jenny had lived in London for thirteen years at the time of the interview and found that over time the balance of her affiliations shifted so that she identified more closely with an 'ethnic' Irishness in London than with Irish identity in Ireland.

> When I go home things have gone on that I have missed out on. And if you don't live in a place your interest in it does begin to slip. Because it's more relevant for me, for example, to read up what is going on in London. And I am quite interested in London as a place anyway. It has become more relevant for me and the longer you are away the greater that feeling becomes. Because I used to buy Irish newspapers, I might buy the *Irish Press* or *Independent* on a Sunday, but somehow, my interest in it has gone . . . I would be interested in . . . studies of Irish people in England, I am quite interested in that . . . It's not that I am not interested in the other, interested in the divorce referendum and the issues that I hear about and I will always ask. But I don't have the background knowledge anymore.
>
> (Jenny, interview, London)

Studies of the profile of the Irish in London in the 1980s and 1990s undertaken by local authorities, voluntary organisations and universities significantly contributed to the constitution of an imagined Irish 'ethnic' community in 'multicultural London' (Gray 2000). Ethnic Irish belonging in London emerges in Jenny's account as the lived experience of a locality that recognises and reproduces Irish ethnic belonging. Jenny can inhabit the hybrid identity 'London-Irish' which suggests claims to belong in both Ireland and London (albeit in different ways). So the hyphenated identity, 'London-Irish', enables 'through the hyphen, the problematic situating of the self as simultaneously belonging "here" and "there"' (Young 1995: 433). Unlike those accounts that articulated a split self produced by attempts to belong simultaneously in Ireland and London, Jenny's account suggests a letting go of some aspects of belonging in Ireland and her identification with 'ethnic' Irishness in London. This kind of hybrid identification brings difference and sameness together in an apparently 'impossible simultaneity' (ibid.: 26),[18] even as it emphasises the locality of London-based Irishness.

Nearly all of the women taking part in this study identified Irish networks and sporadic participation in Irish cultural activities rather than more sustained practices of community-building as characterising their practices of Irishness in London. For some, their work with Irish-identified welfare agencies was their main reference point for Irish belonging in London and one which relied on discourses of 'multicultural' service provision. For others like Ger and Karen, their use of Irish identified social services was their main point of contact with any Irish 'community' in London. Jenny, who lived in London the longest, framed her Irishness within a multicultural discourse of belonging with which she strongly identified. However, most articulated being 'from' Ireland as their mode of Irish identification while also struggling between the occupation of migrant selves in London *and* in Ireland.

Religion and London-Irish identity

While Mary Hickman (1999) argues that the Catholic religion and its institutions, most notably its schools, have been central to the incorporation of Irish Catholics into the British state, they have also facilitated the maintenance of Irish community and belonging in England (Fielding 1993; Lambert 2001; Swift 1999). The significance of the Orange Order in maintaining Irish Protestant identity in some parts of Britain has also been identified, as well as the tendency of middle-class Irish Protestant migrants to be less community-oriented than their Catholic counterparts (Belchem 1999; Kells 1995a; MacRaild 1998; Walker 1991). However, the Irish presence in Britain has been more publicly identified with Catholicism and Irish women have been more visibly identified with Catholic practices (Walter 2001: 87). As in Ireland, the Catholic Church in England concentrated its attention on women who were seen as the guardians of children's souls and responsible for their education (Fielding 1993: 51/60). Indeed, Sharon Lambert identified considerable continuity between Catholic practices amongst women in Ireland and following migration. In my research, the Catholic Church featured mainly in relation to its gendered practices of oppression, which were often responded to by migration.[19] Paradoxically, Catholicism was embraced in some accounts as a cultural marker of Irishness in Ireland and in England (see Chapter 2).

> I am not particularly interested in religion but ... I do go to church when I go home at Christmas and weddings, baptisms, funerals ... So, I would not say I have thrown religion completely out the door ... the Catholic religion belongs to many different cultures and traditions, so I don't see it as being something that's exclusively Irish. Mind you,

judging from some people's attitudes you would think it was. You know, being Catholic and Irish is synonymous ... I don't have a network to do with the Church. A lot of people that do I think who have children, say they are going to a Catholic school and they know other parents and children with the same very much identical backgrounds. But that does not really apply to me.

(Jenny, interview, London)

Although the Catholic Church played a significant role up to the 1960s in incorporating Irish women migrants in England by, for example, arranging time off with their employers for Mass attendance, Lambert identified strategic religious practice amongst many of the women migrants she interviewed. Mass attendance gave their children respectability in Catholic schools and gave the family some standing (2001: 64). Relationships to the Catholic Church were influenced by religious background and whether they had children. Catholic schools tend to have good reputations but only admit children whose parents are actively involved with the Church and are regular church-goers. One of the mothers interviewed suggested that Mass attendance was both an instrumental practice based on getting her children into a Catholic school and a cultural link to Ireland through familiarity.

The church that we go to, there is a sort of an Irish community that also go there ... I think probably not a lot of my generation or emigrants from the eighties are regular churchgoers. Not a lot of my friends are anyway ... we started going in earnest again when we had children because we thought we would like to send them to one of the church schools and here, if you want to do that, you have to put your envelope in every week. So actually at the moment we are, my husband hadn't been practising, but now we go to two different churches to sort of double our chances ... I think for me, it's a sort of a link with Ireland as well that, you know, religion is such a part of life in Ireland.

(Molly, interview, London)

Mass attendance becomes a cultural resource in relation to generational cultural continuity and a link through memory with an Ireland identified with Catholicism. The extent to which Catholicism is lived as a cultural expression of Irish identity also emerges in Joan's account.

I feel being Irish is being Catholic, from a very young age ... you imbibe the whole thing ... What I often find here is that I pit myself against the Catholics here, English Catholics ... I find they are very specialised as Catholics and they have that edge of being slightly above the Anglican churches ... There's a slight superiority about being Catholic here, so in fact Protestantism is the masses. I think it's almost a class thing, even though a lot of aristocratic families would be

Protestant . . . It's very subtle, so I often find myself pitting against the English Catholic because they actually claim Catholicism in the way that the English mentality claim a right to imperialism . . . what I resent about that . . . is that assumption about what Catholic means, I find that there's a huge difference for me, I didn't come from a very religious family, so Catholic just meant something very ordinary, it didn't mean having very strong beliefs about abortion or divorce, and that assumption that if you say you're Catholic that that means that you are anti-divorce, you're anti-abortion, etc. and I resent that . . .

(Joan, group discussion 5, London)

Catholicism 'Irish style' is contrasted with English Catholicism as symbolising cultural difference within the same religion. If in Ireland Catholicism permeated everyday life and 'meant something very ordinary', in England it was identified with strong anti-liberal beliefs. In Joan's account, the 'moral monopoly' of the Catholic Church in Ireland (Inglis 1998a) reproduces Catholicism as a necessary criterion of Irish identity. Maura, an Evangelical Christian, experiences many of the spaces of Irish belonging in London as being explicitly or implicitly Catholic.

I am a born again Christian . . . it will always be a problem, wherever, even down there in Woking. Now, it's part of the culture being Irish I think being Catholic. I have only ever been in Camden once . . . but I am not Catholic, so I did not fit with a lot of it anyway . . . I really miss Irish culture and the music so much . . . maybe North London would have been better, but living in South London, there wasn't much contact, being a woman on your own and you couldn't really go out and then the hall was to do with the Catholic Church so . . . you do have to forget a good bit about being Irish, don't you, you have to put your head down to work . . .

(Maura, group discussion 2, London)

The mapping of Catholicism onto Irish identified spaces in London reproduces 'cultural Catholicism' in the diaspora. Northern Irish Protestant participants in Mary Kells' study of young middle-class migrants in London in the 1990s contested the dominant assumptions about the Irish in London as Catholic and nationalist (Kells 1995a and b). However, Alison, an advice worker with an Irish voluntary organisation in London who was brought up Protestant in Belfast, identifies the commonalities between Protestant and Catholic Irish migrants.

A lot of people . . . sort of my age identify more with being Irish than being Protestant, certainly a lot of my friends would . . . There is a tension between being Irish and being Protestant and I think it is coming out more now with the ceasefire, most of my Protestant friends see themselves as Irish ... I think that there are certain ways that are similar throughout Ireland ... in the ways that you're brought up, a lot of this kind of guilt feeling, it's often associated with Catholic, but its exactly the same when you're brought up as a Protestant, very much around family and personal issues and how you conduct yourself and how you live your life and that kind of thing, I think you're made to feel just as guilty in a Protestant family ...

(Alison, interview, London)

For those, like Alison, who want to escape the religious divisions that mark Irish identity, there may be more possibilities to identify as Irish in London than in Ireland. She is also conscious that the Peace Process has made the identification with Irish identity above Protestant identity easier for her and her friends. As Alison sees it, both Catholic and Protestant migrants bring with them moral values around family and femininity that produce feelings of guilt when transgressed. A banal cultural Catholicism is variously acknowledged, embraced and contested in these accounts but is less institutionally significant than for the earlier generations of migrant women taking part in Sharon Lambert's study (2001). It is possible that were I to return to interview these women ten years later, for some, their children's educational opportunities might have been a factor in their relationships to the Catholic Church in London.

Conclusion

In her book *The Irish in Britain*, Anne Holohan suggests that young Irish people assume a more fluid notion of Irish identity that is related to a context of global Irish cultural production, membership of the transnational European Union and access to global communications, rather than 'to previous narrow nationalistic ideas' (Holohan 1995: 8). Although this chapter offers some evidence to support this view, it is important that such fluid and globalised notions of belonging are not uncritically embraced. There is no doubt that Irish migrant subjectivity at the end of the twentieth century was partly structured by discourses of a global Irish citizenship, but most of the accounts suggest that migration to London is marked by a 'coming and going' between London and Ireland that produces often more anxious modalities of Irish belonging in diaspora.

London is a site of many contradictory, paradoxical and complex migrant moments in the women's accounts discussed above. The accounts discussed in the first section of this chapter point to the intersections of class and 'white' ethnicity in marking out the terms of belonging within and between generations of Irish in London. They also point to the ways in which 'excessive' Irishness operates through the category gender with women's practices surrounding food, Catholic and national/ethnic rituals representing visible sites of Irish ethnic 'excess'. An autonomous mobile sophisticated feminine self is compromised by the threat of an 'excessive' and 'kitsch' Irishness associated with Irish centres, rural and working-class performances of Irish identity in London. Also, a predominantly Catholic, heteronormative and family-oriented Irish community in London is represented in some accounts as actively mis-recognising and de-nationalising Irish non-Catholics, lesbians and feminists. However, this dominant mode of London-based diasporic Irish culture is challenged by those who are actively engaged with multicultural projects in London to create diverse spaces of Irish belonging and to contest established constructions of Irish identity. For the middle classes, networks or 'peg' communities operated to cultivate social and business connections outside of ghettoised centres of Irish belonging. Nonetheless, England continued to be experienced as 'the nearest place that wasn't home' and many women struggled to occupy a coherent sense of self that was not fragmented by daughterly relations to family in Ireland and attempts to live an autonomous life as an adult woman in London.

Both Ireland *and* London, in the different contexts and circumstances of the accounts above, are identified as progressive modern spaces of identity *and* sites of what are seen as 'backward' cultural practices. Ireland, especially its urban centres and the east coast, represent a central node in circuits of movement that constitute some women migrants as global Irish citizens. Globalised mobile Irish citizenship depended on a 'fixing' of earlier generations of migrants and of rural and poor 1980s migrants whose mobilities were more constrained. There is no doubt that mobility and control over mobility structure power relations between different groups of Irish within the diaspora and between the homeland and the diaspora. Migrancy is a symptom, in some women's accounts, of having transgressed familial sexual norms of 'respectability' in 1980s Ireland and offers the potential for occupying independent adult status for others. Gender and family status re-emerge as intensive sites of the 'truth' of Irish migrant women's selves in this chapter. Individual mobility, while holding out a promise of abandoning gender, national and cultural identities, is compromised in the nexus of global capitalist career structures and heteronormative transnational family connections. In the following chapter, I return to questions of 'white' ethnicity which were raised at the beginning of this chapter and locate these within wider discussions of Irish women's migrancy.

6 'The Irish are not "ethnic"'
'Whiteness', femininities and migration

It's an insidious thing. If you talk about anti-Irish racism[1] people look
at you as if you have two heads, like what is the problem? You are
'white', you speak English, they don't understand this huge cultural
difference. (Anne)

A cultural difference between? (Breda)

Between English people, white English-speaking people and Irish
people. And English friends sort of said to me 'Oh you are all, you
know, you do go on a bit about the fact that you are Irish'. And I don't
notice, but possibly I do. But I only do it now because I am living in
these circumstances. Whereas, if I was still at home it would not be an
issue. (Anne)

What do you think the cultural difference is? (Breda)

The Irish psyche is just different. The way we look at things. The way
we approach things. And there again, I am generalising, I am talking
about the people that I know. And there again, they mostly are people
from my generation, mostly from Dublin. Having said that, you know,
they are from different backgrounds, different you know from all over
the place ... you could identify very clearly differences between ourselves as Irish people and English people. English society, if you like, in
terms of like, language is one thing, that's the way of speaking. (Julie)

... People are inclined to forget the struggle that people have in the
North of Ireland. I mean it's fine to be in Dublin and just you are so
far away from it. You are not exposed to it, therefore you sort of take
– a lot of people accuse Dublin people of having sympathy with the
English. So, I don't know, it doesn't affect my life now ... I don't go
around saying 'Oh well, you know, the British are responsible for this
or'. But you say when in Rome, you know. And I find it's easier, as I
said to assimilate. If you are living in a host country you just live the
way everybody else does. Try not to rock the boat. (Fionnuala)

(Group discussion 3, London)

By looking 'white' and speaking English, Anne does not immediately fit the
category of 'prescribed otherness' in England (Ang 1994: 11). Prescribed
performances of Irish otherness do not include the uninvited assertion of

Irish cultural difference and anti-Irish racism. By speaking English (albeit Hiberno-English) and looking 'white', the presence of most Irish migrants is not at first a 'declaration of . . . belonging somewhere else' (ibid.). The declaration has to be articulated, communicated, and asserted even if already indicated by accent. The seeable is not always self-evident but requires narratives that 'tell' what the body may not 'show' (Bell 1996). It is narrative that undoes assumptions of 'pure whiteness' and destabilises the way 'whiteness' and race are understood (Fraser 1999a: 113).

Cronin argues that language in common can

> produce a fiction of cultural immediacy . . . The illusion of understanding is all the greater because translation is not believed to be a problem . . . However, there can result a genuine sense of bewilderment if a seeming transparency of language gives way to cultural opacity.
>
> (M. Cronin 2000: 25)

To draw attention to oneself as Irish and culturally different, as the discussion above suggests, is to be ungrateful when apparently 'getting away with' invisibility and potential inclusion (albeit conditional). Anne, who worked as a part-time administrator/part-time artist in London, suggests that Irish/English cultural differences are partly structured by discourses of anti-Irish racism. Yet she also draws attention to the difficulties of articulating the specificity of Irishness in England, which in turn contributes to non-recognition of experiences of anti-Irish racism. Julie and Fionnuala's accounts also point to the impossibility of specifying 'the' cultural difference between 'English' and 'Irish' with both pointing to the many internal differences that mark these categories. However, Julie identifies the use of language or her Irish ways of speaking as reminders of her difference while Fionnuala locates the negotiation of English/Irish differences in the political realm of cross-border relations in Ireland and Anglo-Irish relations as marked by the conflict in Northern Ireland.

Anne's account suggests that Irish identity can be concealed when necessary, at least until she speaks, so the implied response is – why doesn't she just do that? (Jordon 1996, in Fraser 1999a). Those who might plausibly escape the regime of 'visibility' should honour that privilege and keep their heads down. As Mariam Fraser notes, the implications of this logic is that 'black and white are immediately available to be accessed by sight' (ibid.). In this sense, the assumption is that the signs of Irishness can potentially 'be "separated" from the self' (ibid.). Fraser invokes Sara Ahmed's argument that

> the reduction of race to skin colour ('chromotism') involves investing skin colour 'with the meaning of racial difference', a difference which 'may fix the object of the gaze into a logic of inclusion (you are white like me) or exclusion (you are black like them)'.
>
> (Ahmed 1996, in Fraser 1999a: 111)

In Anne's account above, the assumption 'you are white like me' discredits Irish articulations of difference which challenge the terms of inclusion and exclusion. The articulation of an Irish presence in England by these women destabilises the borders of identity/difference, which are primarily configured in terms of visibility (Fortier 2000: 25). This migrant assertion of cultural difference constitutes a disturbance in a visual field in which 'looking white' promises some commonality.

In this chapter I argue that Irish migrant belongings in London/Luton are mediated by 'whitely scripts'. I examine some of the modalities in which Irish migrant woman subjects living in London and Luton are constituted and constitute themselves as 'white' in relation to other migrant groups and 'white' English nationals.[2] How and when do the women's accounts interpret events and predicaments in racial and ethnic terms? In what social contexts does racial identification as 'white' emerge as central to the ways in which relations of power are negotiated? If political membership represents one important terrain of belonging that operates through notions of citizenship and nationality, how are these categories racialised? How is twentieth-century British immigration policy racialised and with what effects for Irish migrants?

Whitely scripts

In the recent burgeoning literature on 'whiteness', it is constructed variously as a dominating ideology (Giroux 1997); an ontological status (Gabriel 1998; Giroux 1997); symbolic power (De Luca 1999); a product of social relations and everyday practices (Frankenberg 1993 and 1997); and/or as representation (Dyer 1997). Marilyn Frye (1992) uses the term 'whitely' to mean ingrained ways of being in the world as opposed to the physical appearance of whiteness. Those who look 'white' do not necessarily 'act white'. Indeed, Frye highlights the contingent relationships between 'whitely' performances and looking 'white'. Alison Bailey (2000) develops this idea by positing the term 'whitely scripts' to emphasise the performative nature of 'whiteness'. Racism is seen to operate as a socio-political system of domination with particular racial groups being expected to follow 'historically pre-established scripts' (2000: 289). What it means to be 'white' is not determined only by physical appearance but by the script that the individual animates (ibid.). In other words, through the invocation of the convention of 'whiteness', 'whiteness' itself becomes an authoritative norm that appears fixed and 'natural', thereby exercising a binding power on individuals (Butler 1993). Richard Dyer, in his study of mainly visual representations of 'whiteness' in Western cultures, argues that '[r]acial imagery is central to the organisation of the modern world' (Dyer 1997: 1) which includes the performative production of national identities. Attention to 'whiteness' as scripted 'reveals the less visible, structural regulatory function of racial scripts that exclusive attention to appearance overlooks' (Bailey 2000: 289).

To be 'white' only emerged in the USA as part of the process of establishing a US identity in the nineteenth century, which *included* European settlers and *excluded* indigenous Americans and 'black' slaves (Allen 1994). English, Scottish, Irish and other European immigrants to the USA shifted from the various cultural/regional statuses they occupied into the all-inclusive status of 'whites' (see also Jacobson 1998; Morrison 1992; Roediger 1991 and 1994).[3] In relation to 'how the Irish became white' in the mid- and late nineteenth century in the USA, Noel Ignatiev argues that 'while the white skin made the Irish eligible for membership in the white race, it did not guarantee their admission; they had to earn it' (1995: 59). American immigrant belonging was to be negotiated, therefore, on grounds of 'race', and 'white' status was earned in opposition to 'black' workers in the labour market (ibid.).[4]

In a book entitled *Ethnic Options*, Mary Waters argues that white Americans[5] have the option of identifying as ethnic and some choose *which* ethnicity they want to identify as (Waters 1990: 19). White Americans can, she suggests, invoke ethnicity when they wish and in ways that suit them, while groups identified as non-white are subject to imposed racial identity. However, the processes by which some groups are designated 'white' and others are identified as 'non-white' is not investigated. While there are always options as to how those who look 'white' *and* those who look 'non-white' occupy the category 'ethnic' (see Song 2001), it is the techniques and practices that frame these options in different contexts that need to be analysed. 'Whiteness' is not a static formation, so it is necessary to consider the changing technologies by which 'whiteness' comes into being and is increasingly 'constituted as pliable, and as "on the move", rather than fixed' (Ahmed 2000: 189).

In the case of Britain, anti-Irish rhetoric at official and popular levels during the nineteenth century meant that Irish immigrants were excluded from the category 'white' (see Curtis 1984 and Hornsby-Smith and Dale 1988). The Irish, amongst others, 'were collectively figured as racial deviants, atavistic throwbacks to a primitive moment in human prehistory, surviving ominously in the heart of the modern, imperial metropolis' (McClintock 1995: 43). Their evolutionary lateness was figured, according to McClintock, 'by their "feminine" lack of history, reason and proper domestic arrangements' (ibid.). Daniel Jewesbury notes that in Britain, 'whiteness only attained its totalising, totemic status well into this century [twentieth], with the final assimilation of previously separate ethnic groups into the umbrella category "white"' (1998: 23). The category 'white' in England has become a code-word for 'English' (Solomos and Back 1996), and as Britishness is often defined via assumed norms of 'white' middle-class Englishness, it too is produced as a 'white' identity (Walter 1995).

'Whiteness' is maintained as a dominant ideology, according to Dyer (1997) and Frankenberg (1997), by being coded and obliquely referenced in contemporary discourses of 'race', culture, nation and gender identity.

This view is affirmed in the Irish women's accounts below. Yet their accounts also suggest a need to distinguish between 'whiteness' as a dominating ideology and 'white' people across multiple locations of privilege and subordination (Giroux 1997: 383). 'Whiteness' has a 'different exchange value', according to John Gabriel, 'depending on other social locations, including class, gender, ethnicity and abled-bodiedness' (1998: 5).[6] Another important distinction in the critical analysis of 'whiteness' is that between physical traits such as an apparently 'white' skin and 'acting white' (which relates to the cultural value of 'whiteness'), and the contingent relationships between these. For example, those classified as non-white might 'act white' and vice versa. Alison Bailey emphasises the strong 'corporeal element' that emerges in 'whitely scripts', for example 'ladylike' behaviour being implicitly coded 'white' (see also Ahmed 1997 and Fraser 1999a). An important argument in Bailey's essay, which is taken up in this chapter, relates to the idea that 'in a white-centred culture, everyone is more or less expected to follow scripts that sustain white privilege' (Bailey 1998: 36). Both Irish and English national identities are reproduced through racialised and gendered discourses of 'whiteness', which in turn, map onto national 'terrains of belonging' (Fortier 1999: 41–2). Immigration policies also operate as technologies of racialisation which produce differentiated and hierarchised forms of political membership.[7] It is necessary, therefore, to identify some of the historical-political factors that contribute to the British state's classifications of the Irish as an immigrant group in the twentieth century.

Citizenship and migration in proximity

Although 'citizens inhabit the political space of the nation' this space is, 'at once, juridically legislated, territorially situated, and culturally embodied' (Lowe 1996: 2). Lisa Lowe argues that the administration of citizenship can be seen as 'simultaneously a "technology" of racialization and gendering' through which the state classifies different immigrant groups (1996: 11; see also Paul 1997). The state, through its legal procedures of exclusion and inclusion, attempts to reconcile the contradictions between the needs of the global market for mobile labour and the political need of the nation-state 'for "abstract citizens" formed by a unified culture to participate in the political sphere' (Lowe 1996: 13). The British state in the twentieth century identified Irish immigrants as a necessary, accessible and unnoticeable labour force by constituting 'the Irish' as both 'the same as' and 'different from' the British people.

Many writers suggest that the Irish in Britain lost their Irish identity in the nineteenth century due to a high degree of structural assimilation. However, Mary Hickman resists the assimilation thesis and emphasises modes of incorporation by which the state attempted to regulate potentially oppositional ethnic groups in order to reproduce a single nation-state (Hickman 1995: 17). The establishment of Catholic schools in Britain, she argues, was aimed at strengthening Catholic identity, weakening any sense of Irish national identity and transforming students into 'respectable' and loyal British citizens. The thesis is that the Irish were incorporated into Britain via a strategy of 'denationalisation' through state funding for Catholic schools. One of the effects is the production of a homogenous 'white' population in a state in which skin colour has become a marker of national belonging (see also Cohen 1988).[8] However, the Irish in Britain received political attention as a migrant group whose presence was variously described as necessary and undesirable until the early 1990s.

Early in the twentieth century, economic depression, anti-Catholic Irish prejudice and a growth of nationalism in Scotland led to public articulations of fear and official investigations of Irish migration to Scotland (Delaney 2000: 85–9). In the 1930s, Irish migration was raised by the Committee on Empire Migration and later by the Dominions office when Irish migrants were identified as a burden on public funds. The difficulties of agreeing arrangements with the Irish state and the convenience of the Irish labour supply meant that the British official response was a pragmatic one of doing nothing (ibid.: 90). It is noteworthy that questions of labour supply at the time were explicitly gendered. A memo from the Minister for Labour in 1932 in response to the call for repatriation noted that all Irish migrant labour could be replaced with the 'possible exception of those engaged in domestic service' (Glynn 1981 in Walter 2001: 121). Political discourses of immigration assume an abstract masculine citizen and individual mobile workers. However, Irish migrant women until the 1950s at least were less visible immigrants because their traditional work as domestic servants located them at the heart of middle-class English lifestyles in ways that were concealed (Walter 2001). By the end of the Second World War, Delaney (2000) argues that Irish migrants in Britain were accepted as an important addition to the 'home'.

The 1948 British Nationality Act provided that 'an Éire citizen in the United Kingdom gets automatically the same treatment under our existing laws as if he (*sic*) were a British subject' (Attlee speaking in the second reading of the Ireland Bill, *Hansard* 1949, Vol. 464, Col. 1859; quoted in CRE report: 9). The 1952 Common Travel Area agreement allowed for free movement between both states and is now incorporated into the EU Treaties (Meehan 2000). Another debate on immigration, recorded in the 1955 Cabinet reports of the Eden administration, asserted that

> the outstanding difference is that *the Irish are not*, whether they like it or not, *a different race from the ordinary inhabitants of Great Britain.* ... the Irish not only provide *much-needed labour*, but have always done so, and any restoration of the immigration control on the traffic between Great Britain and Ireland would be *tiresome* ... the only way out of this dilemma would appear to be to argue boldly along the lines

that the population of the whole British Isles is *for historical and geographical reasons essentially one.*

(Quoted in Connor 1987: 20; emphasis added)

The suggestion that the lack of immigration controls on the Irish could legitimately be defended on the basis of an historical and geographical oneness constructs the Irish as *the same as* the British in terms of 'race' and geography and ignores state boundaries. Yet, the Irish are constructed as *different* in so far as they represent a source of 'much needed *labour*' – labour that is easily available, rather than requiring 'tiresome' regulation and administration. The labour market requirements for a flexible component of the labour force and the political need to maintain the rights of UK citizens in Northern Ireland came together in the 1950s in debates about immigration (see Hickman 1998). While at an official level the Irish were being 'included' (albeit in an ambivalent manner) within the British state as a source of labour, at a cultural level, in the 1950s, they continued to be the butt of discriminatory and anti-Irish racist behaviour (Connor 1987; Lennon 1988). The state identified a need to use their labour but saw little need to provide for their inclusion in civil society. At a time when immigration laws treated citizens of the Republic of Ireland 'as if' they were British citizens, the Irish were both defined as, and for the most part, saw themselves as different, as Irish in another country (Lambert 2001).

In the 1962 parliamentary debates about immigration, reference was made to the fact that the Irish 'in bringing over tuberculosis, were more likely to create health problems than West Indian immigrants and created worse housing problems' (Hickman and Walter 1997: 10). Although immigration controls were increasingly placed on black immigrants in the latter half of the twentieth century, the Irish remained a 'special case' ambivalently positioned as 'non-immigrants', but yet as a source of social contamination and a drain on public resources. Partly because of their exclusion from the 1962 immigration controls, the Irish became invisible as migrants and as an 'ethnic' presence in Britain (Hickman 1998: 289). Hickman challenges the view that the Irish were excluded from immigration control because they looked 'white' and presents a number of political and economic reasons why they were differentiated from other immigrant groups. The most powerful reason for excluding immigrant control on the Irish was the expected negative reaction from Northern Irish citizens of the United Kingdom (ibid.).[9] While arguing that 'whiteness' was not central to the omission of the Irish from immigration controls, she suggests that the effect was to reinforce a black and white dichotomy in terms of 'race' in Britain.

In a speech given in 1966,[10] Home Secretary Roy Jenkins argued for a policy of 'integration' based on equal opportunity and cultural diversity, which could be seen as inaugurating an officially sanctioned 'multiculturalism'. However, anti-racist activists in the 1970s dismissed notions of 'ethnicity' and 'multiculturalism' as apolitical and eliding relations of power.[11] By the 1980s, culture and ethnicity had assumed some credibility and the Irish were, in some contexts, identified as 'an ethnic minority' (Connor 1987: 22). The terrain of 'multiculturalism', as Lowe (1996) and others have argued, poses culture as a site for the resolution of inequalities and exclusions that cannot or are not effectively addressed in the political domain. Although official multiculturalism tends to aestheticise and dehistoricise 'ethnic' differences, a critical politics of difference operates within the domain of the cultural. Lowe argues that it is 'through culture, rather than government, that alternative forms of subjectivity, collectivity, and public life are imagined' (1996: 22). Yet, as noted in Chapter 3, official multiculturalism marks only some groups as culturally 'different' and has the effect of producing 'the difference' and making the identified groups responsible for regulating the boundaries of their 'difference'. English national belonging is racially and culturally regulated through discourses of 'whiteness' and liberal multiculturalism, with particular effects for Irish women migrants. Culture in this sense becomes a technology of government as well as a space of alternative forms of subjectivity.

Cultural exclusion and racial inclusion

The markers of Irishness identified in the Irish women's accounts and discussed in this section accentuate the women's experiences of being positioned as cultural 'outsiders' and racial 'insiders' in England. Many of the accounts discussed below are framed by discourses of Irishness, which render Irish identity the antithesis of normative notions of 'white' Englishness. They suggest belongings that are negotiated in the contradictions between what are identified as English cultural and racial criteria for belonging. The cultural criteria identified in the accounts mark these Irish women as cultural 'outsiders', while simultaneously positioning them as racial 'insiders' because they look 'white'. Helen, who worked as a journalist in London at the time of the research and was a student nurse before she left Ireland, describes how her imagined interlocutors affect what she feels able to say about Irish identity.

> I feel hugely guilty every time I criticise Ireland over here . . . I spend my life defending it . . . I don't feel constantly under some kind of racist attack, it's not like that . . . I am very aware of the fact that if I criticise Ireland it adds to a whole culture which perceives Ireland in a certain way. So I can't very openly criticise Ireland unless I am with other Irish people.
>
> (Helen, group discussion 4, London)

Helen is conscious of different interlocutors, some English, some Irish, and of the *defensive* and *testimonial* narratives of Irishness that are invoked in relation to these interlocutors respectively (Henderson 1992). Any criticism of Ireland in England might, for her, involve a repetition and reaffirmation of discourses that homogenise 'the Irish' and divest them of subtlety and diversity. Other accounts set out a range of perceived cultural criteria for Englishness and identify the ways in which the markers of their Irishness represent a falling short of legitimated belonging in England. Some felt positioned as unreasonable when compared to the English norm of *reasonableness* (Valverde 1996). Joan, who did community work before leaving Ireland and went into housing support work in London noted that

> my temperament, my humour, all of that was too strong for a lot of people. . . . It's stifling, I hold back, *I hold myself down*, I'm careful . . .

(Joan, group discussion 5, London;
emphasis added)

As in other accounts, Joan describes a disciplining of behaviour in response to her perception that she is viewed as being excessively emotional. This consciousness of what (English) 'people think' is a recurring theme that is linked to a sense of being seen as 'unreasonable'. 'Reasonableness' has been institutionalised as a quintessentially English trait (Valverde 1996). To be reasonable is to be 'moderate, commonsensical and normal, like the man forever sitting on the unexciting Clapham omnibus' (1996: 363). Mariana Valverde notes that English reasonableness has a moral cultural content that is held in higher regard than intellectual skills. In the English tradition, the virtue of 'reasonable men' was most valued and was incorporated in common law, thereby tying political citizenship to 'certain moral "habits"' (ibid.). As Valverde hints here, 'reasonableness', as well as being nationally produced, is also gendered. Joan's temperament and humour fall outside of 'white' English ladylike scripts. Although a discourse of 'freedom to choose' emerges as an important aspect of how migrancy is understood in many accounts, the options for occupying the category 'Irish women' in London and Luton are circumscribed and regulated by competing national imperatives and the repeated identification of gender identity with practices of family. An associated theme is that of *respectability* which is also central to the development of the notion of Englishness (Skeggs 1997). Respectability is identified with family and community in Ireland (see Chapter 2) but is constitutive of the status of 'individual' in England (ibid.). Those failing the respectability test tend to be seen as vulgar and undisciplined and outside the norms of Englishness (ibid.). Respectability and individuality, then, embody a moral authority that endows belonging in England.

IRA violence in England reinforced discourses of the Irish as incapable of 'reason' and attempting to resolve their problems through violence. Many of the accounts described how the women were positioned as *potential terrorists*, or part of a 'suspect community' (Hillyard 1993), which can be contrasted with the assumed civilised and civilising influence of the

English (McClintock 1995). Many women felt as subject to suspicion as they thought Irish men were, and maybe doubly subject to being positioned as 'unreasonable' as both women and Irish.

Josey, who was unemployed before she left Ireland and worked in secretarial work in London before signing up to do a degree, points to the implications of being part of a 'suspect community' in one of the places she worked in London.

> I was working for this boss who was very prejudiced and sort of saw all Irish people in England as . . . in support of the IRA. You just could not get it across to him that the average Irish person abhors what they do, and okay, wants a united Ireland, but in a peaceful manner . . . But he could not accept that. He just had a chip basically . . . He eventually got rid of me . . . he just could not accept that Irish people could be peace-loving and rational and everything.
>
> (Josey, group discussion 5, London)

Suspicion, in this case, meant that Josey lost her job. The individuality associated with reason and reasonableness is denied to Josey when she is lumped together into a homogenous 'mass' of Irish people who are seen as 'suspect'. Anthropologist Marilyn Strathern argues that 'the first fact of English kinship is the *individuality* of persons' (1992; emphasis added). Yet, Josey, Helen and others suggest that their individuality is denied by being made to stand in for the 'mass of Irish people'. Ethnicity is not an 'option' that is expressive of individuality, as Mary Water's study of middle-class white ethnics in the United States indicated, but is experienced as a socially-imposed racialised identity.

Joan identifies use of the English language as a mode of exclusion that she has experienced in London

> I find it an empty battle trying to prove myself to English people . . . because you're agreeing with the terms of the battle . . . what do I want to prove? . . . about whether to say sofa or settee . . .
>
> (Joan, group discussion 5, London)

The invitation to prove herself as worthy is refused by Joan because she sees it as an impossible task when the terms of her Irish positioning are always already established. The invitation to be 'more like us' holds out a promise of belonging that she believes will never be delivered on. Language and the domestic come together in Joan's account in ways that map onto Enoch Powell's definition of Englishness in the late 1960s as 'whiteness, a command of the English language and a certain kind of domestic space' (Baucom 1999: 15). Like Joan, many of the women recounted experiences of being made to feel 'outsiders' by reference to their inadequate grasp of the English language. For example, both Maggie, an unemployed secretary and Sarah, an astrologer and counsellor, describe experiences of having their English corrected.

> I've had my English corrected. I've really resented that . . . because I had used some turn of phrase. I asked someone to pass me a thumbtack one day and he put it into my hand and really smugly said; 'it's a drawing pin'. . . he was gone so fast I couldn't say anything to him.
>
> (Maggie, interview, London)

> I often find that English people will correct a word that I've used . . . there's an assumption that you've said it arseways.
>
> (Sarah, group discussion 5, London)

The Irish accent and manner of speaking is identified as incorrect and inferior to 'the Queen's English'. Templates for the 'proper' way of doing things and English national stereotypes rely on only a small section of the English population, i.e. 'the heartland of south-east England and adherents of the Anglican Protestant established church' (Walter 1995: 41).[12] Bronwen Walter's observation points to the many groups within Britain for whom cultural belonging may be questioned or contested. However, she argues that, in the case of the Irish, the power/knowledge associated with 'Standard English' or 'the Queen's English' is counterposed by 'assumptions of Irish stupidity' and other characteristics such as alcoholism or terrorism. As non-citizens, non-nationals and immigrants in a context of ongoing conflict over Northern Ireland, there is more at stake in the negotiation of cultural belongings for these women than there might be for women from other regions within England.

Constant reminders of the impossibility of meeting the criteria for cultural belonging in London/Luton mean that 'passing' as English/British, or even as 'legitimate' residents, can never be a possibility. In nearly all cases, the women 'always already' knew, via constant cultural reminders, that they would be caught out. Their Irishness could never achieve equal status with the 'authoritative norm' that is middle-class Englishness of the south-east (Skeggs 1997; see also Walter 1995). The grounds of belonging in the accounts discussed here are articulated in relation to what seem to be mutually exclusive and 'reified' criteria for 'Englishness' and 'Irishness'. Although apparently positioned as cultural outsiders and racial insiders, cultural and racial discourses interact in the above accounts to produce racialised subjects. The accounts identify the ways in which cultural differences are naturalised so that 'race' and racism are located within 'ethnic-related discourses of differentiation . . . [in which] some cultural practices are reified and naturalized as "typical expressions" of an ethnic identity' (Fortier 1999: 43).

Cultural categories of belonging are complicated by a colonial history and geography which produce pride in marginality and which feed into a

politics of identity (Probyn 1996: 73). The cultural (un)belonging(s) represented above are partly (re)produced by a hierarchisation of cultural difference in England, but also by compensatory desires to revalorise and even
romanticise Irish identity. In some cases, 'outsider' status is embraced as a
means of revalorising and asserting an oppositional ethnic/national identity.
This move is legitimated by those articulations of identity and belonging
made possible within discourses of multiculturalism. However, notions of
'whiteness' and belonging also structure the ways in which Irish migrant
women are positioned in England. These women's embodiments of Irish
culture are represented as falling short of the 'whitely script' in their apparently 'unladylike' use of language, humour and manners. They lack the
refined 'reasonable' English middle-class femininity that is coded 'white',
yet because they look 'white' the potential to inhabit this femininity is held
out in ways that position them as 'nearly British'.

To draw attention to the terms of cultural difference and exclusion has
the effect of being positioned as unappreciative of the promise of inclusion
held out by looking 'white'. 'Difference', when defined by the Irish women
themselves, is represented as, amongst other things, 'making a fuss', unreasonable, unladylike, a fabrication, or nationalistic. To be excluded from the
terms of difference and yet to make a claim within its terms is 'to utter a
performative contradiction' (Butler 2001: 431) so that such a claim is met
with derision or may (in particular circumstances) work to produce a revi-
sion of the terms of difference. Cath's account below suggests that masculine
racialised stereotypes of the Irish, such as the repeated invocation of 'Paddy',
may position Irish women as having greater potential for inclusion than
Irish men, making their non-acceptance of the terms of that inclusion all the
more transgressive.

> I think discrimination against Irish people is so subtle, bar the statement
> that 'all Paddys are stupid', the rest of it is so subtle that to describe it
> or to say what it's about is just very difficult, and people think you're
> just making a mountain out of a molehill.
>
> (Cath, interview, London)

Cath's account points to the impossibility of articulating these complex
inclusion/exclusion dynamics in tangible terms. To 'make a mountain out
of a molehill' is to magnify that which is hardly visible. It is to give up the
potential 'invisibility' available through looking 'white', but also to expose
the masquerade of a homogenous 'white' English/British 'race'. The aim
expressed by women in these accounts is not to pass as English or British,
but to embrace a form of passing

> where tactics are employed to neutralise one's presentation of self,
> making it as neutral as possible. Avoiding being read . . . is a strategy

in which one attempts to make the body illegible. Under such circumstances, overt symbols of affiliation in the 'wrong' place become
regarded as purposefully provocative.

(Bell 2001: 69)

Overall, the women's accounts discussed above expose the inevitable un-
realisability of a belonging based on looking 'white' when those who identify
as Irish are culturally racialised. Responsibility for belonging is shifted
away from structural modes of exclusion to the excluded group/individual
which/who is represented as self-deluded and self-excluding. Processes of
pathologising and individualising construct these women as misperceiving
the situation. The implication is that it makes more sense to preserve the
privilege of 'invisibility' based on 'whiteness' by colluding with the racial
hierarchy that re-produces it and by mimicking 'ladylike' femininities. Yet
these accounts suggest that a choice between 'invisibility' and 'visibility' is
no choice at all. The promise of belonging based on performing 'whitely
scripts' operates in such a way that belonging can never be achieved and
the failure to belong is cast as individual and cultural pathology. Nonetheless,
these accounts, by revealing the regulation of belonging, begin to challenge
the 'logic' of belongings and the robustness of 'whitely scripts'. Some of
these accounts might be characterised as 'privilege-cognizant white scripts'
(Bailey 2000: 289) in so far as they refuse to animate the whitely scripts
that they are expected to perform and draw attention to a differentiated
'whiteness'. They reveal the ways in which racial scripts are not only regulated by appearance but by bodily gestures and language. The following
section considers an excerpt from a group discussion that took place in Luton
and which focuses specifically on the desire to achieve belonging by acting
'white'. Some of the accounts discussed below might be characterised as
'privilege-evasive scripts' (ibid.: 292) because the enactment of these scripts
can be seen as reproducing white privilege.

A transnational 'white' Irishness?

In a racially-structured society in which categories of 'visibility' largely
establish identity, looking 'white' offers the possibility of 'passing' and,
thereby, exceeding the categories of 'visibility' (Walker 1993). Identities
which are rendered 'invisible', according to Fraser, 'might be absorbed
into the authoritative "norm" – if no one looks black, everyone is white'
(1999a: 112). As noted already, discourses of multiculturalism in Britain
are marked by a sliding from 'race' to 'ethnicity' in ways that both map
onto this black/white dichotomy and in some cases blur it. Differentiated
modes of racialisation persist both alongside and within discourses and
practices of multiculturalism. Official multicultural policies and initiatives,
although represented as acts of inclusion, produce new forms of othering

(Ang 1996). It is in response to these forms of othering that some of the accounts articulate a desire to be absorbed into the authoritative 'white' norm. Mary, who worked in residential social work in England and in casual work before she left Ireland (at eighteen years), suggests a disidentification with the perceived 'visibility' of 'ethnic' identity and a desire to embrace a potential 'invisibility' by looking *and* acting 'white'.

> Did anybody see the TV on Wednesday? . . . they had the Irish people as an ethnic minority . . . in England . . . we are going to be monitored by the Ethnic Minority Commission[13] . . . I think it's disgraceful . . . I don't think I am *an ethnic person* . . . I mean I hate people condemning this country (England) and what not. If you are living here and you are Irish, why bother living in it if you are going to condemn it? That would be my attitude . . .
>
> (Mary, group discussion 6, Luton; emphasis added)

Mary's reaction to the definition of Irishness within a discourse of ethnicity and multiculturalism is to refuse it. The operation of 'ethnicity' within official modes of multiculturalism means that 'people are assigned to an "ethnic minority" without being asked for their consent' (Bauman 2001: 89). Whether embraced or resisted, Zygmunt Bauman argues that this amounts to 'enclosure from outside' (ibid.: 90). Internal differences are elided and the difference that marks 'ethnic' is an 'enforced ascription' (ibid.). Unconditional loyalty is required by all inside this enclosed fortress and the main battles 'are fought on the domestic front' rather than on the 'ramparts of the fortress' (ibid.: 97). However, the markers of ethnic difference and deprivation are sustained in order to access public funds, while those inequalities and injustices that are recast as cultural differences remain unchallenged (ibid.: 107).

Policies of official multiculturalism constitute a regime of power that generates 'visibility' on terms that Mary is not happy with. The 'ethnicisation' of 'the Irish' involves a kind of objectification which Mary refuses – 'I don't think I am an ethnic person'. The imperative to accept the invitation to 'act white', to perform 'whitely scripts' and not to criticise England/Britain is taken up. 'Acting white' in this context does not necessarily translate into 'acting English/British'. It is more like an undertaking not to undo 'white' invisibility and thereby destabilise constructions of 'white Englishness/ Britishness'. To secure the sign 'white' English or British would require more than the appearance of 'whiteness'; as Fraser notes, 'it is also a way of behaving a manner of conduct' (1999a: 122). The desire is less to belong as British or English than to neutralise the presentation of the Irish self through the category of 'whiteness'. The promise of inclusion that is held out by looking 'white' is a seductive one and 'can give rise to all sorts of strategies of self-correction and voluntary assimilation' (Smith 1994: 20).

As discussed in Chapter 3, the multicultural involves 'the construction of assimilable differences' which requires groups to 'appear different'; that is, to be recognised as different in specified ways only (Ahmed 2000: 133). To assume 'ethnic' identity is be positioned as different to 'the English' and other ethnicities, but also as a member (albeit a marked member) of a multi-cultural British state. But Mary refuses assimilation as 'ethnically' different, opting instead for the promise of inclusion as 'equal' and unmarked because she looks 'white'. She identifies as nationally Irish rather than ethnically Irish. The former is seen as having equivalence with all nationalities whereas to identify as 'ethnic' would be to be somehow less than national, a 'differ-ence' to be incorporated as marked. To appear different in the context of British multiculturalism means assuming 'ethnic' identity and may involve inhabiting a non-'white' identity or 'acting black', as Rhona (a pub manager) and Mary go on to suggest.

> All ethnic minorities in England are a different colour. (Rhona)
> Ethnic minorities up until now are people who are a different colour ... we are not classified on any written document in any country in the world as an ethnic minority. We are not. No we are not. (Mary)
> (Group discussion 6, continued)

Mary's absolute refusal of ethnic identity above is based on its association with non-'whiteness'. In this account she can be read as unreflectively animating whitely scripts in order to avoid being marked as 'ethnic' or black. She assumes instead an unmarked Irish 'we' that is 'not classified . . . in any country in the world as an ethnic minority' and resists any marking of Irishness by implicitly appealing to 'white' skin colour. To do this, she also distances the conditions of Irish belonging from those of black belonging in England. Such differentiations have a long and contested trajectory in Irish history (see Howe 2000; Lloyd 1999 and O'Toole 2000).[14]

The project of 'visibility' that structures multicultural policies brings 'to the fore the very assumption that white immigrants have no "ethnicity"' (Fortier 1999: 58). Yet, as noted in the accounts discussed in the previous section, there is always already a gap between how 'white' Irish women immigrants are positioned and the category of 'invisible' 'whiteness'. When coded in terms of cultural inferiority and the embodied and gendered conduct of the self, the signs of 'whiteness' do not always 'fit'. Although these accounts suggest that through their cultural and embodied ways of behaving, Irish women in England emerge as not quite 'white', they are nevertheless invited to preserve the racial superiority of 'whiteness' by 'acting white'. But, how is 'white' Irish identity in England apprehended outside of discourses of ethnicity? This question is raised by June (who worked in an office in England) later in this group discussion.

> Why are we here talking about being Irish if we are not an ethnic
> minority? (June)
>
> I mean people in Northern Ireland, they can all work and earn the
> same currency, we drive on the same side of the road, we basically eat
> the same food. We live our cultures pretty much the same except . . .
> The Irish flag, you have got Irish accents, you have got the Irish dancing,
> you have very little else. (Mary)
>
> (Group discussion 6, continued)

The assumption behind June's question is that national 'difference' only
becomes visible or 'talked about' in England when it is 'ethnicised'. In a
context of multiculturalism, to identify as different from British or English,
is (almost necessarily) to identify as 'ethnic'. In response, Mary points to
the position of Northern Ireland as part of the United Kingdom. Markers of
national identity are refused as significant in the face of a state (UK) and
assumed 'whiteness' in common. British and Irish become equivalent claims
to citizenship and difference, but contestation over national identifications
in Northern Ireland haunts these assertions. Mary's account could be interpreted as what Gabriel calls 'cultural bleaching' as a means of defending
her belonging in Britain via a discourse of 'race' (1998: 5). Interestingly,
it is at the point where the question of what it means to be 'Irish' is raised
that a totalising 'whiteness' begins to be challenged, if only to reassert
belonging in common with (implicitly 'white') British citizens through a
common 'British Isles' culture. However, Mary returns the discussion to the
problems that the category 'ethnic' causes for Irish identity.

> I don't agree with the Irish people becoming an ethnic minority . . . you
> have the religion, you have the divide with Northern Ireland, and you
> have all the other things that are a problem now, but if we have become
> an ethnic minority they are going to be magnified fifty times. And it's
> going to become so bad that . . . when we go back we are going to be
> viewed far differently, especially if it is publicised. As we are, we are
> people who happen to live an hour's flight away, or six hours drive
> away or whatever. We go home, we happen to live in England, we work,
> we earn our money. If we have become an ethnic minority everything
> gets magnified and we become like prats basically.
>
> (Mary)

Although the position of Northern Ireland means that issues of ethnic and
political boundaries of belonging never disappear, the feminised label
'ethnic' is seen as undermining the masculine status of 'citizenship' (Pateman
1992) which provides the grounds upon which equal treatment is demanded.
As noted in Chapter 5, the performance of 'ethnic' Irishness in London is
identified in many accounts with stasis, community and kitsch. These feminised practices contrast with the individualised citizens of nation states who

move freely within and between these nation-states as national citizens instead of being identified with marginalised and collective 'ethnic' spaces within nations of destination. Mary's account suggests that if Irish identity becomes an 'ethnic' identity in England, the current blurring between Irish national identity in Ireland and in England will be called into question. Her concern about the effects of 'ethnicising' Irish identity in England, then, extends back to Ireland where the category 'ethnic' might deny her the more individual status of national citizen and differentiate her from the *Irish in Ireland* – a distinction she wants to avoid.

The official term 'ethnic' is seen as having similar connotations as the inauthentic category 'the Irish abroad' discussed in Chapter 5, both of which identify migrancy as 'emigrant' and abroad and thereby 'inauthentic' – not 'real' citizens of Ireland. Mary's comment brings us back to the act of *em*igration, which seems as significant here as *im*migration. Mary has left a country in which 'whiteness' and Irishness are mutually constitutive. Like in England/Britain, 'whiteness' in Ireland is differently inflected in relation to different groups such as Travellers (see Chapter 3), Protestants, immigrants, refugees and different classes, but establishes a self-identity that is deeply connected to notions of 'white' Europeaness. To become 'ethnic' in England might locate Mary as a potential 'ethnic' in Ireland, stained by her emigration and representing an 'outsider' status in relation to her country of origin. By being defined as 'ethnic' in England, the elements of Irish identity in Britain that are *emigrant*, and visibly different from Irishness in Ireland, are magnified. To become a 'prat' would be to become marked as an 'outsider', or a 'stranger' *in* Ireland rather than a woman *from* Ireland who just happens to live in England.

To be an unmarked 'white' Irish person, a non-'ethnic', is to have claims to belong in Ireland while simultaneously assuming a mobile identity that can move without notice or negative personal effect. Mary's account returns us to the ways in which a global citizenship constituted through mobility is territorialised insofar as individuals are free to move/travel only as national citizens. For example, mobility within Europe is possible 'only to the extent that this limitless travel is firmly grounded in national territory and national identity' and relies on an 'old white nation state project' (Verstraete 2001: 33/28) that continues to racialise, ethnicise and immobilise. To be identified as 'ethnic' is to be stained by movement; to become visible and open to surveillance and containment. Irishness, as an unmarked 'white' identity, is (potentially) an easily transported identity from Ireland to England and back again. This mobility is in danger of being contained by the designation 'ethnic'. The promise of and desire for an unmarked easily transported Irish identity between Ireland and England and vice versa, although not realised in the accounts, is a seductive one that seems to work against any reflexivity about positioning in common and relative positioning of migrant Irish women and other migrant or 'ethnically' marked women in England. Although some Irish identify themselves as 'black' or non-white on the basis of experiences of racism and a history of colonialism, this can elide the specific conditions of racism experienced by those identified as 'black'. This disavowal of 'looking white' can also in some circumstances legitimate a non-reflective and non-critical approach to the social positionings available to those who look 'white'.

Conclusion

Bronwen Walter uses the term 'outsiders inside' to characterise the ambiguous position of Irish women in Britain and in the United States. The paradoxical notion of 'outsiders inside' is seen as expressing the both/and ties to countries of origin and settlement that marks diaspora. Irish migrant women are identified as 'coming from/identifying with an outside and settled/belonging inside' and 'whiteness' is seen as shoring up 'the outside/ inside duality in unspoken ways' (Walter 2001: 9/272).[15] Irish migrant women's potential invisibility is premised, according to Walter, on the operation of 'whiteness' as an unmarked identity in the United States and Britain. However, this location of potential invisibility based on 'whiteness' *outside* of Ireland raises questions about the operation of this category *within* Ireland and how it is negotiated in all of those practices that take place *between* Ireland and the many sites of the diaspora. Further, the status of 'outsider within' is seen by theorists such as Sandra Harding (1991) as having an 'epistemic standpoint' that is particularly advantageous because it offers a broader view of the world than either that of 'insider' or 'outsider' (Bailey 2000: 285). The potential for 'double consciousness' (Du Bois 1994) that enables a perception of themselves through their own eyes and those of insiders are seen as bringing a unique combination of closeness and distance that can maximise objectivity and insight (Bailey 2000: 285). The accounts discussed in this chapter suggest that the status of 'outsider inside' is negotiated in different ways and cannot always be assumed to maximise objectivity. Also, the status of 'outsider/inside' is itself a radically differentiated status that may be inhabited in numerous ways even by the same individual.

I have used 'whiteness' as a category of analysis in this chapter because it seemed to me that assumptions of 'whiteness' as symbolic of national collectivity in common and of access to belonging arose both in the official namings of the Irish as an immigrant group in England and the self-positionings in the women's accounts. Many of the accounts point to the disjunctures between looking 'white', lived experience, aspirations and desires. The analysis considers the discourses that frame claims to 'whiteness' and the negotiation of migrant belongings in England and Ireland. Monolithic notions of 'whiteness' are undone as these accounts suggest that integration or assimilation in England are not available to all of those who look 'white'. The women's accounts identify the ways in which notions of 'whiteness' intersect with gender, so that particular performances of gender can mark these women as 'non-white'. It is clear also that 'whiteness' travels across Irish and English borders in contingent ways. The same 'white' (settled) woman's body is inhabited in Ireland as an unmarked 'white' body while in England the intersections of Irish, gender and racial identities render the same body 'marked' and not quite 'white'. The focus on 'whiteness' in this chapter then illuminates the ethnoracial differentiations and divisions involved in the hegemonic reproduction of national identities as 'white' (Rasmussen *et al.* 2001). It also locates the workings of British multiculturalism in a national context in which many everyday experiences and conditions are lived though 'race'.

Some of the ways in which 'white' belongings are achieved in dialogic relationships between countries of immigration and emigration (and within the wider socio-political horizons of Europe, the US and 'the global') have been analysed in this chapter. The Irish represent an ambiguous and potentially unsettling presence in England, and there is some evidence that they have also occupied a border zone in the United States (see Bayor and Meagher 1996).[16] Because most Irish *immigrants* to England look 'white', they are ambiguously positioned in relation to an Englishness that is largely defined in terms of 'whiteness'. In this context, 'white' immigrant groups such as the Irish are seen as potential agents of 'white remarkability' (Hill 1997: 160) because they are marked as cultural 'outsiders' but look 'white'. Their presence represents a potential threat to the hierarchy of 'race' as currently articulated in England. As *emigrants* from a country that also implicitly defines itself in terms of 'whiteness', some Irish women immigrants draw on discourses that conflate national citizenship, 'whiteness' and belonging and that affirm assumptions of a Euro-American global 'white' mobility. 'Whiteness' is reaffirmed, and 'difference' is produced as 'sameness' in this move to construct 'white' European national identity as a sign of unmarked mobility and belonging. At the same time, border crossing challenges the ideological meanings of racialised codes, potentially producing more self-conscious performances of 'whiteness' as in some of the accounts above. Often contradictory modes of belonging are permitted and desired in the context of the migration of a largely 'white' migrant group to the geographically proximate country (England) which is represented (however inaccurately) as a 'white' nation. The ambivalent rhetoric and practices of the British state with regard to Irish immigration form an important backdrop to these accounts of belonging producing conflicting desires and potentialities. The women's accounts point to the racialised and gendered reproductions of Irish and English/British identities and the contestation about whether migration between Ireland and Britain can be understood in terms of unmarked 'European national and "white" mobility' or coded as 'ethnic'. These racialised and gendered technologies of the self individualise the grounds of belonging often in response to the ways that the code 'ethnic' enforces collectivity and suggests surveillance and a threat to mobility. The 'white'-centred cultures of England and Ireland code particular femininities as 'white' and reproduce scripts that invite Irish migrant women to act 'white', an invitation that is reinforced by the hierarchies of belonging that mark contemporary British 'multiculturalism'.

The slippages between inclusion and exclusion, identification and dis-identification, constitute these women's Irish subjectivities and belongings as simultaneously gendered, classed, raced, migrant, national and trans-national. The performance of 'whitely scripts' by some Irish migrant women locates them within the gendered and racialised constraints and privileges of the category 'white *women*'. However, this category is never completely occupiable because it is rendered impossible by the marked category 'Irish migrant women'. As noted already, the category 'Irish migrant women' is occupied in differentiated ways and is negotiated in relation to the unmarked category 'white women' and the category 'ethnic'. In order to constitute the category 'Irish migrant women' as modern, those designated 'ethnic' are often constituted as not sharing 'modern' characteristics. The simultaneous negotiation of a colonial history, anti-Irish racism and the social location of 'white' European produces all kinds of complex positionings and politics in the accounts above. Irish feminist politics therefore, requires a nuanced and politically sensitive analysis of the paradoxical and contradictory reproduc-tion of the category 'Irish women' in and through differently racialised 'white' Irish femininities. The silence surrounding Traveller and 'black' Irish femininities suggests that they continue to occupy the 'constitutive outside' (Butler 1993) of the category 'Irish women'. How then might Irish femi-nists develop theoretical and political perspectives from their particular (if contradictory) social locations to develop 'alternative scripts capable of disrupting the constant reinscription of whitely scripts' (Bailey 2000: 293)? This question (amongst others) is taken up in the following concluding chapter, which addresses contemporary reworkings of the categories of Irish modernity, diaspora, family, feminism and the global.

7 Women, the diaspora and the 'global Irish family'
Feminist contentions

The debates and struggles around sexuality, migration, Traveller identity, 'whiteness' and feminism that mark the accounts of Irish women in this book offer some 'local' resources for the development of feminist theory and activism in Ireland and the diaspora in the twenty-first century. The global and the diaspora are rarely identified in feminine terms, yet as this book demonstrates, they are occupied and constructed by women who, like men, are agents of diasporisation and globalisation. Through her speeches, global journeys and intercultural encounters, President Mary Robinson imaged the globe as feminine. Her own image as an Irish, but also as a global figure, circulated in media representations of her encounters with women around the world, whether they were starving women in Somalia (understood primarily through their local belonging; see Kelleher 1997), or other women figures of global mobility such as Hillary Clinton. Her subsequent positions as United Nations High Commissioner for Human Rights and director of the Ethical Globalisation Initiative[1] based in New York established her as a global figure. The UN is involved in constituting women as global citizens, Ahmed argues, by locating the well-being of all women in relation to the degree to which they 'are "brought" into modernity by global agencies' (2000: 175).[2] In Hillary Clinton's speech at the 1995 UN conference on women, she implied 'that women become global actors precisely through an *extension* of the activities within the home' (ibid.: 172). The documentation for the conference can be read as identifying the goal of global feminism as the 'developed woman' constituted as an individual who has 'autonomy, rights and freedom': it also defines global citizenship 'in terms of the heterosexual couple and the heteronormative family' (ibid.: 174/176).[3] The family is put forward as 'a form of global nomadic citizenship, which despite its emphasis on movement and the overcoming of boundaries, remains predicated on traditional forms of social differentiation' (ibid.: 176).

Individual women subjects' self-understandings as analysed in this book continue to be identified through the binding forces of habits, sentiments, affections and obligations that are located in the familial, but are also structured by discourses of choice. The accounts of both migrant and non-migrant women suggest ambiguities about gender, maternity, daughterhood and migrancy in the cultural life of Irish global modernity. Migration and staying-put are reworked as potentially equivalent practices of Irish global modernity, even if still marked by assumptions of migration as modernisation, staying as stasis (albeit also a marker of authenticity), and 'ethnic' diaspora as caught in a cultural time warp. The intricate webs of gender and generational relations that comprise families are shifted onto new ground as gendered familial obligations and identities are unsettled in these negotiations of mobility, 'home' and belonging. Equally, the structure and practices of the gendered global labour force are changing, with Irish migrant women taking up new positions of professional, technical and service provision posts in global cities, while many continue to occupy the 'traditional niches' of service and nursing. Questions of Irish women's 'authentic' cultural belonging are structured in many of the accounts through familial relations that are increasingly negotiated through discourses of choice. For women living in Ireland the meanings and implications of social change are frequently projected onto the perceived choices that women make between the largely media constructed positions of 'women in the home', 'feminists' and 'career women'.

If the nation-state is governed through the family (Donzelot 1980), it is possible that the global nation may also be governed through the family. There is a vested interest in cultivating the desire to belong, to be part of a recognisable 'family' that will provide a relatively stable anchor for identity in what is identified as an uncertain and changing world. The transnational family is increasingly an object of academic and political knowledge and posited as a potential vehicle for transnational political and economic strategies. But what kind of family is this global or transnational family? What are the characteristics of the 'global Irish family' as articulated by President McAleese in the late 1990s and early 2000s? What happens when this territorialised discourse of the global Irish family (i.e. produced and circulating in the context of Ireland) meets Irish identified individuals and families in different parts of the world? In what ways might the promise of belonging through 'the global Irish family' be complicit with global neo-liberal power relations? My first aim in this concluding chapter is to consider the figuring of the global Irish nation through the diaspora via the trope of the family by President Mary McAleese who followed Mary Robinson as the second woman President of Ireland in 1997. I examine how Irish familism as a source of national strength and continuity is newly invoked as an ideological framework for articulating a distinctly Irish global modernity. Given the extent to which the women's accounts discussed in this book are marked by family, it is important to consider what might be involved in this move to figure the global Irish nation as a family. This move is also discussed in relation to how feminism is both globalised and reworked by notions of 'the global' and the specific feminist local/global questions raised by this analysis of women and the Irish diaspora. My second aim is to outline the ways in which the parameters of Irish modernity(ies) are redrawn by the women's accounts discussed and analysed in this book.

The 'global Irish family'

In 1980s and 1990s Ireland, migrants and the diaspora were viewed as potential investors in the homeland, as agents of Irish globalisation and symbolic of the persistence of Irish patriotism and kinship. The diaspora was officially represented as 'both the window and the bridge to a distinctive kind of [Irish] affluence and modernity' (Ong 1996: 75). In this section of the chapter I want to consider how the rhetoric of the global nation is discursively structured in the speeches of the current President of Ireland, Mary McAleese. It is evident from many of her speeches since becoming president that her preference is for the trope of the family to figure a simultaneity of the national and the global. The first quote below is an excerpt from the president's lecture on the theme of 'the marginalised child'; the second excerpt is from a speech delivered on the occasion of an emigrant return holiday weekend in County Mayo, and the third is from a speech delivered at the Centre for Migration Studies in Omagh.

> The power to shape destinies is an awesome power indeed. *Families matter.* They come in all sizes from 'The Little House on the Prairie' to 'Angela's Ashes' ... It is remarkably easy to convince ourselves that ... alternative lifestyles are part of some quintessentially modern, futuristic and unstoppable dynamic [...] Its (the family in the past) apparent random, rough and tumble nature often masked *its subtleties, its successes, its foundation on generations of lived life, of distilled, even better wisdom, its capacity to absorb change, to mutate and to adapt.*
> (McAleese 2000a; emphasis added)

> This modern Ireland is faster more sophisticated than many remember it ... its name is debated from one end of the globe to the other. But beneath these changes lie the unchanging *core values* that drive, shape and inform our psyche as a nation – *our sense of family,* our commitment to community, our ability to celebrate life itself even in adversity, our profound sense of responsibility for each other, our compassion, our spontaneous gift for friendship, enduring friendship.
> (McAleese 2001a; emphasis added)

> Today Ireland knows *the strength of a global family,* which has *turned the tragedy of emigration into a huge success story.* So many lives were vindicated once their talents met opportunity. And so they moved the story on from hardship to hope.
> (McAleese 2001c; emphasis added)

In the first quote the family is constructed as a central social institution and, despite its shortcomings,[4] the most effective model for collective belonging. Indeed, bonding through kinship or family is represented as the only significant mode of collective solidarity. The foundational social status of the family is enhanced by its 'generations of lived life' and ability to contain randomness, diversity and change. Although this notion of family incorporates difference, the grammar of the family, as Donna Haraway argues, is one of indifference and the 'multiplication of sameness' (1997: 243). It is the assumed multiplication of sameness that makes 'families matter'. In this speech, the family holds continuity and change together through 'generations of lived life' and accumulated 'wisdom' which in turn render it familiar despite its mutations and adaptations. The second quote identifies 'our sense of family' as a natural core value of the Irish nation. It insulates against the speed of social change because it anchors a dispersed Irish identity and reproduces sameness in spite of change. In the third quote, the president represents the family as the source of strength that underpins an Irish story of success. This attempt to produce an imagined global Irish community relies on the motif of kin to reproduce the narrative of a successful Irish diasporic community.

The trope of the family invoked by President McAleese subsumes the gender, class and racial hierarchies that structure the diaspora to the assumed unity of interests of the global Irish family. The trope of the family suggests a progressive notion of time through genealogy and transmitted memory, but also brings space under control by locating the family in the spaces of Ireland and the global as now equivalent sites of opportunity and success. The narrative of success that attaches to the diaspora extends to the homeland in 2000 through its possessive and kin relationship to the diaspora – 'our global Irish family' (see later speech excerpts). The apparently contradictory impulses of cultural nationalism underlying notions of 'the Irish family' and economic liberalism based on the possessive individual come together in the trope of the global Irish family and its allied success narrative. De Valera's family centred and communal Ireland is recast on a global stage where individual lives meet opportunity. Indeed, cultural nationalist values of the Irish family are deployed as conduits of individualism and materialist values.

However, the Irish diaspora is inhabited and lived by people in a variety of ways and with multiple and contested relationships to Irish identity, so that lived experience always exceeds discourses of the diaspora and kinship. Transnational kin relations, as discussed in this book, are marked by suspicion of the differences produced by the specific familial (and social) conditions and dynamics of migrating and staying put. Legacies of concealment around migration and the potential for more frequent contact render migrant/non-migrant familial relationships more fraught. The intensification of relations between migrants and non-migrants (even as these categories are blurring) is identified in this book with the proliferation of discourses of choice. Transport and communication technologies produce more choices for migrants about levels of involvement in family and community in Ireland and vice versa. In these families, the capacity to absorb change is present but is not always openly negotiated, and the story of migrant success is often double-edged. Tensions between individualism, family obligation and national belonging mark intimate familial relations and the more public domain of feminist politics in the women's accounts. However, these tensions are apparently resolved by the construction of the global Irish family as reproducing core Irish values and mediating individual and collective economic success.

These gendered tensions and contradictions are further elided by invocations of the 'global Irish family'.[5] The first quote below is taken from the president's address to the Joint Houses of the Oireachtas[6] and the second is taken from her speech to the nation to mark the millennium.

> We owe a debt of gratitude too, to those who left this island ... It was our emigrants who globalised the name of Ireland. They brought our culture with them, refreshed and enriched it with the new energy it absorbed from the varied cultures into which it was transplanted ... They gave us that *huge multicultural Irish family* now proudly celebrated and acknowledged in the new Article Two of the Constitution.[7]
>
> (McAleese 1999; emphasis added)

> Our rich cultural and spiritual heritage, today's cultural vibrancy, our membership of the European Union, our legendary missionary and peace-keeping endeavour, we have made an impact on the world far above what might be expected from a small nation. Around the world the *huge global Irish family* joins us in looking at this new Ireland with gratitude and respect ... We need a modern world which is not in the vicelike grip of the past, but which is also not amputated from the past. So there you have another hope, that we will find the right relationship between what has gone and what is.
>
> (McAleese 2000b; emphasis added)

Emigration and emigrants are identified as reproducing global Irishness. Of course, the diaspora is not the only mediator of Irish globalisation. For example, the global Irish nation is also naturalised through discourses of a runaway global economy that identifies specific forms of mobility as an essential attribute.[8] However, the President's speeches suggest that without emigration, the energy and multiculture produced by the global dispersal of Irish people would be absent. The use of 'we' (in Ireland) and 'our' emigrants who have given 'us' this huge multicultural Irish family puts the diaspora to work in the name of those who live in Ireland. Who is imagined as part of this 'multicultural Irish family' and which 'Irish homes' can they occupy? Who/what are the 'others' of this 'global Irish nation'? If the diaspora was once 'the other' of the Irish nation, is it now being incorporated within it? In Chapter 5 'the Irish abroad' are identified with excessive performances of Irishness and are constructed as 'other' to the modern Irish nation. The accounts of Traveller women in Chapter 3 identify how their 'Irish' presence in the diaspora both goes unrecognised and is constructed as 'other', while in Chapter 6, non-white 'ethnic' groups in Luton became the others of a 'white' Irish nation/diaspora. In what ways then can this global Irish family be multicultural?

In the President's speech above, hybridity and multiculture are located at the heart of Irish cultural survival. When multiculturalism is increasingly invoked as a mode of transnational belonging, diasporas are seen as teaching the homeland the skills of 'co-existing with and absorbing the good points of other cultures' (Ong 1996: 82–3). The implication is that Irish migrants and their descendents have remained 'Irish' in some basic and unchangeable way, so that multiculturalism is added on rather than transformative (ibid.). The global family trope articulates Irish particularism and difference in ways that keep both in play but that enable a recognisable Irish identity to persist. The multi-located figure of the 'global Irish family' collects together assumed experiences (or transmitted memories) of migrancy and produces a global Irish belonging in common through the notion of a 'controlled' diversity. Cultural difference becomes a resource to be taken in and assimilated rather than transformative of globalised Irish identity. The idea of the global Irish family posits a culturalised right to identify as Irish and belong to 'the Irish nation'. But this is less about social justice or social inclusion than capitalising on the human potential of the diaspora in the interests of the nation. A global/multicultural Irishness is represented in the President's speech as an enriching and energetic cultural resource for a territorially located Irish identity in Ireland. The different narratives of origin that mark Irishness in the diaspora are seen as generating an 'open-ended potential' that can draw on multiple global locations but also on 'a diffusion of temporality, drawing on past, present and future' (A. Cronin 2000: 147). In the second quote, the past, present and future are brought together in a narrative of achieved global visibility. The global present is identifiable by a spiritual heritage, cultural vibrancy, membership of the EU, missionary work and peace keeping around the world. Through these multi-temporal global activities this small nation is seen as having reproduced itself as a 'huge' global force. Presented as national achievements, these activities are evacuated of politics and contestation. Instead, the ability to overcome 'the past' represents evidence of potential. But in order to achieve this potential there is a suggestion that the contradictions between elements of the country's past and its current global and economic positioning must be addressed. This negotiation of past and present takes place in this speech through a discourse of potential and a reworking of the relationship between the homeland and the diaspora as a site of both potential and hope.

In a speech delivered to launch the new Irish World Heritage Centre in Manchester, the president identified both the diaspora and the homeland in terms of success and prosperity.

> There has always been an invisible yet powerful network of links between the *global Irish family*; today that ancient web of friendship is mirrored and strengthened further by the Internet, and by websites . . . which put Irish people in every part of the globe in constant touch with their heritage and each other . . . The Centre (Irish World Heritage Centre, Manchester) . . . will most certainly have another eye on the remarkable new heritage being forged by a new, successful generation in an Ireland that is today, dynamic and prosperous and by *its high-achieving global Irish family* rooted in cultures the world over.
>
> (McAleese 2001b; emphasis added)

The diaspora does not produce ruins as evidence of its ancient existence; even the links between Irish migrants in the past are constructed in this quote as invisible. Therefore, centres such as the Irish World Heritage Centre are seen as having the potential to give depth of meaning to this diasporic heritage, which although 'rooted in cultures the world over', needs agents of visibility in order to do justice to its achievements. The need of all nations for 'representational labor' to supplement their 'founding ambivalence', lack of self-presence and essence (Parker *et al.* 1992: 5) is made tangible by this physical and virtual centre which provides sites of definition for the 'global Irish nation'. The limits of the global Irish family as a site of cultural maintenance and continuity are performatively reproduced in this speech. Global modernity's visual culture (A. Cronin 2000) renders familial connection even more invisible than in the past and requires the work of the heritage industry to make Irish culture globally significant. New life will be breathed into this global Irish family by networked visual images of its existence including photographs, letters and genealogical data. If globalisation involves the development of global memory located in the space of the global, then this is a project for the construction and circulation of global Irish memories and will support rather than displace the global Irish family.

Despite arguments for a detraditionalisation of culture, the 'tradition' of the Irish family circulates in the trope of the 'global Irish family' which acts as both a utopian image of global community and a normative guide for the global reproduction of Irish identity through kin. John Thompson (1996) argues that the transmission of the symbolic materials which comprise traditions is increasingly detached from local contexts of social interaction. In a media saturated world marked by increased migration there is a consequent nomadism of tradition (ibid.). Traditions, therefore, circulate and are re-embedded in new contexts not least in the diasporic and global spheres. Communication media, globally mediated national commemorations, and cultural products branded and marketed globally provide new ways of sustaining cultural continuity despite spatial and temporal dislocations and dispersal. The global nation cannot be reproduced in a similar way to the public sphere of the nation-state where citizenship is reproduced via enfranchisement, civic acts and face-to-face interaction in the public sphere. In this new context of global Irishness identifications rely on traditional notions of home, family, and community (Berlant 1997: 5). A patriotic traditionalism is at the heart of the invitation to heteronormatively reproduce the global Irish family biologically, culturally and economically.

The institutional family structure, predicated on a presupposed inequality between women and men, parents and children has led feminists to identify new sites of collectivity, care and belonging. Donna Haraway argues for the identification of 'a different primal scene where everything does not stem from the dramas of identity and reproduction' (1997: 265). She calls for affiliation based on other things such as friendship, work, collective pain, or hope (ibid.) The heteronormative notion of the global Irish family constitutively excludes Irish lesbian and gay diasporas because these cannot be accounted for in a familial language of genealogy. Same sex desire in the diaspora constitutes different non-heteronormative spaces and imaginings of diaspora. If public discourses of the diaspora such as 'the global Irish family' exclude other modes of diaspora, we are left with questions of how queer Irish diasporas are made available to memory and part of the national/global story(ies)? The trope of the global Irish family limits imaginings of affiliation and cultures of belonging by privileging notions of kin, a possessive relationship between the 'homeland' and the diaspora, and by locating a narrative of economic success based on multi-location at the heart of Irish global modernity.

President McAleese's 'global Irish family' is implicated in reproducing the global as heteronormative through the trope of kin while 'the global' constructs the Irish family as dispersed, multicultural and mobile. Yet, the global in these speeches is undifferentiated. It does not mark out the uneven conditions of mobility, multiculture and dispersal. It does not identify the patriarchies, racisms, colonialisms and feminisms that structure the reproduction of the local through the global and vice versa. It does not identify the ways in which new circuits of Irish culture, capital and people interact with older circuits or with other cultural circuits. It incorporates Irish women and men into the global via the family as unmarked citizens of the globe. It elides the unequal and uneven ways in which global/local relationships position different groups of Irish women and individual Irish women. The global Irish family floats free of those differences that cannot be assimilated by 'the global' and that have been gestured towards, articulated and/or remain unspoken in the accounts discussed in this book.

At the end of the twentieth century, feminists struggled to produce analyses that acknowledged the conditions of global inequality and the differentiated feminist priorities that these gave rise to. Feminism, as Judith Butler reminds us, is a movement that proceeds precisely by bringing critical attention to bear on its premises in an effort to become clearer about what it means, and to begin to negotiate the conflicting interpretations, the irrepressible democratic cacophony of its identity.

(2001: 415)

Feminism is part of modernity and has appropriated the exclusionary masculinist terms of modernity to open up routes to women's democratic inclusion and to produce a rethinking of modernity that exposes the gendered assumptions that underpin it. The accounts discussed in this book often position 'Irish women' as 'developed women' of global modernity and as individuals who have 'autonomy, rights and freedom' (Ahmed 2000: 174) in opposition to Irish Traveller women and women in the 'Third World'. This Western liberal choosing self is also constituted as a 'white' self in many accounts.

Recent discussions about how best to pursue feminist scholarship and politics in a global frame have focused mainly on women's rights as human rights.[9] Sylvia Walby argues that feminism has 'changed its repertoire and form' due to changes in the gender regime and globalisation (2002: 534). This change is marked by an assertive engagement with the state;[10] the prevalent use of equal rights discourse; the increased significance of the global both in feminist political connection and in the development of new political spaces such as the UN and EU; and finally, the innovative use of coalitions and alliances as modes of feminist organising.[11] Feminist activists, Walby argues, are increasingly incorporated into the governance of liberal democracies and are 'important players in the construction of a newly globalizing world' (ibid.: 549). The 'NGO-ization of feminism' (Kaplan and Grewal 2002: 70) and the proliferation of UN events and activities relating to women and human rights are also implicated in the re-construction of feminist concerns as global.[12] But how effective is the universalising rhetoric of feminist human rights activism when it meets neo-liberal global economics, the momentum of global consumer culture and globalised militarism? Do the overlaps between liberal discourses of individualism and choice and rights undermine the potential of women's rights as human rights? How can the agenda of women's rights as human rights critically engage with the ideological work of the family in constructing global Irish modernity? Despite the evidence of progress in the areas of reproductive rights and violence against women, it is important that feminists critically engage with the proliferation of rights and 'freedom-as-rights' discourses. Wendy Brown, for example, argues that rights discourses represent the 'development less of freedom than of an increasingly administered society' based on proceduralism and litigiousness and asks how rights might be implicated in entrenching rather than redistributing power. (2001: 12). The fact that rights as the means to freedom are now at the heart of discourses of the Left and Right also challenges us to rethink how equality and freedom might best be achieved (ibid.). These are just some of the questions and challenges that frame debates between feminists and feminisms as feminist politics are formulated and reformulated in the contexts of 'the global'.

Technologies of globalisation involve lines of connection amongst a diversity of types of knowledges, forces, capacities and types of judgement as well as aspirations to achieve certain outcomes and conducts (Rose 1999a: 54). Presidential speeches and discourses of the 'global Irish family' become technical insofar as they attach themselves to economic and cultural practices of diaspora in the homeland and beyond (see Chapter 1). The accounts in this book are testimony to the uneven operation of discourses of the global and the diaspora in producing modern Irish selves. In the following section, I offer my readings of the kinds of knowledges and judgements that produce gendered Irish global, national, and migrant selves based on the variety of sites of Irishness and perspectives articulated by the women who took part in this study.

Blurring the migrant/non-migrant dichotomy

Some academic commentators identify the global as a space of 'freedom' that offers a release from the past in Ireland. For example, Rory O'Donnell argues that

> Ireland ends the 20th century in a position of unprecedented potential. It leaves the century free of the two masters that dominated and constrained – London and Rome. It is now free to reinvent itself: an international people in a global world, a negotiated state in a negotiated Union . . .
>
> (2000: 212)

If the research on which this book is based proves anything, it is that the legacy of these 'masters' continues to mark the category 'Irish women' and Irish femininities both in the diaspora and in Ireland, even if newly inflected by the global. Ireland and Irish citizens at home and abroad are constituted by the promise of 'freedom' to invent themselves, but as Franklin *et al.* argue, 'it is the requirement of the exercise of the will which is the decisive means by which the global citizen is established' (2000: 75). In O'Donnell's formulation above this new found 'freedom' is epitomised by the development of the Irish citizenry as 'an international people in a global world', but it is important to examine the ways in which the imposing of a global 'national' imagining identifies choice as its origin and produces new regulatory effects.[13] The women's accounts discussed in this book are testimony to the newly configured inequalities and tensions that this 'global' framing of Irish belonging produces.

Just as the social is reworked in terms of dispersal, mobility and the global, so too are gender, sexuality, 'race' and the family reworked in these terms. The characterisation of the 1980s generation of Irish migrants and non-migrants as 'the Ryanair generation' and 'the young Europeans' contributed to a figuring of their 'selves' as mobile, reflexive and 'white'. Irish modernity is located within a tradition of Euro-American modernity/'white' hegemony through notions of the global. This book argues that the categories 'women' and 'the Irish diaspora' are reworked and hierarchised in new ways in a global modernity marked by a privileging of 'white' Euro-American mobility. The privileged subject of global modernity is a subject with a mobile relationship to the self and to geographic location. Discourses of career advancement through mobility and adaptability make available narratives of the self as self-actualising and self-responsible. There is also an individualisation of the migrant as a career-oriented self and a figuring of migrants as 'the agents of themselves' (Adkins 2002: 118). Even as this construction of the migrant gains legitimacy the non-migrant is also constructed through discourses of individualisation and self-actualisation thereby blurring the boundaries of these categories. Both migrants and non-migrants are 'continuously engaged in a project to shape their lives as autonomous, choosing individuals driven by the desire to optimise the worth of their existence through the constant building and rebuilding of their own resources' (ibid.). As Lisa Adkins argues, this mobile self is central to new forms of categorisation, regulation and hierarchisation. While a re-working of the migrant/non-migrant categories is evident at a discursive level, at the level of lived experience these categories are being re-negotiated in ways that are difficult to articulate. Migration produces differences, distances and new negotiations of gender and national/ethnic identity that are not easily accommodated by family and transnational practices as currently constituted. The accounts discussed in this book are testimony to the 'privatised' emotional management that ensues when this 'mobile self' is negotiated transnationally as a result of migration and in relation to a less mobile familial gender regime.

As Irish national identity is reformulated to conform to a global modernity marked by neo-liberal politics and technologies of individualism new relationships to notions of 'home' and belonging are produced. Migration and staying put represent two modalities of doing 'home' in modernity. Staying in Ireland (as opposed to migration) is increasingly marked by mobility, interconnection, and outernational dependence so that it no longer (if it ever did) represents stasis or being 'left behind'. Constructions of the nation-state as a local facilitator of global flows of capital, labour and culture produce new stratifications between mobilities. For example, the emphasis on global mobilities is often at the expense of more local forms of movement. The rural poor, Travellers and other socially and economically excluded groups are further excluded by an infrastructure shaped for the globally rather than the locally mobile. Questions of 'choice', compulsion and constraint are at stake here. Earlier generations of migrants, working-class migrants, Travellers and young lone mother migrants are identified in fixed terms. They are held in place as 'out of date', static or excessive in order for a flexible Irish middle-class self in the present to be articulated. A knowing relationship to the self is attributed to the young middle-class woman migrant and urban professional stayer, but for this relationship to the self to emerge those who occupy the categories 'Irish abroad', 'working class', or 'Irish Traveller' are constituted in collective terms as having a non-reflexive, immanent relationship to the self. As May Joseph argues, '[w]ithin globalizing discourses of transnational exchange, the seductive metaphors of heightened mobility [are] advanced at the expense of the political [and] generate anxiety around the local' (Joseph 1999: 8).

The forced migrations and diasporas of asylum seekers, refugees and immigrants to Ireland have not, so far, been described in Irish political or media discourses as diasporas. At the same time as Irish migrant and cultural dispersals are celebrated through the figure of the diaspora, immigrants and refugees in Ireland are, for the most part, problematised and pathologised by elements of the state and media alike (Farrell and Watt 2001). Increasingly, immigration, as an effect of some processes of globalisation, produces nationally bounded habits of thinking as the protection of 'our' 'homeland' is invoked against the 'mobilities' and 'foreignness' of immigrants and refugees. The paradox of the global, as Bryan Turner reminds us, is that as 'the world becomes as a single place it intensifies the problem of otherness' (2001: 134). Borders of EU states, including Ireland, are sites of surveillance, criminalisation and locations of death in the interests of immigration control and the protection of national boundaries. These practices are legitimated in the interests of the stability, security and wealth of EU states and involve a re-territorialisation of identity and re-embedding of culture. The invocation of the 'Irish' diaspora in Ireland positions the country in a European 'tradition' of emigration and obscures its collusion with the global conditions that produces forced migrations in the present. Discourses of the Irish diaspora from this perspective operate as another modality of exclusionary nationalism and produce the 'homeland' less as a 'diaspora space' (Brah 1996) than as a determinately national space of the global.

Conclusion

I chose the image of Siobhan Hapaska's sculpture 'Land' for the cover of this book because it suggests surface, speed and hybridity alongside moments of depth, stasis and memory. Speaking about her artwork, Hapaska notes 'there is a suffocating history flowing beneath the skin of the object . . . The reflective surfaces safeguard against a saturation of memory and overload' (1999: 73). Hapaska's comment on her art objects resonates with the tensions that this book addresses between the burdens passed onto Irish women via histories of women in Ireland and the diaspora, and a 1990s global surface culture marked by mobility and choice. Hapaska goes on to speak of her piece called 'Land', noting that she tries 'to ally states of mind with geological forms' so that the little pools of water 'are like rock pools by the ocean. Rock pools, once filled by tide become like reservoirs for the memory of an event. When the water recedes, they are once again left in isolation – cut off from the whole' (ibid.: 76). My aim in this book has not been to provide a definitive or 'whole story' of women and the Irish diaspora, but to attend to some of the pools or moments that offer insights into the workings of these categories in the accounts of Irish women. The transnational focus of the book offers perspectives on identity and belonging that exceed the dichotomisations of staying and going, the local and the global, the national and the diaspora. When physical movement is emphasised, wider fields of relationships are identified as impinging on the local so that the national becomes a vantage point from which the global can be apprehended and vice versa. This book moves beyond debates on women, migration and Irish modernity by examining the changing workings of the category 'Irish women' in constituting late twentieth-century Irish modernity. Irish modernity(ies) are constituted in the accounts of Irish settled and Traveller women living in the Republic of Ireland and in England and through my discussion and analysis of these. Political and media celebrations of geographical mobilities, multiculture, the global and diaspora are critically engaged with via the 'lived' experiences of these women. Irish Traveller women's accounts identify the ways in which different aspects of modernity including nation-state building, multicultural constructions of the nation and diasporic notions of national identity both exclude and incorporate Travellers in circumscribed ways. Traveller women and working-class migrants represent important sites of cultural anxiety and instability in the face of rapid social change. These anxieties cohere around the bodies and familial practices of Traveller women in Ireland and constructions of Irish 'ethnic' communities in the diaspora.

Because the categories 'women' and the 'Irish diaspora' cannot rely on some prior understandings of these terms as cohesive or self-evident, they are never simply assumed in this book. Instead, the discussion acknowledges their circulation as knowledge and interrogates the ways in which they are constructed across multiple discourses, positions and readings. Migration and staying in Ireland are located at the heart of negotiations of Irish femininities and are implicated in the practices of denial, euphemism and silence that continued to mark Irish femininities in the 1990s. The figure of 'the Irish mother' emerges as an ambivalent one marked by regulation, but also resistance. The accounts suggest that stoicism, 'purity' and strength associated with this figure continue to frame notions of 'authentic' settled Irish femininity in Ireland, London and Luton. However, the mother is absent as a key reference point in the accounts of Traveller and Protestant women whose femininities were over-determined by their Traveller and Protestant identities. Although similar attributes of strength and capability attach to these femininities, they were located in Protestant or Traveller culture rather than in relation to the notion of the 'Irish mother'.

Whether in London or in Ireland, the women's accounts challenge perceptions of global modernity as heralding an unimpeded mobility that renders
migration a less uprooting practice. Their accounts poignantly engage with
the idea that migrants today, because they are globally connected, are quali-
tatively different from earlier generations of migrants who were uprooted
because of their broken ties with the homeland (Handlin 1979). Instead of
an unimpeded fluidity of movement and relationships, they suggest that
potential and actual transnational connections produce intensified forms of
uprootedness. This migrancy is marked by the promise of being able to
occupy and maintain multiple 'homes' and the simultaneous revelation
that 'home' is not possible without fulfilling certain (often impossible)
gendered commitments and performances of belonging. The complex and
gendered legacy of past constructions of Irish migration as 'exile' and/or
'national betrayal' intersects with late twentieth-century practices of mobility
and the promise of multilocatedness to produce often anxious and defensive
relations between migrant and staying subjects. Migration has uprooting/
displacing effects for both migrants and non-migrants. The expectation
that women migrants can maintain roles as daughters, sisters and friends
almost as if they were still in Ireland produces the persistent effect of disappointment and mistrust in transnational familial (and some friendship)
relationships. At the same time, the frequent but temporary presences of
migrants in Ireland through their 'coming and going' is unsettling because
it positions them in an 'unrecognised' relationship to family, 'the homeland'
and indeed countries of destination. In the past they were gone and 'settled
down', now they 'come and go'. But if norms, rules and obligations of
'coming and going' have not been established, avoidance and silence rather
than engagement emerge as the response. Ambivalences about the new presences of the diaspora in the 'homeland' are also evident at an official level
in the contradictory celebration and denigration of the diaspora in debates
about votes for emigrants (see Introduction). There are moments in the
accounts when the Irish migrant woman, precisely because of her ability to
move between places is seen as belonging nowhere and without an authentic
cultural identity.

Globalisation is often seen as heralding homogenisation and an emptying
out of cultural content, yet the accounts in this book point to an ethnicisation, or culturalisation of local identities. Discourses of ethnicisation and
indigenisation are central to the rhetoric of globalisation and 'the global'
and are advanced in different ways by transnational or global organisations
such as the UN and EU. A central invitation in a context of global modernity
is to articulate uniqueness and therefore difference (Robertson and Khondker
1998: 30), and this is increasingly articulated via 'ethnicity'. Multiculturalism
in the 1990s became part of what Appadurai calls the global 'ideoscape'
that circulated and materialised in different forms within particular states
and locales (Appadurai 1996; Vertovec 1996). The multicultural nation
or city marks out acceptable terrains of difference. The 'ethnicisation' or

'culturalisation' of social life and politics, not least in liberal discourses of multiculturalism, involves closer regulation of women members of groups designated 'ethnic' because women's bodies and practices tend to symbolise the integrity and uniqueness of 'ethnic' groups (see Chapters 4 and 5).[14] Diaspora and multiculturalism ethnicise culture in ways that re-work gender, class, generational, and racialised power geometries. Although difference is at the heart of multiculturalism and diaspora, the accounts in this book point to the ways in which these operate locally to regulate women. Traveller women embraced multiculturalism as a means of articulating identity and political claims-making, but multiculturalism also revealed a self-regulatory relationship to Traveller culture in order to justify these claims. Multiculturalism imposes a collective responsibility on those designated 'ethnic' for the terms and practices of 'their' difference while simultaneously structuring that difference.

As ethnicity becomes 'the dominant paradigm for political advancement' (Sinfield 1996: 271), some of the accounts in Chapter 5 identify the patriarchal and heteronormative nature of such politics so that Irish lesbian and Irish feminist activists in London found themselves positioned as 'inauthentic' Irish 'ethnics'. Yet this is not a totalising process and these contestations often produced as a result of such regulation led, in the case of Irish women in London, to new feminist and lesbian spaces of Irish cultural belonging in London. A 'deep' Irish global subject is produced by ethnicised references to the self that are at once diasporic (involving multiple points of affiliation and attachment) and multicultural (produced through multicultural relations of belonging in countries of settlement, or indigenous 'minority' relationships to country of origin). However, some of the accounts in this book stage a clash between homogenised notions of 'whiteness' and an 'ethnicised' Irishness. As 'whiteness' becomes ethnicised, and in some cases exoticised, not least by new practices of niche marketing within consumer culture, it is becoming less unified. Yet the workings of 'whiteness' in the lives of Irish migrant and non-migrant women point to the subtle power dynamics that mark the ethnicisation of social life.

Irish women's migration in the 1980s and 1990s was subsumed by the ungendered figure of the educated mobile Irish citizen, or 'young (Irish) European' whose liberation was located in the potential to move/migrate. This citizen subject takes up a charged relationship to mobility, which is marked by the promise of belonging *both* in Ireland and in the country of sojourn/residence. However, the women's accounts discussed in this book betray a mismatch between the promise of ungendered diasporic/global subjectivity and the new modes of gendered, classed, racial and national classifications that mark Irish global modernity. A gendered national distinctiveness was achieved until the mid-twentieth century (at least) through the capacity of the Catholic Church (and the state in similar and different ways) to render itself technical by connecting up with technologies of family, national survival and 'sexual purity'. A strategy of rationalisation in the name of the nation enabled a linking of these values so that they appeared to form a coherent logic of 'common sense'. The accounts discussed in this book emphasise the legacy of these technologies of family, Catholicism and nation for the category 'Irish women', but they also point to new technologies of choice, mobility and 'the global' in re-constituting this category, even if in less categorical ways. Feminist political and theoretical interventions have clearly impacted on Irish women's negotiations of a 'solid' modernity framed by the context of the nation-state. However, the way forward when new inequalities and hierarchies of difference are emerging as a result of globalisation and notions of 'the global' is less clear. The women's accounts discussed in this book suggest some starting points for a more globally conscious feminist agenda in and between Ireland and the diaspora.

Appendix 1

Background demographic information sheet/ interview and group discussion schedule

Demographic background sheet

Each participant was invited to complete a form covering:

Date of birth
Where brought up?
Where live now?
Urban or rural background?
Migrant/non-migrant?
Reasons for leaving area brought up?
Religion brought up in?
Religion now/if any?
Number of children in family of origin?
Location in family?
Number of emigrants in family?
Where they emigrated to?
Do you keep in touch? If so how/frequency?
Other relatives who emigrated?
Where to?
Did you consider emigrating?
Reasons for leaving/deciding against leaving?
Age when left?
Do you think you will stay in London/Luton/Ireland?

Interview/group discussion schedule

Irish identity

Do you see yourself as Irish?
What does it mean to identify as Irish?
What are the things you associate most with being Irish?
How would you describe yourself as Irish?
What is life in Ireland like? was it like prior to emigration?
What do you think others see as Irish identity/culture?

Emigration

Story of leaving
Reasons for departure?
Circumstances of emigration?
Images or views of emigration?
Experience of journey/arriving?
Experience in London/Luton now?
Perceptions of non-emigrants?
How might life be different if stayed?
Return visits?

London/Luton

Arrival in London/Luton?
Impressions?
Experiences of living in London or Luton?
Everyday social activities?
Work?
Recreation?
Irish community activities?
Return visits to Ireland?
Future in London/Luton?

Staying

Decision to stay – circumstances?
Life in Ireland at time when many leaving?
Perceptions of emigrants?
Who stayed and reasons?
How might life be different if emigrated?
Visits to emigrant family/friends?
Return visits of emigrant friends/family?

Ireland

Perceptions of Ireland?
Relationship to the place – local/national?
Future in Ireland?
Events that seem defining of Ireland and living there in 1980s and 1990s?

'Irish women'

Perceptions of the category 'Irish women'?
Identify as Irish woman?

If not, what aspects of this identity do not appeal?
If so, what are the positive aspects of this identity?
How is being an 'Irish woman' different from other nationalities?
What are the main issues for Irish women today?
How might migration/Ireland/London/Luton be different for Irish men?

Images (see Appendix 2)

Brainstorm – what strikes you about these images?
What do they say to you about Ireland, Irishness, migration, Irish women?

Appendix 2

Poster published by the Centre for Research and Documentation (CRD), Belfast, in the mid-1990s and used in this study to prompt discussion.

Appendix 3

Profile of participants Ireland, London and Luton

Ireland: nine individual interviews and nine focus groups (not all participants returned demographic information)

Nos.	Names	Age	Children	Work	Rural/urban	Religion
Individual interviews						
1	Kathleen	38	4	teacher	rural	rc
2	Doreen	36	2	mother	city	rc
3	Suzy	44	0	banking	rural	Church of Ireland
4	Nora	36	0	civil servant	city/suburban	rc
5	Nell	40	0	professional	town and rural	rc
6	Bride	36	0	lecturer	rural	rc
7	Siobhan	39	0	primary school teacher	rural	rc
8	Maria	42	0	student on tourism	city	Church of Ireland
9	Romy	40	0	education officer	city	rc
Group 1 respondents to adverts						
10	Ann	36	0	jeweller	city	sort of Buddhist
11	Lorna	37	0	teacher	rural	rc
12	Sue	35	2	teacher	city	rc
13	Mary	35	1	work in home	city	rc
14	Nola	29	0	part-time free-lance design	city	rc
15	Margaret	34	2	sales	city	
Group 2 respondents to adverts and word of mouth						
16	Camille	33	1	self employed	city	rc
17	Bev	26	0	student	rural	rc
18	Patsy	27	0	employment scheme	rural	rc
19	Mary	31	0	counsellor	rural	rc
20	Trudy	37	2	social worker	city	rc
Group 3 Traveller women						
21	Rita	36	6	work in home/ training	both	rc

Nos.	Names	Age	Children	Work	Rural/urban	Religion
22	Anne	38	7	work in home/ training	both	rc
23	Helen	21	2	work in home/ training	city	rc
24	Deirdre	21	1	work in home/ training	city	rc

Group 4 Traveller women

25	Gerardine	26	0	work in home/ training	both	rc
26	Bernie	20	1	work in home/ training	both	rc
27	Judy	34	6	work in home/ training	both	rc
28	Moyra	37	6	work in home/ training	both	rc
29	Elaine	22	2	work in home/ training	both	rc
30	Mary	36	8	work in home/ training	both	rc
31	Aine	43	5	work in home/ training	both	rc
32	Caroline	25	3	work in home/ training	city	rc
33	Deirdre	27	2	work in home/ training	city	rc
34	Elsie	27	1	work in home/ training	both	rc
35	Fran	23	3	work in home/ training	city	rc
36	Holly	29	5	work in home/ training	both	rc

Group 5 women living in rural areas

37	Carol	37	3	work in home and farmer	rural	rc
38	Jill	40	3	tutor	rural	rc
39	Ada	42	5	work in home	rural/?	rc
40	Moira	37	2	catering	rural	rc
41	Moyra	43	3	work in home	rural/mc	rc
42	Angela	43	6	work in home	town	rc
43	Ida	38	3	work in home	rural	rc

Group 6 women's literacy class in Dublin

44	Joy	46	5	work in home	city	
45	Una	40	2	work in home	city	
46	Cherry	28	0	p/t student	city	
47	Lisa	42	4	work in home	city	
48	Marion	43	3	work in the home cleaner	city	
49	Bernie	72	4	work in the home	city	
50	Rose	68	12	home help	city	

Nos.	Names	Age	Children	Work	Rural/urban	Religion
Group 7 Women's Studies students (Dublin)						
51	Vera	46	6	work in home	city	rc
52	Jan	28	0	student	city	rc
53	Pauline	27	0	student	city	rc
54	Gill	45	3	work in home	city	rc
55	Cathy	30	0	professional	city	rc
56	Martha	35	0	teacher	city	rc
57	Shauna	21	0	student/journalist	city	rc
58	Maureen	47	3	teacher	rural	rc
59	Dervla	23	0	student	city	none
60	Denyse	32	0	statistician	city	rc
61	Mo	58	4	unwaged in home/ voluntary work	rural	rc
62	Aisling	27	0	student	both	rc
63	Esta	41	0	nurse/student	city	Church of Ireland
64	Audrey	43	2	student/writer	city	rc
Group 8 women's workplace group						
65	Rosie			prof/admin		
66	Paula			admin		
67	Celine			admin		
68	Mairead			admin		
69	Joanie			admin		
70	Alison			admin		
71	Sue			admin		
Group 9 – pilot group						
72	Kath	33	0	prof		
73	Corrine	36	3	care worker		
74	Harriet	37	2	work in home		
75	Dora	35	0	prof		
76	Janine	34	0	prof		

London and Luton: nine individual interviews, five focus groups (London) and one focus group (Luton) (not all participants returned demographic information)

Nos.	Names	Age	Children	Work	Rural/urban	Religion
Individual interviews – most took place in the women's homes – one in a café in London						
1	Hazel	41	0	counsellor	city	rc
2	Molly	31	2	work in home/ doctor	rural	rc
3	Jenny	42	0	adult education teacher	rural	rc
4	Heather	38	0	advice worker	city	rc
5	Jane	46	1	administrator	rural	rc

Nos.	Names	Age	Children	Work	Rural/urban	Religion
6	Alison	30	0	office and finance manager	city	protestant
7	Hilda	45	2	work in home	city	rc
8	Cath	29	0	social work	town/ mc	rc
9	Maggie	39	0	unemployed	city/wc	rc

Group 1 – London – Irish lone mother's group –
discussion took place at drop in centre

10	Sue	27	2	carer	rural	rc
11	Kate	25	5	carer	town	rc
12	Trish	25	1	carer	town	rc
13	Ger	25	1	carer	rural	rc
14	Phil	30	1	carer/p/t worker	rural	rc

Group 2 – London – discussion took place
at Hammersmith Irish Club

15	Brigid	31	0	technician	rural	rc
16	Maura	28	0	personal assistant	town	rc
17	Bernie	33	0	secretary	rural	rc

Group 3 – London – discussion took place
in room above bar in central London

18	Julie	32	0	social worker	rural	rc
19	Fionnuala	32	0	business manager	rural	rc
20	Anne	34	3	p/t admin, p/t artist	city	rc

Group 4 – London – discussion took place
in room above bar in central London

21	Josey	29	0	student	city	rc
22	Una	29	0	student	city	rc
23	Helen	28	0	journalist	city	rc

Group 5 – London – discussion took place
at Joan and Sarah's house

24	Joan	46	0	housing support	city	rc
25	Sarah	36	0	astrologer/ counsellor	city	rc

Group 6 – group of Irish friends Luton discussion
took place in backroom of bar in Luton

26	Lucy	36	2	nurse	rural	rc
27	Rhona	37	6	pub manager	rural	rc
28	June	38	2	payroll admin	city	rc
29	Mary	28	0	residential social worker	rural	rc
30	Vicky	44	3	pub manager	city	rc
31	Val	31	0	factory worker	rural	rc
32	Janine	22	0	nurse	rural	rc
33	Miriam	26	0	clerk	rural	rc
34	Sian	25	0	admin (insurance)	town	rc
35	Sara	30	0	social worker	rural	rc

Appendix 4

Summary profiles of the women who took part in this study

A total of 111 women took part in this study. Although not all of the women completed the demographic details forms the following offers a broad overall profile of the women who took part in the study in each of the locations. Thirty-six of these women took part in the London/Luton part of the study.

- This London/Luton group of women were aged between twenty-two and forty-six at the time of the study, but 62 per cent of the group were between twenty-two and thirty-two. Eighty per cent of the group left Ireland between the ages of eighteen and twenty-four.
- Seventy-one per cent had left Ireland between 1985 and 1989.
- Sixty-three per cent had no children, 51 per cent from rural areas in Ireland, 14 per cent from towns and 34 per cent from cities.
- Ninety-seven per cent of this group were brought up Catholic and 49 per cent identified as Catholic at the time of the research.
- For 86 per cent of this group some member of their extended family had emigrated in the past and 60 per cent had siblings who had migrated.
- Only 17 per cent did not have paid employment prior to leaving Ireland and 86 per cent migrated without a job in London.
- Yet the main reason for migration was work in 51 per cent of cases; 27 per cent gave partner as a reason and 23 per cent other reasons including unplanned migration.
- Eighty-three per cent visited Ireland at least once annually and 66 per cent said they would like to return and further 14 per cent said they might return. However, only 49 per cent thought that they would actually return.
- Forty-three per cent said that they did not see themselves as part of an Irish community in London and 17 per cent felt they were partially involved with an Irish community.

In Ireland a total of seventy-five women took part in the study; this included seventeen women who had migrated and returned and sixteen Traveller women eight of whom had lived in Britain at some stage in their lives.

- Ninety-six per cent of this cohort was between the ages of twenty and forty-five at the time of the research with 62 per cent between twenty-seven and thirty-seven.
- Forty-one per cent worked in the home, 28 per cent were in professional work, 16 per cent in other paid work, and 14 per cent were students.
- Forty-seven per cent lived in cities, 28 per cent in rural areas and 25 per cent in rural towns.
- Ninety-one per cent of this group were brought up Catholic, 5 per cent were brought up Protestant and 4 per cent identified religious background and other/none. Sixty-four per cent still identified as Catholic, 4 per cent as Protestant and 20 per cent as none.
- Sixty-three per cent had migrants in their extended family member and the same percentage had sibling migrants.
- Seventy-three per cent said that they had considered migrating, 62 per cent of these for life experience, 8 per cent to get out of Ireland and 23 per cent for work.
- Forty-seven per cent of this group had lived outside of Ireland for some time. For those who did not leave, 32 per cent said that family and friends kept them in Ireland, 16 per cent stayed because of children, 26 per cent because they preferred Ireland, 10 per cent for work and 6 per cent because of a relationship.
- Sixty-eight per cent said that they would probably stay in Ireland and 64 per cent of these said they would stay because they would prefer to live in Ireland than elsewhere.

Notes

Introduction

1 Migration statistics show that over the period 1871–1986 net female emigration was 1,511,550 and net male emigration was 1,502,535 (King and O'Connor 1996: 311). Men migrants outnumbered women migrants during the war years and during the mass out-migration periods of the 1950s and 1980s (ibid.). The 1970s was the first period since records began when net in-migration was recorded. During this decade women 'constituted 75 per cent of the gross outflow but only 39 per cent of the gross return movement' (King and O'Connor 1996: 312; see Kirwan and Nairn 1983).

2 I use the terms 'migration' and 'migrant' mostly instead of 'emigrant' and 'emigration' in this book because of the ideological work that the latter two terms have done in the context of Irish modernity (see Miller 1985 and 1990; and Lloyd 1994).

3 The new Irish state in the south was formed in 1922 despite formidable challenges to its legitimacy and evolved from the Free State to establishment of the Republic of Ireland in 1949. In this book I refer to the twenty-six county state in the south variously as 'Ireland', the Republic of Ireland and the southern state. I refer to the northern six counties as Northern Ireland or 'the North'.

4 Enda Delaney, in a discussion of women's migration to Britain in the 1930s and 1940s argues that women's migration proved humiliating for the country (2000: 134–5).

5 See Miller (1990) and Jacobson (1995) for a discussion of how the idea of emigration as individual initiative was undermined by more communal explanations of Irish migration. See also Blessing (1985) who argues that kin played a significant role in Irish emigration patterns to the US and McCarthy (2000) who argues that kinship ties were central to Irish women's emigration to New Zealand between 1840 and 1925.

6 In 1900, 54 per cent of all Irish born women in the US worked as domestic servants (Nolan 1989: 69).

7 There is some debate as to Irish migrant women's marriage aspirations and patterns in the United States. For example, Nolan (1989) argues that Irish born women took marriage as being a normal part of life, while Diner (1983) identifies a reluctance to marry and Fitzpatrick suggests that marriage in the country of destination represented a challenge to cultural and family unity (see Fitzpatrick 1986 and 1989). Discussing the 1910 US Census, Timothy Guinnane argues (based on those in the 45–9 age-group in 1910) that the Irish-born in the US were more likely to marry than the same cohorts in Ireland but less likely than the 'typical' American. Irish-born women had 'higher never married proportions than their men' (1997: 224). Yet, he notes that people living in large urban centres in the US were less likely to marry and, when compared with this group rather than the 'typical'

American, the Irish marriage pattern was less remarkable. However, he argues that so many variables are involved that comparisons can be misleading.

8 The promise of individual status was held out to women despite the fact that the status of individual is constituted via the exclusion of women from occupying this category (A. Cronin 2000).

9 Miller *et al.* (1995) note that Diner and Nolan provide little evidence to prove that women were avoiding marriage or seeking marriage partners respectively. Fitzpatrick (1987) Jackson (1963) and Miller *et al.* (1995) all argue that the increased migration of women after the Famine can be partly accounted for by the dramatic deterioration in their socio-economic status in rural areas due to the changing agricultural and industrial landscape, the dowry system and falling marriage rates.

10 See Goldthorpe and Whelan (1992), Laffan and O'Donnell (1998) and Walsh (1989) for reflections on how migration significantly shaped the development of industrial society in Ireland and the internationalisation of the Irish economy.

11 It is noteworthy that a range of overt governmental policies including those of Australia, New Zealand and South Africa indicate that Irish women were actively sought to help 'breed an indigenous white population' (Akenson 1993: 183).

12 About 10 per cent of Irish migrants are said to have returned to Ireland. This was a considerably lower rate than for any other migrant groups. See Neville (1995 and 1997) for a discussion of women returning to Ireland from the US with money saved for their dowries.

13 Up to 1921, 84 per cent of emigrants from the southern state went to the United States and only 8 per cent went to Britain (Kennedy 1973). With the introduction of quotas in the US and the establishment of the new state in the south, Britain became the preferred destination for migrants in the twentieth century.

14 In 1851, 42.7 per cent of Irish women in London worked in domestic service (Lennon *et al.*: 1988).

15 The anti-global or anti-globalisation movement demonstrates the extent to which global consciousness prevails (Roberston and Khondker 1998: 31).

16 It is unlikely, given changes in the demographic, industrial and social profile of Ireland since the late 1990s, that the combination of factors that led to mass emigration in the 1980s will be repeated (Mac Éinrí 2001). The year 1980 recorded the highest total number of births in the twentieth century; however, by 1989 the total had fallen to the lowest on record. This figure had fallen further by the mid-1990s though it was still at the upper end of fertility patterns in Europe (Fahey and FitzGerald 1997: 39).

17 Ó Riain argues that Ireland was integrated into the global economy in two distinct ways in the 1990s: first, by the partial local embedding of global corporate networks into Ireland and second, by the integration of local networks of indigenous firms into global business and technology networks. Further he suggests that national social partnership arrangements, which began in 1987, helped to manage 'the relation to the global economy of both the macro economy and of unionised workers' (2000: 158). He sees the state as a central actor in shaping these developments acting as a kind of 'midwife' and mediating the local and global.

18 The 'flexible developmental state' (Ó Riain 2000) (that nurtures post-Fordist networks of production and innovation to attract international investment and link local and global technological and business networks together to promote development) both reproduces and is legitimated by notions of the 'global nation'.

19 Although few studies have been done on the return rates of Irish migrants, those that do exist suggest a lower return rate than for other European countries (Akenson 1993: 14/5). Joe Lee (1993) points to an increase in return migration in the 1980s which was mainly young workers coming back to job opportunities at home.

1980s return migration reached unprecedented levels in the 1990s when the Irish government actively encouraged them to return by running jobs fairs in Britain, the US, Canada, Germany and many other countries. Returning emigrants tend to be mainly early middle-aged adults with children.

20 The 1980s represent a watershed in the politicisation of Travellers in Ireland with two women Travellers (Nan Joyce in 1982 and Margaret Sweeney in 1987) standing as independent candidates in national elections.

21 Between 1850 and 1914, 54 million Europeans left for the Americas, Australia and New Zealand and about 2 million of these were Irish (Cowley 2001).

22 See Drudy (1986) for a discussion of the colonial legacies and relationships between Ireland and Britain since 1922.

23 Migration to the USA remained high until the First World War after which a quota system was introduced in the USA and Irish migrants turned mainly to Britain. The US Quota Acts of 1921 and 1924 and the economic depression in the 1930s led to a shift away from the USA as the predominant destination for Irish migrants. In 2000, there were an estimated 3 million citizens living outside the island about 1.2 million of them having been born in Ireland. Most of these are in Britain and the US (Coogan 2000). It is estimated that the worldwide Irish diaspora (those who identify in some way with Irish identity) is composed of some 70 million people, approximately 40 million of whom reside in America and 13 million in Britain.

24 I am using the term multiculturalism to mean 'the assertion of normative principles that affirm the value of such cultural diversity in terms of equality between groups, and the realization of these values in institutions and politics' (I. Young 2001: 116).

25 The theme of proximity has been a recurring one in debates in Britain about controlling Irish immigration. For example, the Kilmur Committee, appointed by Eden in 1955, asserted that the anomalous position of Irish immigrants 'could be defended on the grounds of proximity and the practical problems which it generates' (in Delaney 2000: 210). Ireland's long-extended common history with Britain and self-perception as part of the wider European context sharing a common European Christian heritage with Britain and other European countries contributes to this context of proximity (Murphy 1999).

26 When all of the Irish born in Britain are considered, nearly half of these live in the southeast of England with the single largest concentration being in the Greater London area. The second largest concentration is in the West Midlands metropolitan area, followed by Greater Manchester and Scotland. Northern Irish-born (im)migrants have a geographical distribution similar to that of the white population as a whole (Owen 1995).

27 I advertised in Irish Networks established in London in the 1980s, at the London Irish Women's Centre, the Camden Irish Centre, in the *Guardian* newspaper, the *Irish Post* and through friends in London. A letter introducing the research and inviting participants was published in the Irish broadsheet national press in Ireland. I posted notices at the offices for the Council for the Status of Women, Lesbians Organising Together, and asked friends in Ireland to circulate notices. In a few cases, women who responded to the newspaper notices facilitated access to these groups. My experience of contacting potential participants by telephone highlighted the shortcuts that were possible for me because of my Irish accent.

28 I am grateful to the Centre for Research and Documentation, Belfast for permission to reproduce this poster in this book.

29 Lancaster is about 250 miles from London and the journey takes a minimum of three hours by train.

1 'Women', the diaspora and Irish modernity(ies)

1 The causes of modernity continue to be much contested with some seeing it as a product of capitalism, others as a product of industrialisation, new technologies, secularisation, slavery, colonialism, imperialism, the public/private divide and new forms of subjectivity (Felski 2000: 73). Giddens (1991) focuses specifically on the consequences of modernity while Appadurai (1996) and Calhoun (1995) emphasise the inevitable partiality and plurality of understandings of modernity. Rabinow argues against defining modernity and advises that the best approach is to track the diverse ways in which claims to the modern are made (1989: 9). Similarly, Foucault tracks practices of normalisation and disciplining in which particular modern relations to the self are produced and through which specific categories of people become the focus 'for intervention and production of discourses about the self and its sexuality' (ibid.).

2 See Clear (2000) who argues against the idea of domesticity and the family as an 'ideology' in Ireland.

3 The conditions of possibility for certain ways of acting on the conduct of women to reproduce a uniquely Irish modernity are discussed in greater detail in Chapter 2.

4 See the government sponsored *Commission on Emigration and other Population Problems 1949–54 Reports* and ethnographic work such as that of Arensberg and Kimball in West Clare in the 1930s, (1940/68), Messenger (1969), Brody (1973) and Scheper Hughes (1979), as well as work by Jenny Beale (1986) and Joe Lee (1989a and b).

5 The migration of Irish women became a matter of great concern for the Catholic Church since the establishment of the southern state and was publicly acknowledged and institutionalised when, in 1942, the then Archbishop of Dublin, John Charles McQuaid, established the 'Emigrant Section of the Catholic Society'. At the opening of the agency Dr McQuaid said: 'I have entrusted to you, as your chief activity in the beginning, the care of emigrants, especially women and girls' (quoted in Kelly and Nic Giolla Choille 1995: 169). One of the functions of the agency was to 'make enquiries as to whether or not the proposed employment in Britain was suitable for Catholics' (ibid.). At the same time, English Catholic women, writing in the journal *Christus Rex,* were advising Catholic Irish women intending to emigrate to consult their parish priest before leaving Ireland 'in order to prevent accepting a job far away from a Catholic Church' (Garrigan 1949: 50).

6 Kerby Miller argues that the development of individual calculation and instrumentality was concealed by fatalism and collective explanatory strategies which helped to cover up psychological and social tensions (1993: 274).

7 Speaking of the period 1856–1921, Miller argues that 'migration at once reflected and reinforced an increasing instrumentalism in family relations' (1993: 282). He also suggests that interfamilial relations in many parts of Ireland 'were characterised by a jealous and secretive competitiveness' in which migration played a role (ibid.: 284). The idealisation of family, marriage and motherhood obscured the distribution of resources within the family between men and women, a matter that 'remained outside the realm of political debate' (O'Dowd 1987: 29).

8 See Finola Kennedy (2001) for a discussion of the continued significance of inheritance systems in structuring gendered belonging in Ireland in the 1990s.

9 The focus on the parental rather than sexual can be understood as a kind of biopolitics, but in many large Irish families, the sibling relationship often operated as a parental one.

10 Humphreys' study of families in Dublin in the early 1960s found that although many aspects of life became more individualised attitudes to sex were not so different in Dublin (1966).

11 Hugh Brody (1973) noted that sexual behaviour was rare and covert in Ireland and that young people often saw emigration as a means to sexual fulfilment. Arensberg and Kimbal (1940) note the confinement of any obvious sexual interest to only those who were married and Messenger (1969) characterises the community he studied as sexually naïve.

12 Grace Neville's study of women's migration as represented in the Irish Folklore Commission Archives found that instances of married women running away to the United States were cited as 'Irish-style divorce'. There was also evidence of women who were pregnant, or who had an illegitimate child emigrating under pressure from relatives, and couples leaving because of family opposition to their relationship (Neville 1995).

13 The first report of the Commission for the Status of Women (1972) noted that the public image of Irish femininity as wife and mother was a harmful cultural stereotype because it led girls to see their lives in terms of a short period of work outside the home followed by marriage and caring for children.

14 During the 1980s and 1990s individual women's experiences revealed the brutal denial of women's status as human beings with rights to determine their own life courses. For example, Eileen Flynn was fired from her job as a teacher because she was pregnant by and living with a man who was married; fifteen-year-old Ann Lovett died giving birth to a baby at a Marian grotto; the X Case, a fourteen-year-old girl, pregnant as a result of a rape was initially refused permission to travel to England to have an abortion; and Lavinia Kerwick spoke out about her experience of being raped and its effects on her life.

15 In 1997 women accounted for 38 per cent of the workforce an increase of 170 per cent since 1971 while the number of men in the workforce had hardly changed in the same period (Galligan 1997: 109).

16 In 1973, the Supreme Court in the *McGee versus the Attorney General* case held that the state ban on contraception for personal use to be unconstitutional, partly because it breached the right to privacy. In the same year, the *Roe versus Wade* case in the US granted the right to choose abortion as a consequence of the right to privacy. This case linked personal choice with the liberal notion of privacy as it was argued that 'within the private sphere, all individuals are free and equal' (MacKinnon 1989: 191). The extension of this individual right to privacy in relation to contraception gave rise to the pro-life movement lobby in Ireland for a referendum to bring about a constitutional amendment to prevent the introduction of abortion (O'Reilly 1995).

17 In 1972 the 'special position' of the Catholic Church was removed from the Constitution by referendum. In 1973 Ireland became a member of the European Economic Community. The marriage bar, introduced in 1933, operated until 1957 for primary school teachers and until 1973 for women in other public service employment. Equal pay legislation was passed in 1974 and employment equality legislation in 1977 both facilitated by directives from the EEC. In 1979 contraception was legalised although in a limited way. However, the Pope's visit to Ireland in the same year focused on issues of sexual morality and family life calling on Irish women to recognise the superior calling of motherhood above 'a secular job'.

18 The journal *Foreign Policy* developed an index of globalisation which identified Singapore as the most globalised country in 1998, followed by the Netherlands, Sweden, Switzerland, Finland, the Irish Republic and Austria (Walker 2001). Based on data from 2000, Ireland was identified as the most globalised country in the world based mainly on economic criteria.

19 Although global modernity or the globalising project cannot be assumed to have a single, stable or unified meaning (Franklin *et al.* 2000), contemporary globalisation is a neo-liberal globalisation that cannot be seen as an inevitable force but

an effect of discourses and practices that are institutionally supported by the IMF, the EU, the World Trade Organisation and other global institutions.

20 Addressing a conference entitled 'Women Mean Business' in Lexington, Kentucky, USA on 2 September 1999, the *Tánaiste* (deputy Prime Minister), Mary Harney, said that women now represented the largest pool of potential entrepreneurs in Ireland. She suggested that economic necessity in itself would enable the achievement of real gender equality in the business world. In her speech, she noted that 'There is no doubt that the provision of child-care options has proved a critical factor in facilitating the participation of many young mothers in various enterprise programmes in Ireland . . . We must do more in the future to assist on child-care'. She noted that gender equality was crucial if best business practice was to prevail.

21 Of course, this relocation of Ireland in relation to the global market is not an undifferentiated process and does not go uncontested. Government ministers have differentiated between the kinds of globalised connection and ideology the country should embrace. The most notable interventions have insisted on Ireland's closer affinity with Boston than Berlin and indicated their preference for the neo-liberal global market economy above the social democracy approaches of the European Union. In a speech to a meeting of the *American Bar Association* on 21 July 2000, Tánaiste Mary Harney emphasised Ireland's relationship with the United States and its attractiveness to American business. 'It is a remarkable fact that a country with just 1 per cent of Europe's population accounts for 27 per cent of US greenfield investment in Europe . . . When Americans come here they find a country that believes in the incentive power of low taxation. They find a country that believes in economic liberalisation. They find a country that believes in essential regulation but not over-regulation. On looking further afield they find also that not every European country believes in all of these things . . . we have sailed closer to the American shore than the European one . . . The people of Europe are not united by common language, common history and common tradition in the way that Americans are'. Minister deValera, in an address to *Boston College*, USA on 18 September 2000 noted that she looked

> forward to a future in which Ireland will exercise a more vigilant, a more questioning attitude to the European Union . . . As we embraced Europe, we seemed at times to forget our close and very important ties with the United States of America . . . .

22 The Progressive Democratic Party's youth policy document in the 1980s argued that migrants should be better prepared for migration and more competent in other languages (Nic Giolla Choille 1989). Mobility was facilitated by the government's interventions to increase the availability of US visas to Irish citizens.

23 Of course, these mobilities were regulated in the 1980s by the operation of the Prevention of Terrorism Act on the British borders and immigration controls in the US.

24 In an ironic piece on this slogan, writer Joseph O'Connor noted that most of those in the poster had left the country because of the economic policies which the poster was promoting and that those still in Ireland at the time were unemployed (O'Connor 1993: 12).

25 TD – Teacha Dála means Dáil deputy or member of parliament. The Progressive Democratic political party was established in 1985 as a result of divisions in Fianna Fáil on Northern Ireland policy and questions about Fianna Fáil party leadership. The Progressive Democratic party represented itself as a liberal and economically conservative party. It won 12 per cent of the vote in the 1987 election but has remained a minor party although it has had considerable influence as a partner in Coalition governments.

26 After loosing his Dáil seat, Michael McDowell was appointed Attorney General in the Fianna Fáil/Progressive Democrat coalition government formed in 1997. On winning his seat back again in the 2001 general election, he was appointed Minister for Justice, Equality and Law Reform in another Fianna Fáil/Progressive Democrat coalition government.

27 See the *Programme for National Recovery 1988–90*; Laffan and O'Donnell (1998) and NESF (1997).

28 Margaret Heckler, US Ambassador to Ireland, noted at a summer school on emigration in 1980s that '[e]migration is about personal liberty ... The simple reality of it today is that emigration has become a fact of life in Ireland'. Making links between the successes of past emigrants, the Ambassador asserted that 'this emigration (the 1980s) will lead, too, to great influence for Ireland. And when the Single European Market becomes a reality in 1992, Irish professionals will be well positioned to take advantage of the free labour flow' (Heckler 1989: 160).

29 Nic Giolla Choille noted that the Fine Gael party policy document recommended responses in Britain to vulnerable Irish migrants, but made no reference to how emigration might be tackled in Ireland or its implications for Irish society. She argues that any initiatives mooted in official circles focused on what should be done outside of Ireland. Piaras Mac Éinrí (1989) notes a similar trend in a discussion of the political and media preoccupation with Irish Illegals in the USA.

30 *The Crane Bag* periodical was published from 1977–85 in two annual editions. Its aim was 'to disseminate modern Irish thinking and culture, while also engaging the critical participation of artists and thinkers from other countries' (Böss 2002: 142). *The Field Day* originally established to stage the plays of Brian Friel culminated with the publication of an anthology of Irish writing. This anthology for the most part excluded Irish women's writing and led to an important debate about women and the canon. This resulted in the publication of Volumes IV and V of the Field Day anthology devoted solely to women's writing in 2002. The Field Day project was concerned with a cultural re-imagining of Ireland in the context of the conflict in the north.

31 The symbol of 'the fifth province' was taken from the Celtic idea that Ireland was divided into four provinces and a spiritual middle province counterbalancing the political centre of Tara (Böss 2002).

32 Thank you to Michael Cronin for drawing this to my attention.

33 These countries include India, Mexico, Columbia, El Salvador and Haiti (see Smith 2001: 19).

34 There had been a move towards the diaspora in the previous decade when, in the early 1980s, the Minister for Foreign Affairs, Peter Barry, included the Irish migrant population in his definition of the nation in the *Forum for a New Ireland* in order to extend the boundaries of Irish nationalism (Kearney 1997). Richard Kearney sees this move as part of the development of what he calls 'new nationalism', which included Irish nationalists north and south of the border as well as elsewhere in the world. The term 'diaspora' has also appeared sporadically in academic work on emigration but cannot be seen to have gained the status of an object of discourse until the 1990s. See Joe Lee (2000) who argues that popular interest in emigration emerged in Ireland in the early 1970s.

35 When President Robinson retired, Taoiseach Bertie Ahern 'paid tribute to the way in which she had "evoked a strong empathy with the Irish Diaspora, giving a new focus to their isolation and their wish to be re-included in national awareness"' (Böss 2002: 155).

36 See also Archdeacon (2002) and Murphy and Singer (2002) for discussions of the introduction of the Irish Famine to American school curricula.

37 Although rarely invoked by politicians in the 1990s, (this might have been because the term was so closely identified with former president Robinson) the term is more evident in political discourse in the 2000s. For example, the Minister for Foreign Affairs, Brian Cowen, emphasised the significant role played by the diaspora in Ireland's gaining a seat on the UN Security Council in 2001.

38 David Lloyd takes a materialist approach to his analysis of the 'peace process' in Northern Ireland, arguing that it is being promoted largely 'by the promise of international investment, specifically from the USA' and also as facilitating Northern Ireland's 'further integration into the European Community's regional system' (1999: 107). In this way, he argues that it is similar to the postwar settlement in which sites of decolonisation were integrated into the capitalist world order (see also O'Hearn 2000). Lloyd asks 'what can be the space for alternative cultural forms in a peace that is to be regulated everywhere by state institutions?' (1999: 107). Yet, neither global capitalist nor state institutions, discourses and practices can be so totalising as to close down spaces for alternative cultural and political formations. For example, official support for the development of the Irish language, Ulster Scots and other cultural developments should be noted, as well as, on the political front, the dialogue across divided constituencies often mediated by the diaspora and the emergence of the Women's Coalition out of these shifting political and cultural spaces.

39 The Belfast/Good Friday Agreement was reached in Multi-Party Negotiations and was signed on 10 April 1998. It recognises the right of the people in Northern Ireland to choose between the union with Britain and a united Ireland if a majority chooses. The Agreement covers a range of issues including rights, equality of opportunity, decommissioning, security, policing, prisoners and agreements between the British and Irish governments. Tom Garvin argues that the Agreement echoes a 'new flexibility in the culture' (2000: 199).

40 In 1972, the 'special position' of the Roman Catholic Church enshrined in article 44.1 of the Irish Constitution was removed by a referendum that had the support of all the political parties and was passed comfortably.

41 Jacqueline Nassy Brown argues that the reliance on the homeland/new land binary in the literature on diaspora arises from the tendency to focus on the initial movement and leads to an overemphasis on displacement and longing for 'home' as well as a downplaying of transnational identifications (1998: 293). Karen Fog Olwig argues for careful ethnography which exposes differences and similarities between migrants including their attachments to their place of origin and suggests that the concept of 'livelihood' offers a less ideologically and politically loaded framework for such research than transnationalism or diaspora (2000: 7). She ultimately rejects the term diaspora because, for her, it 'carries with it problematic implications of an implicit notion of natural places of belonging . . .' (2000: 22). Others argue that the proliferation of scholarship on 'travel' is often at the expense of the study of belonging to polities and relationships to sovereignty (Brennan 1997; Grewal and Kaplan 1994).

42 The London based campaign *Glór an Deoraí* (Irish Emigrants' Voice) was established in 1988 and argued for the right to vote in *Dáil*, presidential and European elections as well as referenda in the Republic of Ireland for up to twenty years following emigration. This campaign was supported by the 'Irish women in London' conference in 1989, which passed a resolution to the effect that

> This conference petitions the Irish government to introduce a facility that will allow Irish emigrants to vote in Irish elections. We are asking the Irish government to acknowledge our position as emigrants. We ask as Irish citizens to be allowed to participate democratically in the affairs of our country.
> (Annual Report of the London Irish Women's Conference, 1989)

The *Glór an Deoraí* pamphlet argued that emigration was an endemic aspect of economic planning in the Republic of Ireland and because emigrants *had to* leave they should have a right to participate in 'their country's progress'. The Irish Emigrant Vote Campaign (IEVC) was formed in the United States in 1991 and demanded a voice in the future direction of the country because many intended to return (*Irish Voice*, 1 October 1991: 4, in Almeida 1992: 206).

43 The *Dáil* (National Assembly of Ireland) is the Lower House of Parliament and, as noted in note 11 above, a member of the *Dáil* is called *Teachta Dála* or *Dáil* Deputy (TD).

44 This bill was introduced by Gerry O'Sullivan TD and called for emigrants' right to vote for up to fifteen years after becoming non-resident. The Minister for the Environment, Pádraig Flynn, responded to the Bill by noting that emigrants would not be politically informed; that it was not clear that emigrants wanted a vote; that Irish citizens in Britain can vote in British elections and the size of the emigrant constituency provided for might be greater than the national electorate (Dáil Éireann, Official Report, Volume 405, Col 2403–5; 5 March 1991). Many of these assertions are highly questionable (see Howard 2002). A later initiative involved the putting forward of an amendment in 1993 to the Presidential Act to include the right to vote in presidential elections. However this was not incorporated on the basis of technicalities.

45 The All-Party Committee on the Oireachtas published its final report in March 2002. It argued that emigrants are a category of Irish citizens that is not fundamentally affected by the actions of the Dáil and that the history of emigration leaves cause for regret while recognising positive initiatives in recent years. It called for more links between Ireland and the Irish abroad but suggested that the fruitfulness of such relations is not an argument for direct emigrant participation in the central institutions of the State. The one positive proposal was that the *Taoiseach*, in nominating senators, should include among his or her nominees a person or persons with an awareness of emigrant issues. Kevin Howard suggests that the Committee asserted the need to draw a boundary around political entitlement and therefore between Irish citizens who are ordinarily resident in the Republic of Ireland and those who are not (2002). 'The political boundary operative within the Irish citizenship regime highlights clearly the ongoing central reality of Irish territoriality, the ongoing centrality of being *in* Ireland to being *of* Ireland' (Howard 2002).

46 An *Irish Times* editorial estimated the potential increase at a potential 900,000, April 5 1996: 13.

47 The campaign pamphlet noted that Ireland is the only European Union country which does not allow emigrants to vote and that over 20 per cent of Irish bank accounts were held by non-residents; remittances from emigrants are said to make up about 1 per cent of national disposable income and 'ethnic' tourism contributes over 1.5 per cent of GNP (60 per cent of the total tourist industry) (*Glór an Deoraí* pamphlet, 1993: 8).

48 The *Irish Post* is an Irish community in Britain newspaper printed weekly and distributed nationally – see discussion of the *Irish Post* in Chapter 5.

2 'Keeping up appearances' and the contested category 'Irish women'

1 Lloyd notes the re-circulation of the figure of 'Mother Ireland' during 'the Troubles' in Northern Ireland where she became 'a site of profound contestations over the meaning and definition of women's struggles and their relation to republicanism and cultural nationalism' (Lloyd 1999: 94).

2 In the early 1980s, a group of right-wing organisations including the newly established Irish version of the Society for the Protection of the Unborn Child (SPUC)

formed the Pro-Life Amendment Campaign (PLAC). They were successful in forcing the government of the day to hold a referendum to amend the constitution in order to protect the right to life of the unborn 'child'. The referendum held in 1983, was passed by a 70: 30 majority, thereby placing a constitutional ban on abortion in the Republic of Ireland. The full implications of this constitutional ban on abortion came to light in early 1992 when a fourteen-year-old girl, who was raped by a family 'friend', was prevented by the Attorney General and the High Court from going to England for an abortion based on the amendment. Anne Speed argues that this ban on travel 'was portrayed locally and internationally as a ' "rapist's charter" and a form of "state rape" ' (1992: 96). When the pregnant girl threatened suicide, the Supreme Court reversed the ban on her right to travel outside the state for an abortion, on the basis of the equal right to life of the mother. This was followed by a further referendum in 1992, which passed amendments to the constitution allowing travel for an abortion and the provision of information on abortion. The absolute duty of giving birth and motherhood regardless of circumstances was unsettled for the first time in Irish society. Divorce was also the subject of referenda in the 1980s and 1990s. In 1986, the proposal to remove the constitutional ban on divorce in certain circumstances was rejected in a referendum by 63.5 per cent of those who voted. In a further referendum on divorce in November 1995 50.3 per cent voted *for* the introduction of divorce and 49.7 per cent voted against. A high level of disquiet about the introduction of divorce was indicated when the referendum was passed by only 50.3 per cent of those who voted. However, the restricted circumstances in which a divorce could be obtained constituted a cultural message that reinforced 'familial and communal obligation' as marriage was not to be abandoned without considerable deliberation (Dillon 1998: 133). Also, the government established a commission on the family with the aim of 'strengthening families for life' (see discussion in final sections of this chapter).

3 The contested nature of Irish Protestant belonging emerges in accounts discussed later in this chapter.

4 The figure of Mrs Doyle, the priest's housekeeper in the comedy series *Father Ted,* which was screened on British Channel 4 and eventually on RTE television in the 1990s embodied this stereotype. Mrs Doyle's deference and need to serve plays on the perceived subservience of Irish women to men in general and to priests in particular. By its patent absurdity it materialises its own impossibility. The gap between stereotype and any actuality is obviated. The act of exaggerated imitation of the stereotype contains the message that something else is going on.

5 Liam O'Dowd argues that while the Catholic clergy sought to police the family and mothers in particular, Protestant clergy were often married themselves and devolved roles of moral guidance to husbands and fathers (1987: 15).

6 Patricia O'Hara argues that farm-based Irish mothers created a separate sphere of influence that is enabling rather than manipulative, ensuring that their children, especially their daughters got a high level of education so that they could move beyond the roles of wife and mother.

7 E. Ann Kaplan (1992) argues that Rousseau inaugurates the first phase of modern motherhood discourse when, in *Émile,* he argues that it is 'women's business to be a mother'. This early modern paradigm of motherhood as *natural* is difficult to dislodge and residually influences discourses of motherhood today (1992: 20).

8 Sayigh's findings are based on her ethnography of a Palestinian camp in Lebanon in the early 1980s.

9 The idea of Irish mothers as icons of domesticity takes a textual and political form in the 1937 Irish constitution which asserts that: 'the State recognises' by her devotion to home and family that 'woman gives to the State a support without which the common good cannot be achieved' (Article 41.2.1). Because of this, the

'State shall endeavour to ensure that mothers shall not be obliged by economic necessity to engage in labour to the neglect of their duties in the home' (Article 41.2.2). Pat O'Connor (2000) argues that during the 1960s and 1970s, the family was an arena in which women's strength and resourcefulness was developed.

10 This post-Catholicism based on following one's own conscience rather than Church teaching is most evident among the younger age groups, the middle-classes and those living in urban areas (Garvin 1998: 152). A recent study by sociologist priests Andrew Greeley and Conor Ward found that although many did not follow Catholic teaching, there was still a high level of religiosity and acceptance of *core* Catholic teachings (Greeley and Ward 2000: 582).

11 The 1995 divorce referendum result was 50.3 per cent *for* the introduction of divorce and 49.7 per cent against.

12 Another group 'Women in the Home' was founded by Norah Gilligan in Dublin to lobby on behalf of these women (Kennedy 2001).

13 See Endnote 2.

14 Headlines included 'Finola and the feminists: Backlash for a true radical', *Sunday Independent*, 10 December 1995; 'Mrs Bruton has split the women's movement – ICA', *Irish Times*, 5 December 1995; 'Why Finola Bruton rained on the feminist parade', *Irish Times*, 7 December 1995; 'Feminists round on the housewife from Meath', *Sunday Independent*, 3 December 1995; 'Speech urges feminists to develop their thinking', *Irish Times*, 7 December 1995; 'Speech sought to redefine feminism', *Irish Times*, 9 December 1995. Letters flowed into the *Irish Times* for over a month after the event mainly supporting Finola Bruton and all were located under the subheading 'Women in the Home'.

15 A European Values study found that 71 per cent of those women taking part in Ireland felt that being a housewife was as fulfilling as paid employment (Whelan and Fahey 1994).

16 Official exclusion of women working in the home, despite the official ideology of the Irish mother and family is not new. See Caitríona Clear (1995) and Finola Kennedy (2001) for discussion of the 1939 Commission on Vocational Organisation chaired by Dr Michael Brown, Bishop of Galway which made no place for 'home makers' in its recommendation for the development of a vocational assembly.

17 Minister Flynn claimed on a radio programme during the election campaign that Mary Robinson 'has to have new clothes and her new look and her new hairdo, and she has the new interest in family, being a mother and all that kind of thing. But none of us, you know, none of us who knew Mary Robinson very well in previous incarnations ever heard her claiming to be a great wife and mother' (quoted in O'Toole 1995: 18).

18 Mary Robinson topped the poll in Limerick East, Cork North Central and South Central and in most of the Dublin constituencies, especially south of the Liffey. She made less of an impact outside urban areas (Pringle 1990: 139). The distribution of first preference votes for Mary Robinson correlated strongly with the patterns of those who voted 'no' in the 1983 Pro-Life referendum and 'yes' in the 1986 Divorce referendum but this time as Dennis Pringle argues those in favour of a 'new' Ireland won (1990: 141).

19 See Chapter 1, Endnote 32.

20 Meaney notes the domestic violence in Gerry Stembridge's film *Guiltrip* and the strains and contradictions of family life in the 1994 TV drama series *Family*. In the 1990s about two thirds of Irish married women between the ages of 25–34 were in paid employment (O'Connor 2000).

21 While 5 per cent of births were outside of marriage in Ireland in 1980, by 1999 32 per cent of all births were outside of marriage (O'Connor 2000).

3   'We haven't really got a set country'

1   While in the 1960s only 5 per cent of Travellers in Ireland were housed, by 1980 this figure had risen to just under 40 per cent (Mac Laughlin 1999: 143). According to a 1986 *Economic and Social Research Institute* report, which is the most recent evidence available, only 5 per cent of Travellers lived to be 50 years old and 1 per cent to be 65 years, compared with 11 per cent of the settled population. Their life expectancy is equivalent to the life expectancy of settled people in the 1940s (Pavee Point Fact Sheet 2001).

2   Irish and Scottish Travellers identify as Travellers and not as gypsies (Okely 1994). Judith Okely notes that the term 'gypsy' is seen as having positive exotic qualities associated with powerful cultural characters such as Bizet's *Carmen*, while no such positive characteristics are associated with Travellers.

3   This language is variously known as Cant, Shelti and Gammon.

4   The writings of Giraldus Cambrensis in the twelfth century noted the particular mobility of Irish society.

5   Some argue that official concern about vagrants arose following the breakdown of the feudal order based on an agricultural manorial system in Britain when a large population of wandering poor was created. In 1572 a vagrancy statute ordered that Irish beggars be sent home after punishment (Beier 1985). Sharon Gmelsh identifies references to 'tinkers' as a distinct class in the 1835 report of *The Commission the Conditions of the Poorer Classes,* which was set up by the British government partly as a result of concerns about Irish immigration to Britain at the time (1975). But this perception of 'tinkers' as a distinct group did not extend to the wider population until over a century later (Helleiner 1995).

6   The *Commission on Itinerancy* was established by the Government in 1963 to address 'problems arising from the presence of itinerants . . . and . . . their way of life' (Kenny 1997: 62–3). This Commission, which did not include any Travellers, represented the first central government attempt to consider the needs of Travellers as a distinct category of people who were named officially at this time as itinerants. By locating the origins of Irish Travellers in a forced nomadism resulting from colonial dispossession and oppression, the Commission Report implied that the 'natural' state of Travellers was sedentary; a position that legitimated official settlement policy at the time. The Commission's Report, which was influenced by developments in the Netherlands at the time, located Travellers' nomadic way of life within a 'subculture of poverty' and the 'solution' was framed in terms of assimilation based on the idea that Travellers had to become sedentary in order to be helped (see Collins 1994; McCarthy 1994; McLoughlin 1994a).

7   A new and critical phase of modernisation in the Republic of Ireland is seen as beginning in 1958, with the publication of *Economic Development* by T. K. Whitaker, then secretary of the Department of Finance (and followed by the first *Programme for Economic Expansion*). The introductory section of *Economic Development* justified economic modernisation on the basis that it would stem emigration which was affecting so many families in the state. Whitaker's economic programme marked a shift away from ideologies of a self-sufficient economy towards initiatives to attract foreign capital investment in export-oriented manufacturing and the development of an agriculture industry integrated into the European market.

8   This body included three Traveller members and was established in 1982 to examine 'the needs of Travellers who wish[ed] to continue a nomadic way of life' and to break down the mistrust that existed between the settled population and Travellers.

9   The report promoted settlement by asserting that 'Travellers who are not so accommodated cannot hope to receive an adequate education. Nor can they avail

satisfactorily of services such as health and welfare which are of such significance in the life of all people' (*Report of the Task Force* 1995: 15).

10 This report recommended that 3,100 units of Traveller-specific accommodation be provided by 2000, but by early 2000 only 123 were in place.

11 See also Kymlica (1995) who argues that 'ethnic' tends to map onto immigrant groups only.

12 This idea of inclusive citizenship is part of a wider EU policy of social inclusion which focuses on the building of social solidarity and equality through cultural recognition and mainstreaming of service provision. In 1997 local partnerships mainstreamed Travellers in all areas of Partnership activities (Area Development Management Ltd. 1998). National committees on Traveller education, accommodation, health and monitoring were established. Also, the Citizen Traveller campaign, a three-year public education programme, grew out of the 1995 *Report of the Task Force* and was launched in 2000. Its target audience included opinion leaders, the judiciary, gardaí and media as well as Travellers themselves. This initiative was ended in 2002 when, amongst other things, it was identified by a government review as not having focused enough on the settled community.

13 For example, when Fine Gael TD Austin Deasy responded to the Task Force recommendations by suggesting that halting sites were 'wishful thinking' and that the only solution lay in birth control, the Minister for Equality and Law Reform Mervyn Taylor, while agreeing that there should be more access to contraception, noted the lawful right of Travellers to have large families and remarked that many of the settled community also had large families (*Irish Times*, 14 June 1996). Traveller women's objections to Austin Deasy's suggestions about contraception focused on their Irish and Catholic identities (Lentin 1999: 135).

14 *Áras an Uachtaráin* is the home of the President of Ireland.

15 These include the Incitement to Hatred Act 1989, the establishment of the Equality Authority in 1999, the Equality Act and the Equal Status Act in 2000.

16 Lentin gives an example of the absence of Traveller women on the National Women's Council of Ireland's Working Party on Violence Against Women and Children in 1996. The report in a tokenistic way recommended an examination of the needs of Traveller women (Lentin 1999: 135).

17 Birth and infant mortality is higher among Travellers and a 1987 survey found that life expectancy for women Travellers was twelve years less than for settled women (and ten years less for men).

18 During the 1980s, sexual and physical abuse was found to have taken place at Trudder House in Co. Wicklow where some Traveller children were placed by Health Boards. The Health Boards had made the decision that these children would be better in the care of this voluntary institution funded by the state than in their own families. One child made a complaint in 1975, but it was not until 1996 that the first conviction was made and the centre was closed. No official report was produced on these incidents of abuse (Raftery and O'Sullivan 1999).

19 The term 'country people' is used by Travellers to describe settled people. According to McVeigh, the term means 'bumpkin or clod hopper' and signifies a sense of pride and privilege in Traveller identity (1997: 12).

20 The numbers of Travellers living on the side of the road rose from 1,148 in 1998 to 1,207 in 1999 (Holland 2001).

21 The 1993 Roads Act empowered Local Authorities and Gardaí to remove temporary dwellings in certain circumstances. Section 24 of the *Housing* (Miscellaneous Provisions) Act 2002 makes trespass a criminal offence. This Act allows the Gardaí to arrest without warrant, impose fines and force Travellers to move on as well as remove property and vehicles without notice (Jameson-Till 2003). This Act breaches all the rights enshrined in international, European and national human rights law (ibid.) and therefore raises key questions about the effectiveness of

legally defined rights in the struggle against hegemonic sedentary cultural values. The Control of Horses Act 1996 introduced to deal with urban horses roaming in the main cities represents another attempt to destroy all traces of Travellers' nomadic way of life.

22 Ten per cent of women in the women's prison in Mountjoy and 5 per cent of the men in Mountjoy prison are Travellers although they constitute only 0.5 per cent of population suggesting high overall rates of criminalisation, but even higher rates for Traveller women.

23 Of course this was also a research context in which the researcher was a settled person and was inviting these women to talk about their lives as Traveller women.

24 Sinead Ní Shuinear identifies three main narratives of origin applied to Travellers; first, that they are 'drop outs' from 'normal society' because of their own inadequacy, for example, after Cromwell or the Famine; second, that they originate from a pre-Celtic group that was relegated to inferior position by Celtic invaders from fifth century; and third, that they are descendents of indigenous nomadic craftsmen who never settled down or acquired land (1994).

25 These women were doing literacy and cultural heritage courses at the Pavee Point Centre in Dublin.

26 The importance of recognition of dignity intensified as a result of a new understanding of individual identity that emerged at the end of the eighteenth century in which the ideal of being true to oneself or what Taylor calls the 'ideal of authenticity' emerged. The rhetoric of diversity and multiculturalism involves claims to originality and authenticity. Taylor argues that authenticity is a child of the Romantic period and a critique of what was seen as the disengaged rationality and atomism of modernity that did not recognise attachment to community.

27 Some Travellers have noted that living in the North was easier than in the south for Travellers (Gmelch 1986; Noonan 1994).

28 Ray Ryan notes the 'intriguing coalition' between the Orange Order in Northern Ireland (and their wish to march where they want to) and the Travelling community in the Republic both of whose mobility is limited by states that designate 'certain forms of behaviour as incompatible with [their] own stability' (2000: 5). He goes on to argue that neither of these states recognise appeals to histories and traditions that existed prior to partition.

29 For a discussion of the use of ethnic cleansing to conceptualise policy towards gypsies and Travellers in Britain see Hawes and Perez (1995). Irish politicians and journalists continue to call for the extermination of Travellers and assert what they see as the valuelessness of Traveller culture. One journalist, following a number of rural burglaries in the mid-1990s for which Travellers were being blamed, characterised Traveller culture as a 'culture of the sewer' and Traveller life as 'ungoverned by intellect'. Traveller life, she suggested was 'without the ennobling intellect of man or the steadying instinct of animals' (Mac Laughlin 1999: 146). Paul Delaney traces the 'trope of being doomed to non-existence' to the experiences of various nomadic cultures, but most powerfully to contemporary reflections on the Roma people and suggests that given the prevalence of this sentiment it should not be surprising to find it being applied to Irish Travellers (2000: 171–2).

30 Julia Kristeva identifies the abject as that which is 'ejected beyond the scope of the possible the tolerable, the thinkable' (1982: 1). Sara Ahmed argues that the abject 'is expelled – like vomit – and the process of expulsion serves to establish the boundary line of the subject. At the same time, the abject holds an uncanny fascination for the subject, demanding its attention and desire … The abject both establishes and undermines the border between inside and outside' (2000: 51).

31 The Home Secretary stated

Now the first thing we have to say is that people have got to stop being sentimental about so-called travellers ... there has been rather too much toleration of travellers and we want to see the policy and local authorities cracking down on them ... Many of these so-called travellers seem to think that it's perfectly okay for them to cause mayhem in an area, to go burgling, thieving, breaking into vehicles, causing all kinds of other trouble including defecating in the doorways of firms ... getting away with it, then their behaviour degenerates.

(Jack Straw in an interview with Annie Oathen, Radio West Midlands 22 July 1999; quoted in Clark and Dearling (2000: 42).

32 Jameson-Till (2003) argues that the presence of Roma in Ireland (about 2,000 in 2003) offers an opportunity for new alliances. She points to the Roma project of bringing together the Roma diaspora as members of a symbolic Roma nation and suggests that this kind of nation based on a nomadic way of life may offer potential for Irish Travellers. Indeed, Roma leaders have expressed a willingness to include Irish Travellers in this project thereby opening up a new space of challenging anti-nomadic values transnationally.

33 A range of strategies is used for globalising products and companies. Note, for example, the significance of Irish musical products such as Enya in 'world music' where Irish difference is exoticised as 'style' in global consumer culture (hooks 1992: 21).

4 'The bright and the beautiful take off ...'

1 See discussion of debates around the enfranchisement of non-resident citizens in the Introduction. Following the introduction of an amendment to the Electoral Bill in 1991 and the inclusion of the issue of votes for emigrants in both of the Coalition government Programmes for Government in 1992, proposals were finally made for limited representation in the Upper House – the *Seanad,* in 1996. A period of consultation culminated in the minister inviting the All Party Committee on the Constitution to examine this issue in their constitutional review report. The committee reported on this issue in 2002 and, in effect, recommended against the extension of enfranchisement to include migrants, based partly on the size of the external citizenry.

2 An American Jesuit sociologist, commissioned to survey attitudes in Dublin to religion and clerical authority by Archbishop of Dublin, John Charles McQuaid in 1962, noted that Ireland was deprived of intellectual energy because it had forced 'young people of energy and mental independence to find a living in other countries' (Garvin 2000: 197).

3 In the latter decades of the nineteenth century, those who did not migrate 'were often stigmatised as indolent, incapable or deformed' (Fitzpatrick 1980: 126). The outflow, according to Roy Foster, enabled archaic patterns of Irish rural life to continue and 'created a particular social composition among the people who stayed' (Foster 1988: 345). Given the high levels of young Irish people leaving in every generation, Foster suggests that those who were 'left behind' could be seen as 'a residual population' (1988: 371). Another historian, F. L. S. Lyons, also emphasised the allegedly selective effects of emigration with 'the young and the vigorous' leaving behind 'those less well fitted to make their way in the world' (Lyons 1963: 665).

4 There is some evidence that those who were able to stay because of class privilege often looked down on migrants from lower classes who had to leave in order to survive (see http://migration.ucc.ie) and Irish Centre for Migration Studies sound archive – *Breaking the Silence: staying 'at home' in an emigrant society* located at Boole Library, National University of Ireland Cork.

5 See the NESC Report (1991). A survey conducted in 1987 in the New York-based newspaper the *Irish Voice* found that amongst the Irish illegals in New York surveyed, 80 per cent had left jobs to go to the US and over a third had third level education (Holland 1988).
6 Paradoxically, Liam Ryan notes that the motivation of many west of Ireland emigrants in the 1950s was to join their 'own people' in England because of the belief that 'one's own can provide one with the greatest pleasure' (1990: 51).

5 'Are we here or are we there?'

1 Gearoid O'Tuathaigh argues that the 1950s and the 1980s in Ireland 'are divided by a considerable cultural difference' noting a cultural de-differentiation between Irish society and British urban society in the 1980s (1991: 23).
2 Lewis Clohessy notes that Dublin's term as European City of Culture in 1991 and Ireland's Presidency of the EU in the previous year brought the city and country in 'from the periphery' (1994: 190). Peter Sutherland, Chair of Goldman Sachs International and British Petroleum PLC (former director general of GATT and Attorney General in Ireland between 1981 and 1984) identified the International Financial Services Centre as central to making Dublin the Centre of 'a new and consistent flow of business visitors that bring their secondary benefits' to Ireland (1997: 30). Also, the Tánaiste, Mary Harney, has noted that this centre would establish Ireland as a world-class centre and underpin the country's 'competitiveness in an increasingly global economy' (Harney 2000).
3 See Corcoran (1993) for a discussion of New York as a 'global city' and the labour market experiences of Irish 'illegals' in the 1980s.
4 The phrase 'more Irish than the Irish themselves' or *'hiberniores hibernis ipsos'* is a medieval phrase which was used to describe the Normans who crossed from England to Ireland in 1169/70. They intermingled with the Irish and were said to have become 'indistinguishably Gaelic' (Kee 1983 (1972): 10). Yet the phrase implied that they were not 'truly' Irish.
5 Fintan O'Toole notes the excessiveness of the show *Riverdance* with its 'too loud music and too fast beat' and suggests that the 'feeling of release was in direct proportion to the repression from which it sprang' (1997: 145). This show produced 'Irish traditional music and dance re-figured as a big Broadway show' and offered a hybrid representation of the entangled relationship between Ireland and the United States (ibid.). *Riverdance* could 'risk kitsch', according to O'Toole, because it acknowledged both the creative life of folk culture and the spectacle of consumer culture (1997: 152).
6 In 1972, the 'Women and Ireland' group was established to discuss and publicise events in Northern Ireland and to highlight women's activism within nationalism (Rossiter 1993: 239). By the early 1980s, a network of 'Women and Ireland' groups was established extending to twelve British cities. The Irish Women's Abortion Support Group came together in 1980/81 primarily as a support group for Irish women travelling to Britain for an abortion. A sister group, the Irish Abortion Solidarity Campaign, was established after the X Case in 1992 with a political campaigning brief as distinct from a support role. For a discussion of the X Case and its implications for the many temporary Irish women migrants see A. Smyth (1992b) and L. Smyth (2000).
7 The London Irish Women's Centre (LIWC) project was initiated in 1983 and opened as a centre in 1986. It was set up to 'counteract the erosion and marginalisation' of the experiences of Irish women (London Irish Women's Centre Report, 1987: 2). *Solais Anois*, a women's refuge specifically for Irish women escaping domestic violence, was set up in London in 1993.

8 *Amach Linn*, which aims to advance the social and cultural welfare of Irish lesbians and gay men in London, was set up in 1995. Many of those involved in setting up these organisations left Ireland in the 1980s.

9 Of course, Ireland's experience of colonialism as well as its participation in projects of empire and the global activities of the Irish Catholic Church mean that it is impossible to separate Irish migration out from questions of empire (Gilley 1984; O'Connor 2001). For example, as the Atlantic economy grew, Irish migrants played a critical role in the last stages of this phase of British imperial expansion in the West Indies and colonial America (Bielenberg 2000). Irish women's migration was facilitated by the official policies of the British colonies and the USA, which included the aim of increasing their populations, ensuring civil order and filling particular labour market niches (Akenson 1993, see also Fitzpatrick 1997). (For a discussion, contra Helen's account, that some Irish migrants were able to recreate 'homeland' in other parts of the world, see Howe 2000: 56; Kane 2001; Richards 1996: 54 and Rolston 1993).

10 Eighty-three per cent of the women migrants taking part in this study visited Ireland at least once a year, 29 per cent visited twice annually and 34 per cent visited three times annually.

11 'The reception accorded Irish women who went to England for their illegitimate pregnancies, for the adoption of their babies, or more recently, for abortions is the hushed under-belly of the Irish tradition in Britain' (Buckley 1997: 120), and their 'forbidden stories map the suppression of feminine experience across every townland of Ireland' (ibid.).

12 The network was founded in 1989 by a number of Irish people who felt a need for a social organisation which would include a wide range of events within the London Irish community. The club is open to people over the age of twenty-one with no upper age limit, but the age group profile is between twenties and forties. Membership has stood at about 200 since it was established. A committee is elected annually from the current membership for day-to-day management of the club. Events include theatre, restaurant/pub/nightclub outings, concerts, comedy, sporting activities and holiday breaks. Special events are usually organised for St Patrick's Day, summer and Christmas.

13 See Mac Éinrí (1989) for discussion of Irish networks in 1980s Paris.

14 This festival was sponsored by the Federation of Irish Societies and Riverside Studios, London.

15 The first copy of *Ballyhoo!* included articles on enjoying life in London, Irish solicitors in London, the development of the new International Financial Services Centre in Dublin, Landmark Trust weekends away, photographs from the LIS Ball, developments at *Bord Fáilte* (the Irish Tourist Board) and the Bank of Ireland; the presentation of a £5,000 cheque (raised at the ball) to the London Irish Centre; an account of the work done for disadvantaged Irish migrants at the Camden Irish centre; a guide to golf around London; a short story, property buying tips and two accounts of changing careers in London.

16 Kilburn is a ward in the borough of Brent which has been identified with Irish migrants to London since the 1950s. Kilburn High Road includes a number of Irish bars, dancing venues, an Irish travel agent, newsagents that sell Irish national and regional newspapers and many other signs of a migrant Irish presence in the area.

17 By invoking a pensioner whose ethnicity is unmarked but whose life is restricted by globalising processes locally, David Parker suggests that Massey implies a 'nostalgia for all that has changed in the pensioner's lifetime' and the cultural transformation of the British nation (2000: 75).

18 Young notes that there is no single hybridity because it changes as it repeats and also repeats as it changes so that hybridity always suggests the impossibility of essentialism (1995: 27).

19 Tim Pat Coogan, in his focus group-based study of the Irish in Britain, noted 'how infrequently the Church was mentioned, save as something whose influence had to be shaken off' (2000: 136).

6 'The Irish are not "ethnic"'

1 The first public institutional acknowledgement of anti-Irish racism is recorded in the London Strategic Policy Unit report on the Irish in Britain in 1984. This report locates anti-Irish racism in the context of colonisation and its legacy of negative images and popular prejudices. Anti-Irish racism is variously explained as a residue of colonialism, in relation to the economic positioning of Irish migrant workers and in relation to the establishment of the British nation-state.

2 I use the term English nationals here rather than British citizens because British citizens include four nationalities including Northern Ireland. The focus is less on questions of citizenship than on cultural differentiations both within Britain and between Ireland and England.

3 Roediger's examination of whiteness in American labour history considers the making of the American working class in the nineteenth century and early twentieth century and identifies whiteness as a destructive ideology (1991 and 1994). There is an assumption in Roediger's work and others that cross-racial working class solidarity was possible and that the public and psychological wage that 'whiteness' earned is the explanation for this lack of working class unity.

4 Ignatiev argues that the American public did not see early nineteenth-century Irish immigrants as 'white' (see Brodkin 1998 for a similar discussion about the position of Jewish immigrants to the US).

5 Waters did in-depth interviews with sixty people of third and fourth generation 'white' ethnic groups (of European extraction and Catholic background) in suburban areas outside of San José and Philadelphia in 1986/7. She notes that by focusing on Catholics she reduced the variables affecting identification. She also suggests that an ethnic resurgence took place in the 1970s mainly amongst Italians, Irish and Poles whom she identifies as mainly Roman Catholic.

6 Gabriel uses the term 'subaltern whites' to differentiate Jews and Irish 'whites' from what he sees as dominant 'white' groups.

7 For example, Kathleen Paul argues that the Attlee government in postwar Britain attempted to limit and even prevent colonial migration to Britain 'even as it passed a nationality act that confirmed the right of colonials to migrate. This conflict between a formal nationality policy that confirmed the right of all members of the British Empire to enter Britain and an informal constructed national identity that reserved that right for people who really belonged reflected separate spheres of nationality that produced different communities of Britishness' (1997: 130). Bronwen Walter notes that Irish immigrants to the United States in 1980s and 1990s gained disproportionately from Donnelly and Morrison lottery visas because they presented 'themselves as desirable white migrants' (Walter 2001: 71).

8 Of course, this is not to suggest that Irish subjects were equally subject to this positioning or took it up in any universal way. As Foucault argues, 'life is never totally integrated into techniques that govern and administer it: it constantly escapes them' (1976: 143).

9 See Delaney (2000) for an alternative view.

10 This was an address given to a meeting of the National Council for Civil Liberties in London on 23 May (Brah 1996: 257).

11 In debates between multiculturalism and anti-racism in the 1980s, multiculturalism was seen as 'woolly liberalism', a discourse and policy that did not take account of power and anti-racist politics as left and radical (Brah 1996: 230; see also Mercer 1994). This debate set up an unhelpful opposition between structure and culture because discrimination, racism and representations of cultural difference are deeply implicated in one another (Donald and Rattansi 1992).

12 Walter notes that although anti-Catholicism constituted a central aspect of anti-Irish racism in the nineteenth century, anti-Muslim sentiment has unified Christianity, which is closely associated with 'whiteness' (2001: 112).

13 Mary is referring here to the Commission for Racial Equality (CRE), which was established by the Race Relations Act of 1976 to work towards the elimination of discrimination and promotion of equality between persons of different racial groups in Britain. The CRE commissioned a report on anti-Irish racism in Britain in 1993 which found that when Irish respondents in London and Birmingham were asked whether they thought the Irish should be recognised as an ethnic group, 59 per cent answered 'Yes'; 28 per cent gave a firm 'No' and the remainder (13 per cent) were ambivalent. Those giving a positive answer emphasised the similarities they perceived between the situation of the Irish and those from the 'visible minorities'; the entitlements given to visible minorities; the contribution to Britain of the Irish as a labour force; and their view that Irish cultural difference is not understood by British people. Those taking a negative stance did so mainly because they feared identification would cause difficulties and preferred a strategy of keeping a low profile (Hickman and Walter 1997: 190–2).

14 Howe notes the strong identification with 'white' European identity of key Irish political actors in the late-nineteenth century and suggests that some Irish saw themselves as 'an ancient, cultured European people who could be demeaned by comparison with non-whites' (2000: 45).

15 Walter also recognises the ways in which the invisibility enabled through 'whiteness' facilitated the movement of Irish women, and through them their second-generation Irish families, towards the centre of the US nation. In particular, she notes the significant part played by Irish women in 'securing a place for their children in the hegemonic white supremacy' (Walter 2001: 66).

16 Throughout their history in New York, Bayorr and Meagher argue that 'the Irish have been at the border of the ins and outs, interpreting one to the other, mediating, sometimes including, sometimes excluding. They have been victim and victimizer, "other" and definer of the "other", and, paradoxically, sometimes played both roles simultaneously' (1996: 6).

7 Women, the diaspora and the 'global Irish family'

1 The Ethical Globalisation Initiative is a fifteen-month project established in 2002 to ensure support for a sustainable movement for ethical globalisation and to address the need of developing countries to secure adequate resources to build national protection systems into human rights. The construction of 'the global' articulated and reproduced by this initiative raises important questions for feminism that cannot be addressed here.

2 See Chamberlain (1996) for an overview of UN literature on women and resources prepared for the UN fourth world conference on women.

3 Clinton's speech included the following passage 'Families rely on mothers and wives for emotional support and care; families rely on women for labor in the home; and increasingly, families rely on women for income needed to raise healthy children and to care for other relatives' (Clinton 1996: 100).

4 Revelations of violence and sexual abuse within families is mentioned but minimised in this attempt to rehabilitate the family as the central mode of collective belonging.

5 This elision is also evident in former President Robinson's use of the diaspora to locate difference at the heart of Irish identity.

6 The houses of the Oireachtas are the houses of parliament.

7 Article 2 of the amended Irish constitution states that 'It is the entitlement and birthright of every person born in the island of Ireland, which includes its islands and seas, to be part of the Irish nation. That is also the entitlement of all persons otherwise qualified in accordance with law to be citizens of Ireland. Furthermore, the Irish nation cherishes its special affinity with people of Irish ancestry living abroad who share its cultural identity and heritage'.

8 See Note 18, Chapter 1.

9 Liberalism and feminism share the concepts of individuals as free and equal human beings who are liberated from the hierarchical and ascribed positions of traditional society. Discourses and practices of the choosing individual are easily subsumed to a liberal theory in which individualism, freedom and rights are seen to complement one another and represent resources for feminist politics. However, the subject who is 'free to choose' needs critical feminist attention as do the notions of freedom and rights and how power works through these. Some feminist writers have approached the significance of 'the global' for feminism by focusing on liberal universalism (Nussbaum 1995) and the need to respect local cultures and politics (Code 2000; Mohanty 1988; Narayan 2000). Nussbaum argues that an emphasis on cultural traditions in different parts of the world prevents women's development and calls for a liberal universalism that ensures equal rights and opportunities for all women. On the other hand, Judith Butler undoes the universalism versus cultural sensitivity/cultural relativism dichotomy by arguing for a non-foundational notion of universalism. The meaning of 'the universal', she argues, is 'culturally variable, and the specific cultural articulations of "the universal" work against its claim to a transnational status' (Butler 2001: 430). In other words, the cultural conditions of the articulation of the universal are not always the same (ibid.). Equally, those who are excluded or rendered outside the universal and definitions of particular cultures constitute 'the contingent limit of universalization' (ibid.: 432). It is evident therefore that notions of rights and equality are used in different Western and non-Western contexts for myriad and not always progressive ends (ibid.). For example, the argument that feminism and sexual rights are Western has been used by church and states often to debunk the claims of women from non-Western cultures and to defend ethnic purities (ibid.). Rights and discourses of equality need to be investigated within particular contexts and cannot be easily mapped onto the West or non-West because they are deployed in differentiated and not necessarily more or less 'modern' ways within both contexts.

10 Feminists are engaging with the formal political sphere so that violence against women, questions of equality and so on are put on the agenda of the state by feminist networks and become part of mainstream policy. For example 'gender mainstreaming is now a global movement' and the EU has adopted this as a core policy albeit unevenly implemented (Walby 2002: 538). Gender mainstreaming means putting a gender equality perspective into mainstream policies. The Council of Europe defines it as 'the (re)organisation, improvement, development and evaluation of policy processes, so that a gender equality perspective is incorporated in all policies at all levels and at all stages, by the actors normally involved in policy-making' (*National Development Plan* Ireland, 2000 to 2006). A Gender Equality Monitoring Committee was set up in 1997 to oversee the implementation of the recommendations of the Second Commission on the Status of Women and the Beijing Platform for Action. The legal framework on equality in Ireland has been

extended and developed by the Employment Equality Act (1998) and the Equal Status Act (2000), with the Equality Authority established to oversee the implementation of these acts (see http://www.equality.ie). Further, the EU regulations on the spending of European Union Structural and Cohesion Funds require that equal opportunities between men and women be taken into account, using the strategy of mainstreaming. Such developments and feminist involvement in them bring Sylvia Walby to suggest that a reframing of feminism is taking place from an anti-system feminist discourse to an inclusionary one (ibid.: 546).

11 While some aspects of what might be called global feminism, for example, feminist input to state policies (even if framed by EU agendas) such as 'gender mainstreaming' and equality initiatives have contributed to improving the position of women in Ireland, this kind of 'advancement' can contribute to the positing of the 'developed woman' of global modernity as the goal of feminism across the globe. As Uma Narayan argues, any interpretation of rights and equality that is framed in terms of Western values will be insensitive to the predicaments of those marginalised groups including women in non-western contexts (2000: 92).

12 The UN General Assembly in 1985 adopted a resolution on domestic violence and by 1993 it had adopted the Declaration on Violence against Women, which acknowledged the roots of violence against women as in their subordination, identified violence as gender-based and recognised that culture and religion should not be used as excuses for these activities. These represent considerable progress in international politics of women's rights (Pettman 1996: 212).

13 There is a tendency in discourses of globalisation and the global to map the 'prospects for a small class of international entrepreneurs under the very favourable market conditions' onto the 'prospects for Irish society as a whole' (Kirby 2002: 186). In this way the 'potential' for those who can most easily occupy the position of 'global Irish subject' comes to stand in for all.

14 For example, see the use of the stereotype of the 'dirty' and undomesticated Traveller woman in Chapter 3 and of the Irish nurse/mammy figure for Irish migrants in England.

References

Abu-Lughod, L. (1998) 'Introduction. Feminist longings and postcolonial conditions', in L. Abu-Lughod (ed.), *Remaking Women: Feminism and Modernity in the Middle East*, Princeton, NJ: Princeton University Press, pp. 3–32.

Adkins, L. (2002) *Revisions: Gender and Sexuality in Late Modernity*, Buckingham: Open University Press.

Ahmed, S. (1996) 'Moving spaces: black feminism and post-colonial theory', *Theory, Culture and Society*, 13 (1), pp. 139–46.

—— (1997) '"It's a sun-tan, isn't it?" Auto-biography as an identificatory practice', in H. S. Mirza (ed.), *Black British Feminism: A Reader*, London: Routledge, pp. 153–67.

—— (1998) *Differences that Matter: Feminist Theory and Postmodernism*, Cambridge: Cambridge University Press.

—— (1999) '"She'll wake up one of these days and find she's turned into a nigger". Passing through hybridity', *Theory, Culture and Society*, 16 (2), pp. 87–106.

—— (2000) *Strange Encounters: Embodied Others in Post-Coloniality*, London: Routledge.

Akenson, D. H. (1993) *The Irish Diaspora: A Primer*, Belfast: Institute of Irish Studies.

—— (1997) *If the Irish Ran the World: Montserrat, 1630–1730*, Liverpool: Liverpool University Press.

—— (2000) 'No petty people Pakeha history and the historiography of the Irish diaspora', in L. Fraser (ed.), *A Distant Shore: Irish Migration and New Zealand Settlement*, Dunedin, New Zealand: University of Otago Press, pp. 13–24.

Allen, T. W. (1994) *The Invention of the White Race: Racial Oppression and Social Control (Vol. 1)*, New York: Verso.

Almeida, L. D. (1992) '"And they still haven't found what they're looking for": a survey of the New Irish in New York City', in P. O'Sullivan (ed.), *Patterns of Migration, Vol. 1, The Irish Worldwide: History, Heritage, Identity*, Leicester: Leicester University Press, pp. 196–221.

Ang, I. (1994) 'On not speaking Chinese: postmodern ethnicity and the politics of diaspora', *New Formations*, 24 (Winter), pp. 1–18.

—— (1996) 'The curse of the smile: ambivalence and the "Asian" woman in Australian multiculturalism', *Feminist Review*, 52, pp. 36–49.

Anthias, F. (1998) 'Evaluating "diaspora": beyond ethnicity?', *Sociology*, 32 (3), pp. 557–80.

Appadurai, A. (1996) *Modernity at Large: Cultural Dimensions of Globalization*, Minneapolis, MN: University of Minnesota Press.

Archdeacon, T. J. (2002) 'The Irish famine in American school curricula', *Éire-Ireland*, XXXVII (I and II), pp. 130–52.

Area Development Management (1998) *Traveller Inclusion: A Compilation of Case Studies on Themes and Issues within the Local Development Programme*, Dublin: Area Development Management.

Arensberg, C. and Kimball, S. T. (1968 [1924]) *Family and Community in Ireland* (second edn), Cambridge, MA: Harvard University Press.

Armstrong, N. (1987) 'The rise of the domestic woman', in N. Armstrong and L. Tennenhouse (eds), *The Ideology of Conduct*, New York: Methuen, pp. 96–141.

Auge, M. (1995) *Non-Places*, London: Verso.

Bailey, A. (1998) 'Locating traitorous identities: toward a view of privilege-cognizant white character', *Hypatia*, 13 (3), pp. 27–42.

—— (2000) 'Locating traitorous identities: toward a view of privilege-cognizant white character', in U. Narayan and S. Harding (eds), *Decentering the Center: Philosophy for a Multicultural, Postcolonial, and Feminist World*, Bloomington, IN: Indiana University Press, pp. 283–98.

Bakhtin, M. (1981) *The Dialogic Imagination*, Austin, TX: University of Texas Press.

Banton, M. (1997) *Ethnic and Racial Consciousness*, London: Longman.

Barker, D. K. (2000) 'Dualisms, discourse, and development', in U. Narayan and S. Harding (eds), *Decentering the Center: Philosophy for a Multicultural, Postcolonial, and Feminist World*, Bloomington, IN: Indiana University Press, pp. 178–88.

Baucom, I. (1999) *Out of Place: Englishness, Empire and the Locations of Identity*, Princeton, NJ: Princeton University Press.

Bauman, Z. (1993) *Postmodern Ethics*, Oxford: Blackwell.

—— (2000) *Liquid Modernity*, London: Polity Press.

—— (2001) *Community: Seeking Safety in an Insecure World*, Cambridge: Polity Press.

Bayor, R. H. and Meagher, T. J. (eds) (1996) *The New York Irish*, Baltimore, MD: The Johns Hopkins University Press.

Beale, J. (1986) *Women in Ireland: Voices of Change*, Basingstoke: Macmillan.

Beaumont, C. (1999) 'Gender, citizenship and the state in Ireland, 1922–1990', in V. Crossman, S. Brewster, F. Becket and D. Alderson (eds), *Ireland in Proximity History, Gender, Space*, London: Routledge, pp. 94–108.

Beck, U. and Beck-Gernsheim, E. (2002) *Individualization*, London: Sage.

Beier, A. L. (1985) *Masterless Men*, London: Methuen.

Belchem, J. (1999) 'Class, creed and country: the Irish middle class in Victorian Liverpool', in R. Swift and G. Sheridan (eds), *The Irish in Victorian Britain: The Local Dimension*, Dublin: Four Courts Press, pp. 190–211.

Bell, V. (1995) 'Bio-politics and the spectre of incest: sexuality and/in the family', in M. Featherstone, S. Lash and R. Robertson (eds), *Global Modernities*, London: Sage, pp. 225–43.

—— (1996) 'Show and tell: passing and narrative in Toni Morrison's *Jazz*', *Social Identities*, 2 (2), pp. 221–36.

—— (1999) 'Performativity and belonging, an introduction', *Theory, Culture and Society*, 16 (2), pp. 1–10.

—— (2001) 'Negotiating and narrating emplacement: belonging and conflict in Northern Ireland', *New Formations*, 43, pp. 61–86.

Benjamin, W. (1973) *Illuminations*, London: Fontana.

Berlant, L. (1993) 'The theory of infantile citizenship', *Public Culture*, 5 (3), pp. 395–410.

—— (1997) *The Queen of America goes to Washington City: Essays on Sex and Citizenship*, Durham, NC: Duke University Press.

—— and Warner, P. (2000) 'Sex in public', in L. Berlant (ed.), *Intimacy*, Chicago, IL: University of Chicago Press, pp. 311–30.

Berman, M. (1983) *All that is Solid Melts into Air*, London: Verso.

Bhabha, H. (1987) 'Of mimicry and man: the ambivalence of colonial discourse', in J. Donald and S. Hall (eds), *Politics and Ideology*, Milton Keynes: Open University Press, pp. 198–205.

—— (1990) 'The third space', in J. Rutherford (ed.), *Identity, Community, Culture, Difference*, London: Lawrence & Wishart, pp. 207–21.

—— (1994) *The Location of Culture*, London: Routledge.

Bhreathnach, A. (2002) 'Irish Travellers. A question of gender', *Re-searching Irish Women*, Women on Ireland Conference, University of Liverpool, 16–17 March.

Bielenberg, A. (2000) 'Irish emigration to the British empire, 1700–1914', in A. Bielenberg (ed.), *The Irish Diaspora*, Harlow, England: Longman, pp. 215–34.

Blessing, P. (1985) 'Irish emigration to the United States, 1800–1920', in P. J. Drudy (ed.), *The Irish in America: Emigration, Assimilation and Impact*, Cambridge: Cambridge University Press, pp. 11–38.

Bordo, S. (1990) 'Feminism, postmodernism and gender-scepticism', in L. Nicholson (ed.), *Feminism/Postmodernism*, London: Routledge, pp. 133–5.

Böss, M. (2002) 'The postmodern nation: a critical history of the "Fifth Province" discourse', *Etudes Irlandaises*, 27 (1), pp. 139–59.

Bourke, A., Kilfeather, S., Luddy, M., MacCurtain, M., Meaney, G., Dhonnchadna, N., O'Dowd, M. and Wills, C. (eds) (2002a) *The Field Day Anthology of Irish Writing, Vol. IV: Irish Women's Writing and Traditions*, Cork: Cork University Press in association with Field Day.

—— (2002b) *The Field Day Anthology of Irish Writing, Vol. V: Irish Women's Writing and Traditions*, Cork: Cork University Press in association with Field Day.

Bourke, J. (1993) *Husbandry to Housewifery: Women, Economic Change, and Housework in Ireland, 1890–1914*, Oxford: Clarendon Press.

Boym, S. (2000) 'On diasporic intimacy: Ilya Kabakov's installations and immigrant homes', in L. Berlant (ed.), *Intimacy*, Chicago: Chicago University Press, pp. 226–52.

Brah, A. (1996) *Cartographies of Diaspora: Contesting Identities*, London: Routledge.

Braidotti, R. (2001) 'Becoming-woman: rethinking the positivity of difference', in E. Bronfen and M. Kavka (ed.), *Feminist Consequences: Theory for the New Century*, New York: Columbia University Press, pp. 381–413.

Breen, R., Hannon, D. F., Rottman, D. B., and Whelan, C. T. (eds) (1990) *Understanding Contemporary Ireland: State, Class, and Development in the Republic of Ireland*, Dublin: Gill & Macmillan.

Brennan, T. (1997) *At Home in the World: Cosmopolitanism Now*, Cambridge, MA: Harvard University Press.

Brewster, S. (1999) 'Introduction', in V. Crossman S. Brewster, F. Becket and D. Alderson (eds), *Ireland in Proximity: History, Gender, Space*, London: Routledge, pp. 125–8.

Brodkin, K. (1998) *How the Jews became White Folks and What That Says About Race in America*, New Brunswick, NJ: Rutgers University Press.

Brody, H. (1973) *Inishkillane: Change and Decline in the West of Ireland*, London: Allen Lane.

Brown, J. N. (1998) 'Black Liverpool, black America, and the gendering of diasporic space', *Cultural Anthropology*, 13 (3), pp. 291–325.

Brown, W. (2001) *Politics Out of History*, Princeton, NJ: Princeton University Press.

Buckley, M. (1997) 'Sitting on your politics: the Irish among the British and the women among the Irish', in J. Mac Laughlin (ed.), *Location and Dislocation in Contemporary Irish Society: Emigration and Irish Identities*, Cork: Cork University Press, pp. 94–132.

Burchell, G., Gordon, C. and Miller, P. (eds) (1991) *The Foucault Effect: Studies in Governmentality*, London: Harvester Wheatsheaf.

Butler, J. (1990) *Gender Trouble: Feminism and the Subversion of Identity*, New York and London: Routledge.

—— (1993) *Bodies That Matter On the Discursive Limits of Sex*, New York and London: Routledge.

—— (2001) 'The end of sexual difference?', in E. Bronfen and M. Kavka (eds), *Feminist Consequences: Theory for the New Century*, New York: Columbia University Press, pp. 381–413.

Byrne, P. (1995) 'Emigration: the great non-issue', *The Furrow*, LIII (12), April, pp. 224–69.

Calhoun, C. (1995) *Critical Social Theory: Culture, History and the Challenge of Difference*, Oxford: Basil Blackwell.

Callanan, C. (2002) *Catholic Rescue and Repatriation: Irish Unmarried Mothers in England 1950s–1970s*, unpublished Ph.D. thesis, National University of Ireland, Cork.

Casey, E. B. (1989) 'Emigration: the reality – the Catholic Church's response', in J. Mulholland and D. Keogh (eds), *Emigration, Employment and Enterprise*, Cork: Hibernian University Press, pp. 34–45.

Casey, M. R. (1996) '"From the East Side to the seaside": Irish Americans on the move in New York City', in R. H. Bayor and T. J. Meagher (eds), *The New York Irish*, Baltimore, MD: The Johns Hopkins University Press, pp. 395–418.

Chamberlain, M. K. (1996) 'A review of resource volumes prepared for the United Nations Fourth World Conference on Women', *Women's Studies Quarterly*, XXIV (1 and 2), pp. 290–98.

Chambers, I. (1994) *Migrancy, Culture, Identity*, London and New York: Routledge.

Clancy, P., Drudy, S., Lynch, K. and O'Dowd, L. (eds) (1995) *Irish Society: Sociological Perspectives*, Dublin: Institute of Public Administration in association with the Sociological Association of Ireland.

Clark, C. and Dearling, A. (2000) 'Ethnicity, nomadism and "Traveller" identity', *Social Work in Europe*, 7 (1), pp. 42–50.

Clear, C. (1995) 'The women can not be blamed . . .', in M. O'Dowd and S. Wichert (eds), *Chattel, Servant or Citizen: Women's Status in Church, State and Society*, Belfast: Institute of Irish Studies, pp. 179–86.

—— (2000) *Women of the House: Women's Household Work in Ireland 1922–1961*, Dublin: Irish Academic Press.

Clifford, J. (1992) 'Traveling cultures', in C. Nelson, P. A. Treichler and L. Grossberg (eds), *Cultural Studies*, New York: Routledge, pp. 107–20.

—— (1994) 'Diasporas', *Cultural Anthropology*, 9 (3), pp. 302–38.

Clinton, H. R. (1996) '"Women's rights are human rights" excerpts, remarks 5 September 1995', *Women's Studies Quarterly*, XXIV (1 and 2), pp. 98–101.

Clohessy, L. (1994) 'Culture and urban tourism: "Dublin 1991" – European city of culture', in U. Kockel (ed.), *Culture, Tourism and Development: The Case of Ireland*, Liverpool: Liverpool University Press, pp. 189–95.

Code, L. (2000) 'How to think globally: stretching the limits of imagination', in U. Nayaran and S. Harding (eds), *Decentering the Center: Philosophy for a*

Multicultural, Postcolonial, and Feminist World, Bloomington, IN: Indiana University Press, pp. 67–79.

Cohen, P. (1988) 'The perversions of inheritance: studies in the making of multi-racist Britain', in P. Cohen and H. S. Bains (eds), *Multi Racist Britain*, London: Macmillan, pp. 9–18.

Cohen, R. (1995) 'Rethinking "Babylon": iconoclastic conceptions of the diasporic experience', *New Community*, 21 (1), pp. 5–18.

Collins, M. (1994) 'The sub-culture of poverty – a response to McCarthy', in M. McCann, S. O Síocháin and J. Ruane (eds), *Irish Travellers: Culture and Ethnicity*, Belfast: Institute of Irish Studies, pp. 130–3.

Collins, P. (1988) 'Sense of Ireland', *Ballyhoo!*, 1 (1), p. 4.

Commission on Emigration and Other Population Problems 1948–54 *Reports* (1955), Dublin: Government Stationery Office.

Commission on the Status of Women (1972) *Report to the Minister for Finance*, Dublin: Stationery Office.

Connolly, L. (1996) 'The women's movement in Ireland 1970–1995: a social movement analysis', *Irish Journal of Feminist Studies*, 1 (1), pp. 43–77.

Connor, T. (1987) *The London Irish*, London: London Strategic Policy Unit.

Coogan, T. P. (2000) *Wherever Green is Worn: The Story of the Irish Diaspora*, London: Hutchinson.

Coombes, A. E. and Brah, A. (2000) 'Introduction: the conundrum of "mixing"', in A. Brah and A. E. Coombes (eds), *Hybridity and its Discontents Politics, Science, Culture*, London: Routledge, pp. 1–16.

Corcoran, M. P. (1993) *Irish Illegals: Transients Between Two Societies*, Westport, CT: Greenwood Press.

—— (1998) 'Heroes of the diaspora?', in M. Peillon and E. Slater (eds), *Encounters with Modern Ireland*, Dublin: Institute for Public Administration, pp. 135–42.

—— (2002) 'The process of migration and the reinvention of self: the experiences of returning Irish migrants', *Eire-Ireland*, XXXVII (I and II), pp. 175–91.

Coughlan, P. (1991) '"Bog queens": the representation of women in the poetry of John Montague and Seamus Heaney', in T. O'Brien Johnson and D. Cairns (eds), *Gender in Irish Writing*, Milton Keynes: Open University Press, pp. 88–111.

Coulter, C. (1993) *The Hidden Tradition: Feminism, Women and Nationalism in Ireland*, Cork: Cork University Press.

—— (1995) 'Feminism, nationalism, and the heritage of the enlightenment', in T. P. Foley, L. Pilkington, S. Ryder and E. Tilley (eds), *Gender and Colonialism*, Galway: Galway University Press, pp. 195–209.

Cowley, U. (2001) *The Men Who Built Britain: A History of the Irish Navvy*, Dublin: Wolfhound Press.

Crickley, A. (ed.) (1992) 'Feminism and ethnicity', in Dublin Travellers Education and Development Group, *Irish Travellers: New Analysis and New Initiatives*, Dublin: Pavee Point Publications, pp. 101–8.

—— (2001) 'Women and racism', in F. Farrell and P. Watt (eds), *Responding to Racism in Ireland*, Dublin: Veritas Publications, pp. 88–9.

Cronin, A. (2000) *Advertising and Consumer Citizenship: Gender, Images and Rights*, London: Routledge.

Cronin, M. (2000) *Across the Lines: Travel, Language, Translation*, Cork: Cork University Press.

Cummins, M. (1996) *The Best of About Women*, Dublin: Marino Books.

Curtis, L. (1984) *Nothing But The Same Old Story*, London: Information on Ireland.

——, O'Keefe, J. and Keatinge, C. (1987) *Hearts and Minds: Anam agus Intinn: The Cultural Life of London's Irish Community*, London: London Strategic Policy Unit.

De Luca, K. (1999) 'In the shadow of whiteness. The consequences of constructions of nature in environmental politics', in T. K. Nakayama and J. N. Martin (eds), *Whiteness: The Communication of Social Identity*, Thousand Oaks, CA: Sage, pp. 217–48.

Delaney, E. (2000) *Demography, State and Society: Irish Migration to Britain, 1921–1971*, Liverpool: Liverpool University Press.

Dillon, M. (1998) 'Divorce and cultural rationality', in M. Peillon and E. Slater (eds), *Encounters with Modern Ireland*, Dublin: Institute of Public Administration, pp. 127–34.

Diner, H. (1983) *Erin's Daughters in America*, Baltimore, MD: The Johns Hopkins University Press.

Donald, J. and Rattansi, A. (1992) 'Introduction', in J. Donald and A. Rattansi (eds), *'Race', Culture and Difference*, London: Sage, pp. 1–10.

Donzelot, J. (1980) *The Policing of Families*, London: Hutchinson.

Dorcey, M. (1995) 'Interview with Mary Dorcey', in I. O'Carroll and E. Collins (eds), *Lesbian and Gay Visions of Ireland: Towards the Twenty-first Century*, London: Cassell, pp. 25–44.

Douglas, S. J. (1994) *Where the Girls Are: Growing Up Female with the Mass Media*, London: Penguin.

Drudy, J. (ed.) (1986) *Ireland and Britain Since 1922*, Cambridge: Cambridge University Press.

Duara, P. (1996) 'Historicizing national identity, or who imagines what and when', in G. Eley and R. G. Suny (eds), *Becoming National: A Reader*, Oxford: Oxford University Press, pp. 151–78.

—— (1998) 'The regime of authenticity: timelessness, gender, and national history in modern China', *History and Theory*, 37 (3), pp. 287–308.

Du Bois, WEB (1994 [1903]) *The Souls of Black Folk*, New York: Dover.

Dyer, R. (1997) *White*, London: Routledge.

Fahey, T. (1995) 'Family and household in Ireland', in P. Clancy, S. Drudy, K. Lynch and L. O'Dowd (eds), *Irish Society: Sociological Perspectives*, Dublin: Institute of Public Administration, pp. 205–34.

—— and FitzGerald, J. (1997) *Welfare Implications of Demographic Trends*, Dublin: Oaktree Press.

Farrell, F. and Watt, P. (ed.) (2001) *Responding to Racism in Ireland*, Dublin: Veritas.

Featherstone, M. and Lash, S. (1995) 'Globalization, modernity and the spatialization of social theory: an introduction', in M. Featherstone, S. Lash and R. Robertson (eds), *Global Modernities*, London: Sage, pp. 1–24.

Felski, R. (1995) *The Gender of Modernity*, Cambridge, MA: Harvard University Press.

—— (2000) *Doing Time: Feminist Theory and Postmodern Culture*, New York: New York University Press.

Fielding, S. (1993) *Class and Ethnicity: Irish Catholics in England, 1880–1939*, Milton Keynes: Open University Press.

Fitzgerald, G. and Gillespie, P. (1996) 'Ireland's British question', *Prospect Magazine*, (October), pp. 14–19.

Fitzpatrick, D. (1980) 'Irish emigration in the later nineteenth century', *Irish Historical Studies*, XXII (86), pp. 126–43.

—— (1986) '"A share of the honeycomb": education, emigration and Irishwomen', *Continuity and Change*, 1, pp. 217–34.

—— (1987) 'The modernization of the Irish female', in P. Ferguson, K. Whelan and P. O'Flanagan (eds), *Rural Ireland 1600–1900: Modernisation and Change*, Cork: Cork University Press, pp. 167–9.

—— (1989) 'A curious middle place: the Irish in Britain, 1871–1921', in R. Swift and S. Gilley (eds), *The Irish in Britain 1815–1939*, Savage, MD: Barnes & Noble Books, pp. 10–59.

—— (1994) *Oceans of Consolation: Personal Accounts of Irish Migration to Australia*, Ithaca, NY: Cornell University Press.

—— (1997) 'Ireland the empire, 1810–1921', *The Scattering: Ireland and the Irish Diaspora: A Comparative Perspective* Conference, Irish Centre for Migration Studies, National University of Ireland, Cork, 27–30 September.

Fortier, A. M. (1999) 'Re-membering places and the performance of belonging(s)', *Theory, Culture and Society*, 16 (2), pp. 41–64.

—— (2000) *Migrant Belongings: Memory, Space, Identity*, Oxford: Berg.

Foster, R. F. (1988) *Modern Ireland 1600–1972*, London: Penguin Books.

Foucault, M. (1972) *The Archaeology of Knowledge* (trans. A. M. Sheridan Smith), London: Tavistock.

—— (1976) *The History of Sexuality: An Introduction, Vol. 1*, London: Penguin.

—— (1979) 'Governmentality', *I and C*, 6, pp. 5–21.

—— (1980) 'Two lectures', in C. Gordon (ed.), *Power/Knowledge: Selected Interviews and Other Writings 1972–1977*, Brighton: Harvester.

—— (1982) 'The subject of power', afterword to H. L. Dreyfus and Paul Rabinow, *Michel Foucault: Beyond Structuralism and Hermeneutics*, Brighton: Harvester.

—— (1985) *The Use of Pleasure: The History of Sexuality, Vol. 2*, London: Penguin.

—— (1990) *The Care of the Self: The History of Sexuality, Vol. 3*, London: Penguin.

Frankenberg, R. (1993) *The Social Construction of Whiteness: White Women, Race Matters*, London: Routledge.

—— (1997) 'Local whiteness, localizing whiteness', in R. Frankenberg (ed.), *Displacing Whiteness: Essays in Social and Cultural Criticism*, Durham, NC: Duke University Press, pp. 1–34.

Franklin, S. (2000) 'Global nature and the genetic imaginary' in S. Franklin, C. Lury and J. Stacey (eds), *Global Culture, Global Nature*, London: Sage, pp. 188–27.

——, Lury, C. and Stacey, J. (2000) 'Units of Genealogy', in S. Franklin, C. Lury and J. Stacey (eds), *Global Culture, Global Nature*, London: Sage, pp. 68–93.

Fraser, M. (1999a) 'Classing queer. Politics in competition', *Theory, Culture and Society*, 16 (2), pp. 107–31.

—— (1999b) *Identity without Selfhood: Simone de Beauvoir and Bisexuality*, Cambridge: Cambridge University Press.

Fraser, N. (2000) 'Rethinking recognition', *New Left Review*, 3 (May/June), pp. 107–20.

Friedman, J. (1994) *Cultural Identity and Global Process*, London: Sage.

Frye, M. (1992) *Wilful Virgin: Essays in Feminist Theory*, Freedom, CA: Crossing Press.

Gabriel, J. (1998) *Whitewash, Racialized Politics and the Media*, London: Routledge.

Galligan, Y. (1997) 'The changing role of women', in W. Crotty and D. E. Schmitt (eds), *Ireland and the Politics of Change*, London: Longman, pp. 107–21.

Garrett, M. (2000) 'The abnormal flight: the migration and repatriation of Irish unmarried mothers', *Social History*, 25 (3), pp. 330–43.

Garrigan, O. M. (1949) 'So you are going to England', *Cristus Rex*, 111 (2), pp. 49–57.

Garvin, T. (1998) 'Patriots and republicans: an Irish evolution', in W. Crotty and D. E. Schmitt (eds), *Ireland and the Politics of Change*, London: Longman, pp. 144–55.

—— (2000) 'A quiet revolution: the remaking of Irish political culture', in R. Ryan (ed.), *Writing in the Irish Republic: Literature, Culture, Politics 1949–1999*, Basingstoke: Macmillan, pp. 187–203.

Gaul, L. (2000) 'Traditional music and the "master" performers from the Traveller community', in E. Sheehan (ed.), *Travellers: Citizens of Ireland*, Dublin: The Parish of the Travelling People, pp. 65–70.

Gibbons, L. (1996) *Transformations in Irish Culture*, Cork: Cork University Press in association with Field Day.

Giddens, A. (1991) *Modernity and Self-Identity: Self and Society in the Late Modern Age*, Cambridge: Polity Press.

—— (1998) *The Third Way: The Renewal of Social Democracy*, Cambridge: Polity Press.

Gillespie, P. (1997) 'As Irish as it is possible to be in the circumstances: aspects of contemporary Irish political identity construction', paper presented at *The Scattering. Ireland and the Irish Diaspora: A Comparative Perspective* Conference, Irish Centre for Migration Studies, National University of Ireland, Cork, 27–30 September.

—— (2000) 'Diaspora: a resource to the Celtic tiger', *Irish Times*, 22 January.

Gilley, S. (1984) 'The Roman Catholic Church and the nineteenth-century Irish diaspora', *Journal of Ecclesiastical History*, 35 (2), pp. 188–207.

Gilroy, P. (1990/1991) 'It ain't where you're from, it's where you're at . . .: the dialectics of diasporic identification', *Third Text*, 13 (Winter), pp. 3–16.

—— (1993a) *The Black Atlantic: Modernity and Double Consciousness*, London: Verso.

—— (1993b) 'It's a family affair: black culture and the trope of kinship', in P. Gilroy (ed.), *Small Acts: Thoughts on the Politics of Black Cultures*, London: Serpent's Tail, pp. 192–207.

—— (2000) *Between Camps: Race, Identity and Nationalism at the End of the Colour Line*, London: Allen Lane Penguin.

Giroux, H. (1997) 'White squall: resistance and the pedagogy of whiteness', *Cultural Studies*, 11 (3), pp. 376–89.

Glynn, S. (1981) 'Irish immigration to Britain, 1911–1951: patterns and policy', *Irish Economic and Social History*, 8, pp. 50–69.

Gmelch, S. (1975) *Tinkers and Travellers*, Dublin: O'Brien Press.

—— (1986) *Nan. The Life of an Irish Travelling Woman*, London: Souvenir.

Goldthorpe, J. H. and Whelan, C. T. (eds) (1992) *The Development of Industrial Society in Ireland*, Oxford: Oxford University Press.

Gray, B. (2000) 'From "ethnicity" to "diaspora": 1980s emigration and "multicultural" London', in A. Bielenberg (ed.), *The Irish Diaspora*, Harlow, Essex: Longman, pp. 65–88.

—— (2002) '"Whitely Scripts": Irish women's racialised belongings in London', *European Journal of Cultural Studies*, 5 (3), pp. 257–74.

—— (2003a) 'The Irish diaspora – globalised belongings', *Irish Journal of Sociology*, 11 (2) pp. 123–44.

—— (2003b) 'Global modernity and the gendered epic of the Irish empire' in S. Ahmed, C. Castaneda, A.-M. Fortier and M. Sheller (eds), *Uprootings/Regroundings*, London: Berg.

Greeley, A. M. and Ward, C. (2000) 'How "secularised" is the Ireland we live in?', *Doctrine and Life*, 50 (10), pp. 581–618.

Grewal, I. (1994) 'Autobiographic subjects, diasporic locations', in I. Grewal and C. Kaplan (eds), *Scattered Hegemonies: Postmodernity and Transnational Feminist Practices*, Minneapolis, MN: University of Minnesota Press, pp. 231–54.

—— (1996) *Home and Harem: Nation, Gender, Empire and the Cultures of Travel*, London: Leicester University Press.

—— and Kaplan, C. (1994) 'Introduction: transnational feminist practices and questions of postmodernity', in I. Grewal and C. Kaplan (eds), *Scattered Hegemonies: Postmodernity and Transnational Feminist Practices*, Minneapolis, MN: University of Minnesota Press, pp. 1–33.

Grossberg, L. (1989) 'On the road with three ethnographers', *Journal of Communication Inquiry*, 13 (2), pp. 23–6.

Guinnane, T. (1997) *The Vanishing Irish: Households, Migration, and the Rural Economy of Ireland 1850–1914*, Princeton, NJ: Princeton University Press.

Hall, S. (1990) 'Cultural identity and diaspora', in J. Rutherford (ed.), *Identity: Community, Culture, Difference*, London: Lawrence & Wishart, pp. 222–37.

—— (1991) 'Old and new identities, old and new ethnicities', in Anthony King (ed.), *Culture, Globalization and the World System: Contemporary Conditions for the Representation of Identity*, Basingstoke: Macmillan, pp. 41–68.

—— (1996) 'Who needs "identity"?', in S. Hall and P. du Gay (eds), *Questions of Cultural Identity*, London: Sage Publications, pp. 1–17.

Handlin, O. (1979) *The Uprooted* (second edition), Boston, MA: Little, Brown and Company.

Hanlon, G. (1991) 'The emigration of Irish accountants: economic restructuring and producer services in the periphery', *Irish Journal of Sociology*, 1 (1), pp. 52–65.

Hannon, D. (1979) *Displacement and Development: Class, Kinship and Social Change in Irish Rural Communities*, Dublin: Economic and Social Research Institute.

—— and Katsiaouni, L. (1977) *Traditional Families? From Culturally Prescribed to Negotiated Roles in Farm Families*, Dublin: Economic and Social Research Institute.

Hapaska, S. (1999) 'Shooting the breeze', interview by Suzanne Cotter in P. Murray (ed.), *0044 Irish Artists in Britain*, Cork: Crawford Municipal Art Gallery, pp. 72–9.

Haraway, D. J. (1997) *Modest_Witness@Second_Millennium. FemaleMan_Meets_ OncoMouse. Feminism and Technoscience*, New York: Routledge.

Harding, S. (1991) *Whose Science, Whose Knowledge?: Thinking from Women's Lives*, New York: Cornell University Press.

Harney, M. (2000) 'Biotechnology to become major sector for worldwide growth and innovation', speech to National Agri-Food Biotechnology Conference, UCD, 1 June.

Harris, R. A. (1994) *The Nearest Place that Wasn't Ireland: Early Nineteenth Century Labour Migration*, Iowa, IA: Iowa State University Press.

Hawes, D. and Perez, B. (1995) *The Gypsy and the State: The Ethnic Cleansing of British Society*, Bristol: Bristol University, School of Advanced Urban Studies.

Heckler, M. (1989) 'Take a risk for success', in J. Mulholland and D. Keogh (eds), *Emigration, Employment and Enterprise*, Cork: Hibernian University Press, pp. 157–69.

Heelas, P. (1996) 'Introduction: detraditionalization and its rivals', in P. Heelas, S. Lash and P. Morris (eds), *Detraditionalization*, Cambridge, MA: Blackwell.

Helleiner, J. (1995) 'Gypsies, Celts and tinkers: colonial antecedents of anti-Traveller racism in Ireland', *Ethnic and Racial Studies*, 18 (3), pp. 532–54.

—— (1997) '"Women of the itinerant class": gender and anti-Traveller racism in Ireland', *Women's Studies International Forum*, 20 (2), pp. 275–87.

—— (2000) *Irish Travellers: Racism and the Politics of Culture*, Toronto: University of Toronto Press.

Hemmens, B. (1996) Letter, *Irish Times*, 17 October.

Henderson, M. G. (1992) 'Speaking in tongues: dialogics, dialectics and the black woman writer's literary tradition', in J. Butler and J. W. Scott (eds), *Feminists Theorise the Political*, New York: Routledge, pp. 144–66.

Herr, C. (1990) 'The erotics of Irishness', *Critical Inquiry*, 17 (Autumn), pp. 1–34.

Hickman, M. J. (1995) 'The Irish in Britain: racism, incorporation and identity', *Irish Studies Review*, 10 (Spring), pp. 16–20.

—— (1998) 'Reconstructing deconstructing "race": British political discourses about the Irish in Britain', *Ethnic and Racial Studies*, 21 (2), pp. 288–307.

—— (1999) 'Alternative historiographies of the Irish in Britain: a critique of the segregation/assimilation model', in R. Swift and S. Gilley (eds), *The Irish in Victorian Britain: The Local Dimension*, Dublin: The Four Courts Press, pp. 236–353.

—— and Walter, B. (1997) *Discrimination and the Irish Community in Britain (CRE Report)*, London: Commission For Racial Equality.

Hill, M. (1997) 'Can whiteness speak? Institutional anomies, ontological disasters, and three Hollywood films', in M. Wray and A. Newitz (eds), *White Trash: Race and Class in America*, New York: Routledge, pp. 155–73.

Hillyard, P. (1993) *Suspect Community: People's Experiences of the Prevention of Terrorism Acts in Britain*, London: Pluto Press/Liberty.

Holland, K. (2001) 'Campaign on attitudes to Travellers fails to make impression', *Irish Times*, 17 July, p. 5.

Holland, M. (1988) 'The New Wave Irish in the Bronx', *Observer Magazine*, 30 October, pp. 34–40.

Holohan, A. (1995) *Working Lives: The Irish in Britain*, Hayes, Middlesex: The Irish Post.

hooks, b. (1992) 'Representing whiteness in the black imagination', in C. Nelson, P. A. Treichler and L. Grossberg (eds), *Cultural Studies*, New York: Routledge, pp. 338–46.

Hornsby-Smith, M. P. and Dale, A. (1988) 'The assimilation of Irish immigrants in England', *The British Journal of Sociology*, XXXIX (4), pp. 519–44.

Howard, K. (2002) 'The Irish state, citizenship and the ethnic diaspora', *Recycling the State Conference*, University College Dublin, 20 April.

Howe, S. (2000) *Ireland and Empire: Colonial Legacies in Irish History and Culture*, Oxford: Oxford University Press.

Howes, M. (2002) 'Public discourse, private reflection, 1916–70' in Bourke, A., Kilfeather, S., Luddy, M., MacCurtain, M., Meaney, G., Dhonnchadna, N., O'Dowd, M. and Wills, C. (eds), *The Field Day Anthology of Irish Writing, Vol. IV: Irish Women's Writing and Traditions*, Cork: Cork University Press in association with Field Day, pp. 923–30.

Hughes, E. (1992) 'Art, exiles, Ireland and icons', *Fortnight Supplement – Voyages of Discovery*, 295, pp. 9–11.

Humphreys, A. J. (1966) *The New Dubliners: Urbanisation and the Irish Family*, London: Routledge & Kegan Paul.

Ignatieff, M. (1985) 'Is nothing sacred? The ethics of television', *Daedelus*, 114 (4), pp. 57–78.

Ignatiev, N. (1995) *How the Irish Became White*, New York: Routledge.

Inglis, T. (1997) 'Foucault, Bourdieu and the field of Irish sexuality', *Irish Journal of Sociology*, 7, pp. 5–28.

—— (1998a) *Moral Monopoly: The Rise and Fall of the Catholic Church in Modern Ireland*, Dublin: University College Dublin Press.

—— (1998b) 'A religious frenzy', in M. Peillon and E. Slater (eds), *Encounters with Modern Ireland*, Dublin: Institute of Public Administration, pp. 73–80.

—— (2002) 'Sexual transgression and scapegoats: a case study from modern Ireland', *Sexualities*, 5 (1), pp. 5–24.

Jackson, J. A. (1963) *The Irish in Britain*, London: Routledge & Kegan Paul.

Jacobson, M. F. (1995) *Special Sorrows: The Diasporic Imagination of Irish, Polish, and Jewish Immigrants in the United States*, Cambridge, MA: Harvard University Press.

—— (1998) *Whiteness of a Different Color: European Immigrants and the Alchemy of Race*, London: Harvard University Press.

Jameson-Till, J. (2003) 'Roma women in Ireland: breaking down barriers or creating new ones?', *Women's Movement: Migrant Women Transforming Ireland Conference*, Trinity College, Dublin, 20–1 March.

Jewesbury, D. (1998) 'Race isn't an Irish issue', *Circa*, 83, pp. 23–7.

Jordon, J. (1996) 'A new politics of sexuality', in S. Rose and C. Stevens (eds), *Bisexual Horizons: Politics, Histories, Lives*, London: Lawrence & Wishart, pp. 10–19.

Joseph, M. (1999) *Nomadic Identities: The Performance of Citizenship*, Minneapolis, MN: University of Minnesota Press.

Joyce, N. and Farmer, A. (2000 [1985]) *My Life on the Road*, Dublin: Gill & Macmillan.

Kane, K. (2001) '"Will come forth in tongues and fury": relocating Irish cultural studies', *Cultural Studies*, 15 (1), pp. 98–123.

Kaplan, C. (1996) *Questions of Travel: Postmodern Discourses of Displacements*, Durham, NC, and London: Duke University Press.

—— and Grewal, I. (2002) 'Transnational practices and interdisciplinary feminist scholarship: refiguring women's and gender studies', in R. Wiegman (ed.), *Women's Studies on its Own*, Durham, NC: Duke University Press, pp. 66–81.

Kaplan, E.A. (1992) *Motherhood and Representation: The Mother in Popular Culture and Melodrama*, London: Routledge.

—— (1997) *Looking for the Other: Feminism, Film and the Imperial Gaze*, New York and London: Routledge.

Kaufmann, E. (2000) 'Liberal ethnicity: beyond liberal nationalism and minority rights', *Ethnic and Racial Studies*, 23 (6), pp. 1086–119.

Kearney, R. (ed.) (1988a) *Across the Frontiers: Ireland in the 1990s*, Dublin: Wolfhound Press.

—— (1988b) 'Migrant minds', in R. Kearney (ed.), *Across the Frontiers: Ireland in the 1990s*, Dublin: Wolfhound Press, pp. 185–204.

—— (ed.) (1990) *Migrations: The Irish at Home and Abroad*, Dublin: Wolfhound Press.

—— (1997) *Postnationalist Ireland: Politics, Culture, Philosophy*, London: Routledge.

Kee, R. (1983/1972) *Volume One of the Green Flag – The Most Distressful Country*, London: Quartet Books.

Kelleher, M. (1997) *The Feminization of Famine: Expressions of the Inexpressible?*, Cork: Cork University Press.

Kells, M. (ed.) (1995a) *Ethnic Identity Amongst Young Irish Middle Class Migrants in Landscape London*, London: University of North London Press.

Kelly, K. and Nic Giolla Choille, T. (1995) 'Listening and learning: experiences in an emigrant advice agency', in P. O'Sullivan (ed.), *Irish Women and Irish Migration*, Leicester: Leicester University Press, pp. 168–91.

Kennedy, F. (2001) *Cottage to Crèche: Family Change in Ireland*, Dublin: Institute of Public Administration.

Kennedy, K. (1986) *Ireland in Transition*, Dublin: The Mercier Press.

Kennedy, R. E. J. (1973) *The Irish: Emigration, Marriage and Fertility*, Berkeley, CA: University of California Press.

Kenny, M. (1997) 'Who are they? Who are we? Education and travellers', in E. Crowley and J. Mac Laughlin (eds), *Under the Belly of the Tiger: Class, Race, Identity and Culture in the Global Ireland*, Dublin: Irish Reporter Publications, pp. 53–60.

Keohane, K. (1997) 'Traditionalism and homelessness in contemporary Irish music', in J. Mac Laughlin (ed.), *Location and Dislocation in Contemporary Irish Society: Emigration and Irish Identities*, Cork: Cork University Press, pp. 274–304.

King, R. (1995) 'Migrations, globalization and place', in D. Massey and P. Jess (eds), *A Place in the World? Places, Cultures and Globalization*, Milton Keynes: Open University Press, pp. 6–32.

—— and O'Connor, H. (1996) 'Migration and gender: Irish women in Leicester', *Geography*, 81, pp. 311–25.

—— and Shuttleworth, I. (1995) 'The emigration and employment of Irish graduates: the export of high-quality labour from the periphery of Europe', *European Urban and Regional Studies*, 2 (1), pp. 21–40.

Kirby, P. (2002) *The Celtic Tiger in Distress: Growth with Inequality in Ireland*, Basingstoke: Palgrave.

Kirwan, F. X. and Nairn, A. (1983) 'Migrant employment and the recession: the case of the Irish in Britain', *International Migration Review*, 17 (4), pp. 672–81.

—— (1995b) 'Ethnicity in the 1990s: contemporary Irish migrants in London', in U. Kockel (ed.), *Heritage and Identity: Case Studies in Irish Ethnography*, Liverpool: Liverpool University Press, pp. 223–36.

Kristeva, J. (1982) *Powers of Horror: An Essay on Abjection*, New York: Columbia University Press.

Kymlica, W. (1995) *Multicultural Citizenship: A Liberal Theory of Minority Rights*, Oxford: Oxford University Press.

Laffan, B. and O'Donnell, R. (1998) 'Ireland and the growth of international governance', in W. Crotty and D. E. Schmitt (eds), *Ireland and the Politics of Change*, London: Longman, pp. 156–77.

Lambert, S. (2001) *Irish Women in Lancashire 1922–1960: Their Story*, Lancaster: Centre for North-West Regional Studies.

Larner, W. (1998) 'Hitching a ride on the tiger's back: globalisation and spatial imaginaries in New Zealand', *Environment and Planning D: Society and Space*, 16 (5), pp. 599–614.

Lawler, S. (2000) *Mothering the Self: Mothers, Daughters, Subjects*, London: Routledge.

Lee, J. J. (1985) 'Centralisation and community', in J. J. Lee (ed.), *Ireland: Towards a Sense of Place*, Cork: Cork University Press, pp. 84–101.

—— (1989a) *Ireland 1912–1985: Politics and Society*, Cambridge: Cambridge University Press.

—— (1989b) *The Modernisation of Irish Society 1848–1918*, Dublin: Gill & Macmillan.

—— (1990) 'Emigration: a contemporary perspective', in R. Kearney (ed.), *Migrations: The Irish at Home and Abroad*, Dublin: Wolfhound, pp. 33–44.

—— (1993) 'Dynamics of social and political change in the Irish Republic', in D. Keogh and M. H. Haltzel (eds), *Northern Ireland and the Politics of Reconciliation*, New York: Woodrow Wilson Center Press and Cambridge University Press, pp. 117–40.

—— (2000) 'Millennial reflections on Irish American history (Ernie O'Malley Lecture Series No. 1)', *Radharc*, 1, pp. 5–75.

Lee, R. (2002) 'Notes from the (non) field: teaching and theorizing women of color', in R. Wiegman (ed.), *Women's Studies on its Own*, Durham, NC: Duke University, pp. 82–105.

Lees, L. H. (1979) *Exiles of Erin: Irish Migrants in Victorian London*, Manchester: Manchester University Press.

Lennon, M., McAdam, M. and O'Brien, J. (1988) *Across the Water: Irish Women's Lives in Britain*, London: Virago.

Lentin, R. (1999) 'Constitutionally excluded: citizenship and (some) Irish women', in P. Werbner and N. Yuval-Davis (eds), *Women, Citizenship and Difference*, London: Zed Books, pp. 130–44.

Levine, J. (2002) 'The women's movement in the Republic of Ireland, 1968–80', *Field Day Anthology*, Cork: Cork University Press, pp. 177–87.

Levitt, P. (2001) *The Transnational Villagers*, Berkeley, CA: University of California Press.

Litton, F. (ed.) (1982) *Unequal Achievement: The Irish Experience 1957–1982*, Dublin: Institute of Public Administration.

Lloyd, D. (1994) 'Making sense of the dispersal', *Irish Reporter*, 13 (First Quarter), pp. 3–4.

—— (1999) *Ireland After History*, Cork: Cork University Press.

London Irish Women's Centre (1987) *Annual Report*, London: London Irish Women's Centre.

—— (1993) *Roots and Realities: A Profile of Irish Women in London 1993*, London: The London Irish Women's Centre.

—— (1995) *Annual Report*, London: London Irish Women's Centre.

—— (1997) *Annual Report*, London: London Irish Women's Centre.

Lowe, L. (1996) *Immigrant Acts. On Asian American Cultural Politics*, Durham, NC, and London: Duke University Press.

—— and Lloyd, D. (1997) 'Introduction', in Lisa Lowe and David Lloyd (eds), *The Politics of Culture in the Shadow of Capital*, Durham, NC: Duke University Press, pp. 1–32.

Lyons, F. S. L. (1963) *Ireland Since the Famine*, London: Fontana.

Luibheid, E. (1997) 'The nod and the wink, white solidarity within Irish immigrants in the USA', in E. Crowley and J. Mac Laughlin (eds), *Under the Belly of the Tiger: Class, Race, Identity and Culture in the Global Ireland*, Dublin: Irish Reporter Publications, pp. 79–88.

—— (1999) 'Queer circuits: the construction of lesbian and gay identities through emigration', in R. Lentin (ed.), *Emerging Irish Identities*, Trinity College, Dublin: Ethnic and Racial Studies, Trinity College, Dublin, pp. 54–64.

—— (2000) 'The pink tide: narrating Ireland's lesbian and gay migrations', *Journal of Commonwealth and Postcolonial Studies*, 7 (1), pp. 149–68.

Lury, C. (1995) 'The rights and wrongs of culture: issues of theory and methodology', in B. Skeggs (ed.), *Feminist Cultural Theory: Process and Production*, Manchester: Manchester University Press, pp. 33–45.

—— (1998) *Prosthetic Culture: Photography, Memory and Identity*, London: Routledge.

McAleese, M. (1999) 'Address to joint houses of the Oireachtas', Dublin, 16 December.

—— (2000a) 'Fourth millennium lecture on the marginalised child', address for the Lillie Road Centre Group, Jury's Hotel, Dublin, 28 February.

—— (2000b) 'Hopes for the new millennium', address in St Patrick's Cathedral, Dublin, 11 June.

—— (2001a) 'Remarks at the official opening of an emigrant holiday weekend', Castlebar, Co. Mayo, 18 September.

—— (2001b) 'Remarks at the Irish World Heritage Centre', Manchester, England, 22 February.

—— (2001c) 'Remarks at the Centre for Migration Studies', Ulster American Folk Park, Omagh, 6 December.

McCarthy, A. (2000) '"In prospect of a happier future". Private letters and Irish women's migration to New Zealand, 1840–1925', in L. Fraser (ed.), *A Distant Shore: Irish Migration and New Zealand Settlement*, Dunedin: University of Otago Press, pp. 105–16.

McCarthy, C. (2000) *Modernisation, Crisis and Culture in Ireland, 1969–1992*, Dublin: Four Courts.

McCarthy, P. (1994) 'The sub-culture of poverty reconsidered', in M. McCann, S. O'Síocháin and J. Ruane (eds), *Irish Travellers: Culture and Ethnicity*, Belfast: Institute of Irish Studies, pp. 121–29.

McClintock, A. (1993) 'Family feuds: gender, nationalism and the family', *Feminist Review*, 44, pp. 61–80.

—— (1995) *Imperial Leather: Race, Gender and Sexuality in the Colonial Context*, London: Routledge.

McCullagh, C. (1991) 'A tie that binds: family and ideology in Ireland', *The Economic and Social Review*, 22 (3), pp. 199–211.

McDonagh, M. (2000) 'Nomadism', in Erica Sheehan (ed.), *Travellers, Citizens of Ireland*, Dublin: The Parish of the Travelling People, pp. 33–46.

McDonald, W. (2000) 'Time-warp danger if Travellers do not get chance to develop', *Irish Times* (2 March), p. 7.

McDowell, M. (1989) 'Economic participation – the real index of social justice', in J. Mulholland and D. Keogh (eds), *Emigration, Employment and Enterprise*, Cork: Hibernian University Press, pp. 124–28.

Mac Éinrí, P. (1989) 'The new Europeans: the Irish in Paris today', in J. Mulholland and D. Keogh (eds), *Emigration, Employment and Enterprise*, Cork: Hibernian University Press, pp. 58–80.

—— (2001) 'Immigration policy in Ireland', in F. Farrell and P. Watt (eds), *Responding to Racism in Ireland*, Dublin: Veritas Publications, pp. 46–87.

MacKinnon, C. (1989) *Toward a Feminist Theory of the State*, Cambridge, MA: Harvard University Press.

Mac Laughlin, J. (1994a) *Ireland: The Emigrant Nursery and the World Economy*, Cork: Cork University Press.

—— (1994b) 'Emigration and the peripheralization of Ireland in the global economy', *Review*, XVII (2), pp. 243–73.

—— (1995) *Travellers and Ireland: Whose Country, Whose History?*, Cork: Cork University Press.

—— (1996) 'The evolution of anti-Traveller racism in Ireland', *Race and Class*, 37 (3), pp. 47–63.

—— (1997) 'The new vanishing Irish. Social characteristics of "new wave" Irish emigration', in J. Mac Laughlin (ed.), *Location and Dislocation in Contemporary Irish Society: Emigration and Irish Identities*, Cork: Cork University Press, pp. 133–57.

—— (1999) 'Nation-building, social closure and anti-Traveller racism in Ireland', *Sociology*, 33 (1), pp. 129–51.

McLoughlin, D. (1994) 'Ethnicity and Irish travellers: reflections on Ni Shuinear', in M. McCann, S. O'Síocháin and J. Ruane (eds), *Irish Travellers: Culture and Ethnicity*, Belfast: Institute of Irish Studies, pp. 78–94.

McNay, L. (1999) 'Gender, habitus and the field: Pierre Bourdieu and the limits of reflexivity', *Theory, Culture and Society*, 16 (1), pp. 95–117.

MacRaild, D. (1998) *Culture, Conflict and Migration: The Irish in Victorian Cumbria*, Liverpool: Liverpool University Press.

McVeigh, R. (1992) 'The specificity of Irish racism', *Race and Class*, 33 (4), pp. 31–45.

—— (1997) 'Theorising sedentarism: the roots of anti-nomadism', in T. Acton (ed.), *Gypsy Politics and Traveller Identity*, Hatfield: University of Hertfordshire Press, pp. 7–25.

—— (1998) 'Irish Travellers and the logic of genocide', in M. Peillon and E. Slater (eds), *Encounters with Modern Ireland*, Dublin: Institute of Public Administration, pp. 155–64.

Maguire, A. (1997) 'Personal story', in B. Cant (ed.), *Invented Identities? Lesbians and Gays talk about Migration*, London: Cassell, pp. 163–75.

Mahon, E. (1995) 'From democracy to femocracy: the women's movement in the Republic of Ireland', in P. Clancy, S. Drudy, K. Lynch, and L. O'Dowd (eds), *Irish Society: Sociological Perspectives*, Dublin: Institute of Public Administration, in association with the Sociological Association of Ireland, pp. 675–708.

Malkki, L. (1992) 'National geographic: the rooting of peoples and the territorialization of national identity among scholars and refugees', *Cultural Anthropology*, 7 (1), pp. 24–44.

Marshall, B. (1994) *Engendering Modernity: Feminism, Social Theory and Social Change*, Cambridge: Polity Press.

Martin, A. K. (2000) 'Death of a nation. Transnationalism, bodies and abortion in late twentieth-century Ireland', in T. Mayer (ed.), *Gender Ironies of Nationalism: Sexing the Nation*, London: Routledge, pp. 65–88.

Mason, J. (1996) *Qualitative Researching*, London: Sage.

Massey, D. (1994) *Space, Place and Gender*, Cambridge: Polity Press.

—— (1995) 'Making spaces: or, geography, is political too', *Soundings*, 1 (Autumn), pp. 193–208.

Meaney, G. (1998) 'Landscapes of desire: women and Ireland on film', *Women: A Cultural Review*, 9 (3), pp. 237–51.

Meehan, E. (2000) *Free Movement between Ireland and the UK: from the 'common Travel Area' to The Common Travel Area*, Dublin: The Policy Institute.

Mercer, K. (1994) *Welcome to the Jungle: New Positions in Black Cultural Studies*, London: Routledge.

Messenger, J. C. (1969) *Inis Beag: Isle of Ireland*, Rome: Italiana Technico-Economica de Cementis.

Miller, K. A. (1985) *Emigrants and Exiles: Ireland and the Irish Exodus to North America*, Oxford: Oxford University Press.

—— (1990) 'Emigration, capitalism, and ideology in post-famine Ireland', in R. Kearney (ed.), *Migrations: The Irish at Home and Abroad*, Dublin: Wolfhound, pp. 91–108.

—— (1993) 'Paddy's paradox: emigration to America in Irish imagination and rhetoric', in D. Hoerder and H. Rossler (eds), *Distant Magnets: Expectations and Realities in the Immigrant Experience, 1840–1930*, New York: Holmes & Meier, pp. 264–93.

Miller, K. A. with Doyle, D. N. and Kelleher, P. (1995) ' "For love and liberty": Irish women, migration and domesticity in Ireland and America, 1815–1920', in P. O'Sullivan (ed.), *Irish Women and Irish Migration*, Leicester: Leicester University Press, pp. 41–65.

Mitchell, K. (2001) 'Transnationalism, neo-liberalism, and the rise of the shadow state', *Economy and Society*, 30 (2), pp. 165–89.

Mohanty, C. T. (1988) 'Under Western eyes: feminist scholarship and colonial discourses', *Feminist Review*, (30), pp. 61–88.

—— (1997) 'Women workers and capitalist scripts: ideologies of domination, common interests, and the politics of solidarity', in M. J. Alexander and C. T. Mohanty (eds), *Feminist Genealogies, Colonial Legacies, Democratic Futures*, New York: Routledge, pp. 3–29.

Moore, J. (1994) 'One person, one vote', *Fortnight*, 330 (July/August), pp. 24–5.

Morley, D. (2000) *Home Territories: Media, Mobility and Identity*, London: Routledge.

Morrison, T. (1992) *Playing in the Dark – Whiteness and the Literary Imagination*, London: Picador.

Moser, P. (1993) 'Rural economy and female emigration in the west of Ireland, 1936–1956', *UCG Women's Studies Centre Review*, 1, pp. 41–51.

Murphy, A. (1999) *But the Irish Sea Betwixt Us: Ireland, Colonialism, and Renaissance Literature*, Kentucky: University of Kentucky Press.

Murphy, M. and Singer, A. (2002) 'New York state's "great Irish famine curriculum": a report', *Éire-Ireland*, XXXVII (II), pp. 109–29.

Narayan, U. (2000) 'Essence of culture and a sense of history: a feminist critique of cultural essentialism', in U. Narayan and S. Harding (eds), *Decentering the Center: Philosophy for a Multicultural, Postcolonial, and Feminist World*, Bloomington, IN: Indiana University Press, pp. 80–100.

—— and Harding, S. (2000) 'Introduction', in U. Narayan and S. Harding (eds), *Decentering the Center: Philosophy for a Multicultural, Postcolonial, and Feminist World*, Bloomington, IN: Indiana University Press, pp. 1–25.

Nash, C. (1993a) ' "Embodying the nation" – the west of Ireland landscape and Irish identity', in B. O'Connor and M. Cronin (eds), *Tourism in Ireland: A Critical Analysis*, Cork: Cork University Press, pp. 86–112.

—— (1993b) 'Remapping and renaming: new cartographies of identity, gender and landscape in Ireland', *Feminist Review*, (44), pp. 39–57.

—— (1997a) 'Looking commonplace: gender, modernity and national identity', *Renaissance and Modern Studies*, pp. 61–77.

—— (1997b) 'Embodied Irishness: gender, sexuality and Irish identities', in B. Graham (ed.), *In Search of Ireland: A Cultural Geography*, London: Routledge, pp. 108–27.

—— (2002) 'Genealogical identities', *Environment and Planning D: Society and Space*, 20 (1), pp. 27–52.

National Economic and Social Forum (1997) *A Framework for Partnership – Enriching Strategic Consensus Through Participation (Forum Report No. 16)*, Dublin: NESF.

National, Economic and Social Research Council (1991) *The Economic and Social Implications of Emigration*, Dublin: NESRC.

Negra, D. (2001) *Off-White Hollywood: American Culture and Ethnic Female Stardom*, London: Routledge.

Neville, G. (1995) 'Dark lady of the archives: towards an analysis of women and emigration to North America in Irish folklore', in M. O'Dowd and S. Wichert (eds), *Chattel, Servant or Citizen: Women's Status in Church, State and Society*, Belfast: The Institute of Irish Studies, pp. 200–14.

—— (1997) 'Land of the fair, land of the free? The myth of America in Irish folklore', in A. Coulson (ed.), *Exiles and Migrants: Crossing Thresholds in European Culture and Society*, Brighton: Sussex Academic Press, pp. 57–71.

Nic Giolla Choille, T. (1989) 'Emigration is no accident', in J. Mulholland and D. Keogh (eds), *Emigration, Employment and Enterprise*, Cork: Hibernian University Press, pp. 52–7.

Ni Shuinear, S. (1994) 'Irish travellers, ethnicity and the origins question', in M. McCann, S. O'Síocháin and J. Ruane (eds), *Irish Travellers: Culture and Ethnicity*, Belfast: Institute of Irish Studies, pp. 54–77.

Nolan, J. (1989) *Ourselves Alone: Women's Emigration From Ireland, 1885–1920*, Lexington: Kentucky University Press.

Noonan, P. (1994) 'Policy-making and Travellers in Northern Ireland', in M. McCann, S. O'Síocháin and J. Ruane (eds), *Irish Travellers: Culture and Ethnicity*, Belfast: Institute of Irish Studies, pp. 170–8.

Nussbaum, M. C. (1995) 'Human capabilities, female human beings', in M. C. Nussbaum and J. Glover (eds), *Women, Culture and Development*, Oxford: Clarendon Press, pp. 61–104.

O'Brien, O. and Power, R. (1997) *HIV and a Migrant Community. The Irish in Britain*, London: Action Group for Irish Youth.

O'Carroll, Í. (1990) *Models for Movers: Irish Women's Emigration to America*, Dublin: Attic Press.

—— and Collins, E. (eds) (1995) *Lesbian and Gay Visions of Ireland: Towards the Twenty-first Century*, London: Cassell.

O'Cathain, D. (1989) 'Marketing – not the panacea, but could help the three Es', in J. Mulholland and D. Keogh (eds), *Emigration, Employment and Enterprise*, Cork: Hibernian University Press, pp. 179–86.

O'Connor, J. (1993) 'Introduction', in D. Bolger (ed.), *Ireland in Exile: Irish Writers Abroad*, Dublin: New Island Books, pp. 11–18.

O'Connor, P. (1998) *Emerging Voices: Women in Contemporary Irish Society*, Dublin: Institute of Public Administration.

—— (2000) 'Changing places: privilege and resistance in contemporary Ireland', *Sociological Research Online*, 5 (3). http://www.socreesonline.org.uk/5/3/o'connor. html>

O'Connor, T. (2001) *The Irish in Europe 1580–1815*, Dublin: Four Courts Press.

O'Donnell, R. (1999) 'Reinventing Ireland: from sovereignty to partnership', *Jean Monnet Inaugural Lecture*, University College Dublin, 29 April.

—— (2000) 'The new Ireland in the New Europe', in R. O'Donnell (ed.), *Europe: the Irish Experience*, Dublin: IEA, pp. 161–214.

O'Dowd, L. (1987) 'Church, state and women: the aftermath of partition', in C. Curtin, P. Jackson and B. O'Connor (eds), *Gender in Irish Society*, Galway: Galway University Press, pp. 3–36.

O'Hara, P. (1997) 'Interfering women – farm mothers and the reproduction of family farming', *The Economic and Social Review*, 28 (2), pp. 135–56.

O'Hearn, D. (1998) *Inside the Celtic Tiger: The Irish Economy and the Asian Model*, London: Pluto Press.

—— (2000) 'Peace dividend, foreign investment, and economic regeneration: the Northern Irish case', *Social Problems*, 47 (2), pp. 180–200.

Okely, J. (1994) 'An anthropological perspective on Irish Travellers', in M. McCann, S. O'Síocháin and J. Ruane (eds), *Irish Travellers: Culture and Ethnicity*, Belfast: Institute of Irish Studies, pp. 1–19.

O'Leary, O. and Burke, H. (1998) *Mary Robinson: The Authorised Biography*, London: Hodder & Stoughton.

Olwig, K. F. (2000) 'Place, movement and identity: the cultural construction of livelihoods', paper delivered at the Conference on *Locality, Identity, Diaspora* Institute of Social Anthropology, University of Hamburg, 10–13 February.

O'Malley, M. (1991) 'Emigration of Irish Travellers', in Galway Labour History Group (ed.), *The Emigrant Experience*, Galway: Galway Labour History Group, pp. 102–10.

Ong, A. (1996) 'Anthropology, China and modernities: the geopolitics of cultural knowledge', in H. L. Moore (ed.), *The Future of Anthropological Knowledge*, London: Routledge, pp. 60–1.

O'Reilly, E. (1995) *Masterminds of the Right*, Dublin: Attic Press.

O'Riain, S. (2000) 'The flexible developmental state: globalization, information technology, and the "Celtic tiger"', *Politics and Society*, 28 (2), pp. 157–93.

O'Toole, F. (1994) *Black Hole, Green Card: The Disappearance of Ireland*, Dublin: New Island Books.

—— (1995) 'The President's progress', in *Fortnight*, 344 (November), pp. 17–19

—— (1997) *The Ex-Isle of Erin Images of Global Ireland*, Dublin: New Island Books.

—— (1998) 'Hail to the patron saint of gays and refugees', *Irish Times*, 9.

—— (2000) 'Green, white and black. Race and Irish identity', in R. Lentin (ed.), *Emerging Irish Identities – Proceedings of a Seminar (November 1999)*, Dublin: Department of Sociology, Trinity College Dublin, pp. 17–23.

O'Tuathaigh, M. A. G. (1991) 'The historical pattern of Irish emigration: some labour aspects', in Galway Labour History Group (ed.), *The Emigrant Experience*, Galway: Galway Labour History Group, pp. 9–28.

Owen, D. (1995) *Irish-Born People in Great Britain: Settlement Patterns and Socio-Economic Circumstances*, Coventry: ESRC and CRE.

Palmer, P. (1989) *Domesticity and Dirt*, Philadelphia, PA: Temple University Press.

Parker, A., Russo, M., Sommer, D. and Yaegar, P. (eds) (1992) *Nationalism and Sexualities*, New York: Routledge.

Parker, D. (2000) 'The Chinese takeaway and the diasporic habitus: space, time and power geometries', in B. Hesse (ed.), *Un/settled Multiculturalisms: Diasporas, Entanglements, Transruptions*, London: Zed Books, pp. 73–95.

Pateman, C. (1992) 'Equality, difference, subordination: the politics of motherhood and women's citizenship', in G. Bock and S. James (eds), *Beyond Equality and Difference: Citizenship, Feminist Politics, Female Subjectivity*, London: Routledge, pp. 17–31.

Paul, K. (1997) *Whitewashing Britain: Race and Citizenship in the Postwar Era*, London: Cornell University Press.

Peillon, M. (1982) *Contemporary Irish Society*, Dublin: Gill & Macmillan.

Pettman, J. J. (1996) *Worlding Women: A Feminist International Politics*, New York: Routledge.

Pieterse, J. N. (1995) 'Globalization as hybridization', in M. Featherstone, S. Lash and R. Robertson (eds), *Global Modernities*, London: Sage, pp. 45–68.

Popham, P. (1990) 'The London Irish', *The Independent Magazine*, 11 August (101), pp. 22–8.

Pringle, D. (1990) 'Changing Ireland. The 1990 presidential election', *Irish Geography*, 23 (2), pp. 136–41.

—— (1993) *Sexing the Self: Gendered Positions in Cultural Studies*, New York: Routledge.

Probyn, E. (1996) *Outside Belongings*, New York: Routledge.

Rabinow, P. (1989) *French Modern*, Cambridge, MA: MIT Press.

Raftery, M. and O'Sullivan, E. (1999) *Suffer the Little Children: The Inside Story of Ireland's Industrial Schools*, Dublin: New Island Books.

Rapport, N. and Dawson, A. (1998) 'Opening a debate', in N. Rapport and A. Dawson (eds), *Migrants of Identity: Perceptions of Home in a World of Movement*, Oxford: Berg, pp. 3–20.

Rasmussen, B. B., Klinenberg, E., Nexica, I. J. and Wray, M. (2001) 'Introduction', in B. B. Rasmussen, E. Klinenberg, I. J. Nexica and M. Wray (eds), *The Making and Unmaking of Whiteness*, Durham, NC: Duke University Press, pp. 1–24.

Report of the Task Force on the Travelling Community (1995) Dublin: Government Publications Office.

Reynolds, P. (1995) 'Interview with Anne Holohan', in A. Holohan (ed.), *Working Lives: The Irish in Britain*, London: The Irish Post, pp. 105–9.

Rich, A. (1977) *Of Woman Born: Motherhood as Experience and Institution*, London: Virago.

Richards, J. (1996) 'Ireland, the empire, and film', in K. Jeffrey (ed.), *An Irish Empire? Aspects of Ireland and the British Empire*, Manchester: Manchester University Press, pp. 25–56.

Riley, D. (1988) *Am I That Name? Feminism and the Category 'Women' in History*, London: Macmillan.

Robertson, R. (1992) *Globalization: Social Theory and Global Culture*, London: Sage.

—— (1995) 'Globalization: time-space and homogenity-heterogenity', in S. Lash and R. Robertson (eds), *Global Modernities*, London: Sage, pp. 25–44.

—— and Khondker, H. H. (1998) 'Discourses of globalization. Preliminary considerations', *International Sociology*, 13 (1), pp. 25–40.

Robinson, M. (1995) 'Cherishing the Irish diaspora', address to the Houses of the Oireachtas, Dublin, 2 February 1995.

—— (1997) 'Address by the President at the lighting of the great Irish famine candle – commemoration ceremonies, Mill Street, Co. Cork, 31 May.'

Roediger, D. (1991) *The Wages of Whiteness: Race and the Making of the American Working Class*, London: Verso.

—— (1994) *Towards the Abolition of Whiteness*, London: Verso.

Rojek, C. and Urry, J. (1997) 'Transformations of travel and theory', in C. Rojek and J. Urry (eds), *Touring Cultures. Transformations of Travel and Theory*, London: Routledge, pp. 1–22.

Rolston, B. (1993) 'The training ground: Ireland conquest and decolonisation', *Race and Class*, 34 (4), pp. 13–34.

Rose, G. (1995) 'The interstitial perspective: a review essay on Homi Bhabha's *The Location of Culture*', *Environment and Planning D: Society and Space*, 13 (3), pp. 365–73.

Rose, N. (1989) *Governing the Soul: The Shaping of the Private Self*, London: Routledge.

—— (1996) 'Authority and the genealogy of subjectivity', in P. Heelas, S. Lash and P. Morris (eds), *Detraditionalization: Critical Reflections on Authority and Identity*, Cambridge, MA: Blackwell, pp. 294–327.

—— (1999a) *Powers of Freedom: Reframing Political Thought*, Cambridge: Cambridge University Press.

—— (1999b) 'Preface to the Second Edition', *Governing the Soul. The Shaping of the Private Self*, London: Free Association Books, pp. vii–xxvii.

Rossiter, A. (1993) 'Bringing the margins into the centre: a review of aspects of Irish women's emigration from a British perspective', in A. Smyth (ed.), *Irish Women's Studies Reader*, Dublin: Attic Press, pp. 177–202.

Ryan, L. (1990) 'Irish emigration to Britain since World War II', in R. Kearney (ed.), *Migrations: The Irish at Home and Abroad*, Dublin: Wolfhound, pp. 45–67.

—— (1994) 'Women without votes: the political strategies of the Irish suffrage movement', *Irish Political Studies*, 9, pp. 119–39.

—— (1998) 'Constructing "Irishwoman": modern girls and comely maidens', *Irish Studies Review*, 6 (3), pp. 263–72.

—— (2001) 'Irish female emigration in the 1930s: transgressing space and culture', *Gender, Place and Culture*, 8 (3), pp. 271–82.

—— (2002) 'Sexualising emigration: discourses of Irish female emigration in the 1930s', *Women's Studies International Forum*, 25 (1), pp. 51–65.

Ryan, R. (2000) 'Introduction: state and nation: the Republic and Ireland, 1949–99', in R. Ryan (ed.), *Writing in the Irish Republic: Literature, Culture, Politics 1949–1999*, Basingstoke: Macmillan, pp. 1–16.

Sayigh, R. (1996) 'Researching gender in a Palestinian camp: political, theoretical and methodological problems', in D. Kandiyoti (ed.), *Gendering the Middle East: Emerging Perspectives*, London: I. B. Tauris, pp. 145–68.

Scheper-Hughes, N. (1979) *Saints, Scholars and Schizophrenics: Mental Illness in Rural Ireland*, Berkeley, CA: University of California Press.

Scott, J. W. (1993) 'The evidence of experience', in H. Abelore, M. Barade and D. M. Halpenn (ed.), *The Lesbian and Gay Studies Reader*, New York: Routledge, pp. 397–415.

—— (2001) 'Fantasy echo: history and the construction of identity', *Critical Inquiry*, 27 (2), pp. 284–304.

Sedgwick, E. K. (1994) *Tendencies*, London: Routledge.

Sinfield, A. (1996) 'Diaspora and hybridity: queer identities and the ethnicity model', *Textual Practice*, 10 (2), pp. 271–93.

Skeggs, B. (1997) *Formations of Class and Gender: Becoming Respectable*, London: Sage.

Smith, A. M. (1994) *New Right Discourse on Race and Sexuality*, Cambridge: Cambridge University Press.

Smith, M. P. (2001) *Transnational Urbanism: Locating Globalization*, Malden, MA: Blackwell.

Smyth, A. (1991) 'The floozie in the jacuzzi', *Feminist Studies*, 17 (1), pp. 7–28.

—— (1992a) '"A great day for the women of Ireland ..." the meaning of Mary Robinson's presidency for Irish women', *Canadian Journal of Irish Studies*, 18 (1), pp. 61–75.

—— (ed.) (1992b) *The Abortion Papers: Ireland*, Dublin: Attic Press.

—— (ed.) (1993a) *Irish Women's Studies Reader*, Dublin: Attic Press.

—— (1993b) 'The women's movement in the Republic of Ireland 1970–1990', in A. Smyth (ed.), *Irish Women's Studies Reader*, Dublin: Attic Press, pp. 245–69.

—— (1994) 'Paying our disrespects to the bloody states we're in: women, violence, culture and the state', in M. Hester G. Griffin, S. Rai and S. Roseneil (eds), *Stirring It: Challenges for Feminism*, London: Taylor & Francis, pp. 13–39.

Smyth, C. (1995) 'Keeping it close: experiencing emigration in England', in I. O'Carroll and E. Collins (eds), *Lesbian and Gay Visions of Ireland: Towards the Twenty-first Century*, London and New York: Cassell, pp. 221–33.

Smyth, L. (2000) *Abortion, Politics and National Identity: The X Case, Irishness and the Nation-State*, unpublished Ph.D. thesis, University of Warwick.

Solomos, J. and Back, L. (1996) *Racism and Society*, London: Macmillan.

Song, M. (2001) 'Comparing minorities' ethnic options. Do Asian Americans possess "more" ethnic options than African Americans?', *Ethnicities*, 1 (1), pp. 57–82.

Southwark Travellers Women's Group (1992) *Moving Stories: Traveller Women Write*, London: Traveller Education Team.

Soysal, Y. N. (1997) 'Changing parameters of citizenship and claims-making: organised Islam in European public spheres', *Theory and Society*, 26, pp. 509–27.

—— (2000) 'Citizenship and identity: living in diasporas in post-war Europe', *Ethnic and Racial Studies*, 23 (1), pp. 1–15.

Speed, A. (1992) 'The struggle for reproductive rights: a brief history in its political context', in A. Smyth (ed.), *The Abortion Papers*, Dublin: Attic Press, pp. 85–98.

Spivak, G. C. (1996) 'Diasporas old and new: women in the transnational world', *Textual Practice*, 10 (2), pp. 245–69.

Squires, J. (1999) *Gender in Political Theory*, Cambridge: Polity Press.

Stacey, J. (2000) 'The global within. Consuming nature, embodying health', in S. Franklin, C. Lury and J. Stacey (eds), *Global Nature, Global Culture*, London: Sage, pp. 97–145.

Steedman, Carolyn (1986) *Landscape for a Good Woman*, London: Virago.

Stolcke, V. (1995) 'Talking culture: new boundaries, new rhetorics of exclusion in Europe', *Current Anthropology*, 36 (1), pp. 1–18.

Stone-Mediatore, S. (2000) 'Chandra Mohanty and the revaluing of "experience"', in U. Narayan and S. Harding (eds), *Decentering the Center: Philosophy for a Multicultural, Postcolonial, and Feminist World*, Bloomington, IN: Indiana University Press, pp. 110–27.

Strathern, M. (1992) *After Nature: English Kinship in the Late Twentieth Century*, Cambridge: Cambridge University Press.

Sutherland, P. (1997) 'Ireland and the challenge of globalisation', in F. Ó Muircheartaigh (ed.), *Ireland in the Coming Times*, Dublin: Institute for Public Administration, pp. 19–35.

Sweeney, G. (1997) 'The kind of white trash culture: Elvis Presley and the aesthetics of excess', in M. Wray and A. Newitz (eds), *White Trash: Race and Class in America*, New York: Routledge, pp. 249–66.

Swift, R. (1999) 'Historians and the Irish: recent writings on the Irish in nineteenth-century Britain', *Immigrants and Minorities*, 18 (2 and 3), pp. 14–39.

Synge, J. (1966) *Collected Works*, London: Oxford University Press.

Taylor, C. (1989) *Sources of the Self: The Making of the Modern Identity*, Cambridge, MA: Harvard University Press.

—— (1994) 'The politics of recognition', in D. T. Goldberg (ed.), *Multiculturalism: A Critical Reader*, Oxford: Blackwell, pp. 75–106.

—— (2000) 'Modernity and difference', in P. Gilroy, L. Grossberg and A. McRobbie (eds), *Without Guarantees in Honour of Stuart Hall*, London: Verso, pp. 364–74.

Taylor, L. J. (1996) '"There are two things that people don't like to hear about themselves": the anthropology of Ireland and the Irish view of anthropology', *South Atlantic Quarterly*, 95 (1), pp. 213–26.

Thompson, J. (1996) 'Tradition and self in a mediated world', in P. Heelas, S. Lash and P. Morris (eds), *Detraditionalization*, Cambridge: Polity Press, pp. 89–108.

Tololyan, K. (1991) 'The nation-state and its others: in lieu of a preface', *Diaspora*, 1 (1), pp. 3–7.

Tovey, H. and Share, P. (2000) *A Sociology of Ireland*, Dublin: Gill & Macmillan.

Travers, P. (1995) '"There was nothing for me there": Irish female emigration, 1922–71', in P. O'Sullivan (ed.), *Irish Women and Irish Migration*, Leicester: Leicester University Press, pp. 146–67.

Trinh, T. M. (1988) '*Reassemblage*: sketch of a soundtrack', *Camera Obscura*, 13–14, pp. 105–12.

Turner, B. (2001) 'Cosmopolitan virtue: on religion in a global age', *European Journal of Social Theory*, 4 (2), pp. 131–52.

Urry, J. (2000) *Sociology Beyond Societies: Mobilities for the Twenty-first Century*, London: Routledge.

Valiulis, M. G. (1995) 'Power, gender and identity in the Irish free state', *Journal of Women's History*, 6/7 (4/1), pp. 117–36.

Valverde, M. (1996) '"Despotism" and ethical liberal governance', *Economy and Society*, 25 (3), pp. 357–72.

Verstraete, G. (2001) 'Technological frontiers and the politics of mobilities', *New Formations*, (43), pp. 26–42.

Vertovec, S. (1996) 'Berlin Multikulti: Germany, "foreigners" and "world-openness"', *New Community*, 22 (3), pp. 381–99.

Walby, S. (2002) 'Feminism in a global era', *Economy and Society*, 31 (4), pp. 533–57.

Walker, D. (2001) 'Global's good side', *The Guardian*, 2 May, p. 15.

Walker, G. (1991) 'The Protestant Irish in Scotland', in T. Devine (ed.), *Irish Immigrants and Scottish Society in the Nineteenth and Twentieth Centuries*, Edinburgh: pp. 44–66.

Walker, L. (1993) 'How to recognize a lesbian: the cultural politics of looking like what you are', *Signs*, 18 (4), pp. 866–91.

Walsh, B. (1989) 'Emigration: an economist's perspective', in J. Mulholland and D. Keogh (eds), *Emigration, Employment and Enterprise*, Cork and Dublin: Hibernian University Press, pp. 14–27.

Walter, B. (1988) *Irish Women in London*, London: London Strategic Policy Unit.

—— (1989) *Gender and Irish Migration to Britain*, Cambridge: Anglia Higher Education College, Geography Working Paper No. 4.

—— (1995) 'Irishness, gender, and place', *Environment and Planning D: Society and Space*, 13, pp. 35–50.

—— (2001) *Outsiders Inside: Whiteness, Place and Irish Women*, London: Routledge.

Ward, M. (1983) *Unmanageable Revolutionaries: Women and Irish Nationalism*, Worcester: Pluto Press.

Waters, M. (1990) *Ethnic Options*, Berkeley, CA: University of California Press.

Whelan, C. T. (1994) 'Irish social values: traditional or modern?', in C. T. Whelan (ed.), *Values and Social Change in Ireland*, Dublin: Gill & Macmillan, pp. 212–15.

—— and Fahey T. (1994) 'Marriage and the family', in C. T. Whelan (ed.), *Values and Social Change in Ireland*, Dublin: Gill & Macmillan.

Whelan, T. (1987) 'The new emigrants', *Newsweek*, 10 October.

White, T. J. (2002) 'Nationalism vs. Liberalism in the Irish context: from a post-colonial past to a postmodern future', *Eire-Ireland*, XXXVII (III + IV), pp. 25–38.

Wills, C. (2001) 'Women, domesticity and the family: recent feminist work in Irish cultural studies', *Cultural Studies*, 15 (1), pp. 33–57.

Winston, N. (2000) *Between Two Places – A Case Study of Irish-Born People Living in England*, Dublin: Irish National Committee of the European Cultural Foundation.

Wolff, J. (1993) 'On the road again: metaphors of travel in cultural criticism', *Cultural Studies*, 7 (2), pp. 224–39.

—— (2000) 'The feminine in modern art. Benjamin, Simmel and the gender of modernity', *Theory, Culture and Society*, 17 (6), pp. 33–53.

Woolf, V. (1984 [1928]) *A Room of One's Own*, London: Penguin.

Young, I. M. (2001) 'Thoughts on multicultural dialogues', *Ethnicities*, 1 (1), pp. 116–22.

Young, R. J. C. (1995) *Colonial Desire: Hybridity in Theory, Culture and Race*, London and New York: Routledge.

Index

Ryanair generation 159
Ryan, L. 2, 22, 24, 27, 92

St Patrick's Day 34, 37–8, 110, 121
Sayigh, R. 44
Scotland 134
Seanad 36–7, 38
Second World War 134
Sense of Ireland Festival 121
servants 1–4, 134, 150
sexuality 24–9, 38–9, 49; appearances
    59; diaspora 149; familism 159;
    London Irish 112, 118; negotiation
    88, 93; Travellers 63, 66
Smyth, A. 10, 54
Somalia 149
staying put 1, 87–91, 102; familism
    150, 152, 159, 161
Steedman, C. 46
Strathern, M. 138
Sunday Independent 36, 185 n. 14
Sweeney, G. 110
Synge, J. M. 63

Taoiseach 34, 50
taxation 36, 86
Taylor, C. 74
teachers 26
television 30
terrorism 137–9
Third World 157
Thompson, J. 155
Tololyan, K. 6
Tory Island 101
tradition 21–2, 28, 33; appearances 43,
    45, 51–3; familism 156, 160; London
    Irish 110; negotiation 88–9, 93;
    Travellers 62
transcription 13–14
transnationality 116–20, 141–6, 150

Travellers 1, 9, 12; appearances 59;
    diaspora 149; familism 154, 157,
    159–62; London Irish 113; mobilities
    60–83; *Report of the Task Force*
    64–5, 77–8, 82, 187 nn. 9, 13;
    whiteness 145
Travelling Review Body 64
Tricycle Theatre 122–3
Trudder House 67
Turner, B. 160

Unionists 76
United Nations (UN) 149, 157, 162
United States 1–4, 24, 30–2;
    appearances 44, 48; diaspora 9–10;
    identity 105–7; modernities 34, 36–7;
    negotiation 99–100; Travellers 61;
    whiteness 132, 138, 146–7
urbanisation 21, 30, 64
Urry, J. 15

valium 40–1
Valverde, M. 137
Victorians 41
vote 30, 35–6, 38, 162

Walby, S. 157
Walter, B. 4, 139, 146, 192 n. 7
Waters, M. 132, 138
welfare 36, 64, 108, 120
West Indies 135
Westernisation 23
whitely 131–3, 140–2, 148
whiteness 3, 11, 16; familism 157, 159,
    163; femininities 129–49
Wills, C. 25–6, 41
women in the home 49, 59, 150
Women's Movement 9, 28, 113
Woolf, V. 46
working women 49–54, 59